Camino Portugués

Lisbon – Porto – Santiago

Camino Central / Camino de la Costa

*A Practical & Mystical Manual
for the Modern Day Pilgrim*

John Brierley

First published in 2005. This revised and extended **7th** edition published in **2016**.

ISBN: 978-1-84409-681-7

All maps © John Brierley 2016

All photographs © John Brierley 2016

Printed and bound in the European Union

Published by
CAMINO GUIDES
An imprint of Findhorn Press Ltd.
117-121 High Street
Forres IV36 1AB
Scotland
Tel: +44(0)1309-690582
Fax: +44(0)131-777-2711

Email: info@findhornpress.com
www.findhornpress.com
www.caminoguides.com

Pontesampaio – The modern camino, part of the original Roman Road *Via Romana*

Front Flap & Pagemarker: Map of Stages Lisbon – Porto – Tui – Santiago

Rear Flap & Pagemarker: Map of 12 Waymarked Caminos de Santiago

"We walk to God. Pause and reflect on this.
Could any way be holier, or more deserving of your
effort, of your love and of your full intent?...
Look not to ways that seem to lead you elsewhere."

A Course in Miracles.

Notes to the 7th Edition:

Several improvements have been incorporated into this latest guide including its smaller format. The biggest change is the addition of the Coastal route from Porto to supplement the main Camino Central. Facilities for pilgrims along the section from Lisbon to Porto continue to improve with the addition of several new pilgrim hostels. This section still carries relatively few pilgrims with 1,435 commencing their camino in Lisbon (0.6% of the total). Accordingly it should only be undertaken by seasoned pilgrims with an adventurous and flexible approach and an ability to speak Portuguese. The pilgrim association **Via Lusitana** based in Lisbon offer a 24 hour help line (**+351) 915 595 213** which shows a remarkable commitment. Pilgrims starting from Porto increased again last year to 10,636 (4.5%) and those starting from Tui/Valença 16,126 (6.8%) making it the third most popular starting point (after Sarria and St. Jean Pied de Port).

Contrary to popular belief the Portuguese Way is one third by earthen tracks and woodland pathways. This is true for both the Lisbon (33.2%) and Porto (32.5%) sections. While over half the first stage out of Lisbon is on pathways (much of it along the rio Tejo estuary) the waymarked route out of Porto has no natural pathways. Accordingly detailed options are given as to how to avoid the busy road network around Porto city itself.

Acknowledgements:

I would like to thank *Joana Castro, Antonio Martins Ferreira, Fernanda* and *Jacinto Gomes Rodrigues* and their families, all of whom have welcomed me into their hearts and homes and provided me with a sound basis for my love and deep appreciation for Portugal and her people. Gratitude is also due to all those pilgrims who have walked this path over the centuries. Each one has helped to shape and make this path what it is today. From St. James himself who risked life and limb to carry the message of love and forgiveness to the Iberian peninsular and now — some two thousand years later, the Friends of the Way in Portugal who voluntarily give of their time to waymark the route so that we might find our way safely to Santiago de Compostela. I would like to acknowledge the help of the pilgrim association Via Lusitana including *José Luis Sanches, Natércia and Helena Bernardo* who provided invaluable help in the early stages. *Emídio Almeida* of Associação Portuguesa dos Amigos de Apóstolo Santiago, *Nuno Ribeiro, Ilídio Silva, João Moreiro, Ana Castro, Kirsten Kleinfeldt, Alison Raju, Paul Crocker, Rodney Asher, António Pires* and *Pedro Macedo* from the Mosteiro de Vairão all offered valuable feedback. And let us not forget all those people who live along the *caminho* and offer welcome and shelter to us as we pass by... *muito obrigado.*

John Brierley

Foreword:

In the beginning was the Word... John 1.1

We live in a dualistic world of past and future, left and right, right and wrong. This world of time and space, of judgment and condemnation often feels contradictory and threatening. How do we honour our worldly commitments and make time to go on pilgrimage? How do we balance work and play and still find time to pray? How do we resolve a world of seeming opposites and our prejudice and judgement of others?

Perhaps pilgrimage, the Path of Enquiry, will lead us to that point of understanding where there is no longer any separation between path and goal, where life itself is pilgrimage and every step a prayer. In the meantime, we stumble along in dark clouds of unknowing and that is, perhaps, the essential beginning place; to have the courage to admit we are lost and the humility to ask directions.

When I was stumbling around wondering how best to start this guide, a neighbour appeared with a newspaper cutting with the heading, *what is the best guide to the camino?* The instant I asked for help I was handed the answer. The words and timing were perfect: *The best guide to* **what** *camino?* There are many guides to the physical path but if we attend only to the practical we miss the mystical and perhaps we miss the whole point. We walk down a cul-de-sac called despair with only our own mortality waiting for us at the end. There is no way out of our conundrum but in — through the inner landscape of soul.

So suddenly I was prompted to write a foreword, a beginning. And it occurred to me that unless I put God first in everything I do, I will not find my way out. If I look on the world through my lower self with my physical eyes alone I see an image of divisiveness and chaos with the only certainty being death and decay. From the perspective of lower mind the world itself is already half way through its biological life — even the sun will die. I find these thoughts wonderfully liberating because it frees me from my bondage to the material and opens a way to knowledge of Higher Worlds.

Synchronicity was also working when, after walking for five days in perfect weather along the peaceful pathways that make up the Camino Portugués, I arrived in town and was confronted with a televised image of three Western kidnap victims in Iraq with their Islamic guards standing ominously in the background and the imminent threat of beheading. It was a dreadful image of intense pain and suffering that left me feeling shocked and nauseous. I wandered out into the sunlight in a vain effort to erase the terrifying image. An hour later, I found myself in a chapel before an image of St. James the Slayer of the Moors *Santiago Matamoros* occupying the central position over the altar. This was a place of modern Christian worship and the nausea returned as I realised that I was kneeling before an image of St. James with sword raised decapitating Islamic 'Infidels'. The way to forge peace can never be achieved through jihad and crusade.

There are many gods, but one God and whatever term we use to describe what cannot be described seems immaterial. God or Allah will do just fine, provided we direct our prayers towards an image of Love and Light. Words are powerful symbols and we need to be careful how we frame them. We may need to alter our images and think twice before we ask our questions and to whom we direct them. A loving God may provide a very different answer to a vengeful one. We need to watch our terminology, mindful that those who look for separation and dissent will find it, but those who seek the truth and a unified purpose will find that also.

Along every Path of Enquiry there comes a point that requires a leap of faith. A point where we have to abandon the security of outdated dogma handed down to us over millennia. To let go of the familiar story taught to us by our tribe and develop the courage to dive instead into the mysteries – this is the story of the Grail Knights and the heart of modern day pilgrimage too. When we meet that void no one else can cross it for us. We have to let go the safety of the familiar and dive into the unknown, with nothing but our faith in God to support us.

That is why I call these guides A Practical *and* Mystical Manual for the Modern Day Pilgrim. That we might find a place to eat and sleep at the end of a long days walking – but also, and crucially, that we might support each other to dive into the mysteries of our individual soul awakenings, without which all journeying is purposeless. We have a sacred contract, a divine function, and a reason why we came here. Perhaps your calling to go on pilgrimage will be the opportunity to find out what that purpose is and to provide the necessary space to re-orientate your life towards its fulfilment. Maybe this is the point in your life where all your neat and tightly held beliefs get shattered so that you can begin to piece together Who you really are and what your part in God's plan for salvation really is. We don't really have a choice, except to delay. Why wait for the inevitable?

So I end this foreword by giving the last word to the great mystic poet, Kabir.

> *Friend, hope for the truth while you are alive.*
> *Jump into experience while you are alive!*
> *Think... and   think... while you are alive.*
> *What you call 'salvation' belongs to the time before death.*
> *If you don't break your ropes while you are alive,*
> *Do you think ghosts will do it after?*
>
> *The idea that the soul will join with the ecstatic*
> *Just because the body is rotten —*
> *That is all fantasy.*
> *What is found now is found then.*
>
> *If you find nothing now,*
> *You will simply end up with an apartment in the city of death.*
> *If you make love with the divine now, in the next life*
> *You will have the face of satisfied desire.*
> *So plunge into the truth, find out Who the Teacher is,*
> *Believe in the Great Sound!*

The Portuguese Way *Camino Portugués* Caminho Português

The Towers of the West *Torres del Oeste*

Along this route lies Monte Santiaguiño where St. James first preached Christ's great lesson of unconditional love and forgiveness thus helping to write the first pages of Christian history. This pivotal event is represented on the front cover. Sant Iago returns to Jerusalem to face martyrdom and his body is returned to this self-same spot – the boat carrying his mortal remains sailing up past the Towers of the West *Torres del Oeste* at Catoira to fetch land again at Padrón, his body finally being transported to Libredon – now renamed Santiago de Compostela. The Camino Portugués is thus both a starting point and an end point in the legendary Santiago story.

Much of the route follows the original Roman military road that connected Portugal with Spain and then France via the major 'crossroads' town of Astorga *Asturica Augusta*. You will pass by Roman milestones *miliários* to confirm that you are, indeed, directly on this ancient way. We will cross Roman bridges built 2,000 years ago, but this period, which marks St. James life and teaching, was to fade into obscurity for 800 years until the discovery of his tomb in the Roman town of *Liberum Donum*. The legend of the 'Field of Stars' *Compo-Stellae* was born just in time for the Christian re-conquest *reconquista* of the Iberian peninsular from the Islamic caliphate based in Córdoba. The renaming of Libredon to *Santiago de Compostela* was to follow. And here we also see the emergence of the terrible image of St. James the Slayer of the Moors *Santiago Matamoros*. This was an ideal image to spearhead the re-conquest but one far removed from the message of love of God, self, and stranger that is portrayed in the image of St. James the Pilgrim *Santiago Peregrino*. It is this latter figure that was to lead the revival of Christian pilgrimage as early as the 10th century and was to make Santiago de Compostela the third greatest pilgrim destination after Jerusalem and Rome. Most of the bridges that we walk over today were built during this medieval period, sometimes using the earlier Roman foundations. But it is at the dawn of the 21st century that we witness an extraordinary revival of pilgrimage that now places the Camino de Santiago at the forefront of this extraordinary modern phenomena and the most popular Christian pilgrimage route in the world today.

However, this brief overview is only part of the story, for there is not one camino, but many (see map on back cover). Today the Camino Francés accounts for 68% (down from 85% 10 years ago) and the Camino Portugués has become the second most popular route carrying 15% of the total (up from 6% in the same period) but still leaving the Portuguese Way relatively uncrowded. Here you follow in the footsteps of Pagan, Celtic, Roman, Islamic and Christian wayfarers going back over millennia. Today we seek the very same treasure they looked for – to find and embrace that loving Presence that offers us the gifts of joy and peace. In this fearful and war-torn world our mission has never been clearer or more urgent – every step now becomes a prayer for peace. The Way is open again for everyone, irrespective of gender or generation, colour, class or creed and from every religion, or none. This inclusivity marks it apart from virtually every other pilgrim itinerary around the world.

Alternative routes: Before setting off you should at least hold an overview of the alternative routes that come under the general heading *O Caminhos Portugueses.* Not all of these are waymarked but enough have been painted with the familiar yellow arrows to cause possible confusion at certain points where they merge and branch off again. What follows is not an exhaustive list but it contains the major routes that have been used over the centuries and which are still in existence today in some form or another. It is an indication of the popularity of the cult of St. James in Portugal during the Middle Ages that so many routes were available at that time. There are, perhaps, two contrasting reasons for its decline – the arrival of the industrial revolution in the 19th century and the apparition at Fátima in the early 20th century which changed the focus of attention. The early 21st century witnesses a marvellous awakening and renewal. Gratitude is due directly to you for being part of its re-emergence and I trust that it will feed and nourish you to the extent that you feed and nurture it.

❶ **Central Way** *Caminho Central Caminho Real* – the main historic route described in this guidebook from Lisbon to Porto and Porto to Tui which lies just over the border in Spain where more than half of all the pilgrims start the 'Portuguese' way. Also referred to as the *Caminho Medieval*

❷ **Coastal Way** *Caminho da Costa.* This route is gaining in popularity and has now been well waymarked and is included in this guide for the first time. It also includes the variant known as:

❸ **Seashore Path** *Senda Litoral* which is haphazardly waymarked but basically follows the seashore and beaches offering a distinctly tourist vibe. Both routes converge at Caminha to cross the Minho estuary into Spain at A Guarda and then via Baiona and Vigo to rejoin the main Central Camino at Redondela.

❹ **Braga Way** *Caminho por Braga* a little used variant from Porto to Ponte de Lima via Braga. It is mostly along busy roads which deters many pilgrims. Braga can also be visited easily by bus from Barcelos with regular daily schedule (see Barcelos for details).

❺ **Interior Way** *Caminho Interior* from Viseu and Vila Real to Chaves joining up with the camino Sanabrés in Verín. A variant crosses in Lamego to rejoin the central way in Ponte de Lima via Braga which remains the ecclesiastical heart of Portugal and is rich in religious monuments. Churches & museums with religious artefacts and iconography abound. The most widely visited 'tourist' site in Portugal is the intriguing church of Bom Jesus, which lies on a hill overlooking Braga. The extent and wealth of its historical monuments is, perhaps, one of its biggest drawbacks for the modern day pilgrim. Its popularity as a tourist destination means that the roads into and out of Braga are busy and accommodation is relatively expensive.

Braga – *Hospital São Marcos*

❻ The Lamego Way *Caminho Português de Lamego* a variant of the Interior Way from Coimbra to Lamego is now largely obsolete although there is *talk* of re-waymarking. The original route continued north on what is now the waymarked route from Chaves.

❼ The Way of the Star *Caminho de Via de Estrela* from Caceres to Braga. This route follows (in theory) the line of a Roman road that branched off from the Via de la Plata. While it has ancient roots it is only now re-emerging as a possible viable alternative pilgrim route. It crosses the remote and beautiful Monte Estrela. It will, in time, connect with Viseu and the Interior Way.

❽ The Northern Way *Caminho do Norte* via Lanheses. This route is poorly waymarked and appears largely obsolete and the lack of accommodation makes it difficult to negotiate. It combines the early stages of the Coastal route and then swings eastwards towards the Central route before branching off again near Barcelos. It then climbs steeply through the Serra de Padela *Parque de Valinhas* to descend sharply to cross the Rio Lima into Lanheses. From here it is another steep climb up through the Serra de Arga before dropping down to join the Coastal route at Vila Nova de Cerveira and thence to Valença or A Guarda. This route is arduous, taking in the steep mountains of the Serra de Arga.

❾ Sea Route 'Spiritual Variant' *Ruta del Mar 'Variante Espiritual'*. This follows the historical sea route. Commencing in Pontevedra and heading to the coast at Vilanova de Arousa. Here you can take a boat up the river Ulla past Catoira to Pontecesures along the unique maritime *Via Crucis* with the stone crosses rising from the seabed. An alternative is to walk the path alongside the river estuary into Padrón.

❿ Fátima: *Caminho de Tejo* This route follows the camino de Santiago from Lisbon as far as Santarém where it branches off to the west. To pilgrimage in Portugal we need to understand that Fátima and Portugal are synonymous. Since the vision of the Blessed Virgin appeared to three young shepherd children (Lucia, Francesco and Jacinta) in Fátima in 1917, it has become a major pilgrimage centre and place of veneration in its own right and one of the great Marian Shrines in the Catholic world. While the thousands who travel there every year do so mostly by bus, you may well come across happy bands of pilgrims walking to Fátima, sometimes as many as 100 in a group. Lucia was the only one to survive the flu epidemic that ravaged Europe after the First World war and the one to whom the *Three Secrets* were revealed. The first was a horrifying vision of hell and a call for repentance. The second was similar and concerned the threat of world war and persecution. The third was the most prophetic but has never been fully revealed. The Vatican has suggested it concerns the attempted assassination and death of Pope John Paul II (*A bishop dressed in white who falls to the ground as if dead*) but others suggest it prophesies the fall of the Church itself (*due to scandals at the very heart of the hierarchy*). The bullet extracted from the Pontiff has now been inserted into the crown of the statue of the Virgin at Fatima. Lucia died near Coimbra in 2005 and the Congregation of the Doctrine of the Faith will publish the full text of her message in due course and after suitable preparation.

However we might individually interpret such prophecies, the fact remains that in order to breakthrough to a new reality we have to allow old thought-forms and dogma to die. The death of the old is generally experienced as painful, but the emergence of the new often brings elation. As we begin to shift from an imperfect outer authority to our innate inner wisdom we might experience an intensity of both anxiety and a sense of freedom. Fátima struggles with this self-same acceleration of both negative and positive forces. A headline in a Portuguese newspaper declared: *'Another Interfaith Outrage Blessed by Fátima Shrine Rector. Appearing on Portuguese television, Msgr. Guerra regurgitated the long-discredited ecumenical slogan that different religions should concentrate on what we have in common and not on what separates us.'* Pilgrimages

Fátima – *Basilica*

of reparation still take place to atone for this outrage – and what, pray, is this defilement? A Hindu priest was permitted by Msgr. Guerra to offer a prayer for peace and reconciliation at the Catholic altar in the Little Chapel of the Apparitions!

Fátima clearly struggles with a traditional and more progressive faith. This snapshot of Fátima will hopefully provide a context to understand the general lack of interest, even suspicion within Portugal, towards Santiago. The town of Tomar on the historic Santiago route lies 35 km east of Fátima and represents the Gnostic perspective held by the Order of the Knights Templar. This is no less threatening today as it was in 1312 when the Order was outlawed by the Vatican for it proclaims the sanctity of the God that lies within every individual and is therefore less dependent on external authority. It is, perhaps, one of the reasons why no official pilgrim hostels were available on the Lisbon section until 2012, although they were everywhere in the medieval period. However, this lack of any single authority trying to take sole responsibility for the camino permits a more open and eclectic orientation. It might also help us understand why the familiar yellow arrow pointing to Santiago is often accompanied by a blue arrow pointing in the *opposite* direction – to Fátima.

If you intend to detour to Fátima contact the tourist office in the town *Turismo* ℂ 249 531 139. The route can be walked in 2 days from Santarém (56 km). A route continues via Caxarias to rejoin the Caminho Central in either Ansião or Alvaizere (44 km or another 2 days). A popular alternative is to take a 2 night stay in either Santarém or Tomar and take a day return visit by bus. Both have a regular service throughout the day. The journey takes around 1 hour / €9.

Pilgrimage is experienced on many different levels. At one end is the physical challenge of walking a long distance route with a group of friends in a limited time frame, always with an eye on the calendar. Perhaps now is an opportunity for you to experience pilgrimage at the other end, at a pace that allows for the inner alchemy of introspection. How deep you choose to make the experience is, of course, up to you. Nevertheless the basic counsel is to go on foot, alone. The extended periods of silence will open up space to reflect on your life and its direction. Go alone and you may find that you are never alone and that may prove a pivotal turning point.

The Camino Portugués is shaking off centuries of slumber and ready to play its part in the great flowering of human imagination, cooperation and consciousness. In the oft-repeated words of Christopher Frye from *A Sleep of Prisoners*, "… Affairs are now soul sized. The enterprise is exploration into God. Where are you making for? It takes so many thousand years to wake, but will you wake for pity's sake."

… And so, like a latter-day Rip Van Winkle we rise to dust off our boots and join the merry band of pilgrims making their way up through the welcoming beauty and peace of northern Portugal to the city of St. James in neighbouring Galicia. You will meet other fellow wayfarers and the native folk whose lands you pass over, but above all you may meet your Self, and that may make all the difference. Whatever you do, don't forget to begin. Journey well, *buen viaje, boa viagem!*

Historical Snapshot and Brief Chronology:

What follows is not intended as an authoritative discourse on the history of Portugal or its pilgrim routes. It merely seeks to draw together some of the innumerable strands that make the Portuguese Way central to an understanding of the Santiago story. From St. James first landing at Padrón to convert the pagan inhabitants in his guise as *Santiago Peregrino* to his re-invention to spearhead the crusades to vanquish Islam as *Santiago Matamoros* the memory of St. James is indelibly linked to these shores. The route has remained in obscurity for too long and deserves to be more widely discovered and acknowledged.

• Palaeolithic period c. 20,000 B.C.

1992 saw one of the great archaeological discoveries of the modern era in Vila Nova de Foz Côa, in the Douro valley 120 km due East of Porto. Here we find one of the oldest and largest displays of Palaeolithic art dating back some 22,000 years. It was declared a UNESCO World heritage site in 1998. The Douro river valley has been a cradle of civilisation long before the Age of Discoveries was launched from her harbours.

• Megalithic period c. 4000 B.C.

This period is best known for the building of great *mega* stone structures sometimes referred to as Dolmens or Mamoas. They generally had evidence of human remains and have been linked to prehistoric graves. They were also aligned to the winter solstice sun and so are connected to sun worship. An example lies on our route near Arcos (see stage 2 for details). Petroglyphs or rock carvings are another feature of this period. This megalithic culture was deeply religious in nature and left a powerful impact on the peoples who followed.

• Early Celtic period c. 1,000 B.C.

Central European Celts settled in north-western Portugal and Spain intermarrying with the Iberians and giving rise to the Celtiberian tribes. Remains of their Celtic villages *castros* or *citânias* can be seen dotted around the remote countryside especially in the Minho area. These fortified villages were built in a circular formation usually occupying some elevated ground or hillock. They are found today in place names on maps, but one of the most

Monte Tecla – Castro

striking examples can be visited just off our route at Monte de Santa Tecla overlooking the mouth of the Minho. The extensive mineral deposits of this area gave rise to a rich artistic movement and bronze and gold artefacts of Celtic design and origin can be admired in museums all across Europe. The Phoenicians established a trading centre in Lisbon around 900 B.C.

• Early Roman period c. 200 B.C.

The Roman occupation of the Iberian peninsular began in the 2nd century BCE and they too were attracted by the rich mining potential of the Northern region. In

Ponte de LIma *(Lethe)*

136 B.C. the proconsul Decimus Junius Brutus led his legions across the Lima and Minho rivers where he met resistance not only from the fierce inhabitants but also from his own soldiers wary of crossing the river that was thought to represent one of the rivers of Hades – the river of forgetfulness *Lethe*. Brutus became the first Roman general to make it across and on to the end of the known world at Finis Terrae. A Roman garrison was established there that would, in time, become the Roman city of Dugium – present day Duio. This early Roman settlement played host to pilgrims from many different traditions and it was to the king (governor) of Dugium that St. James' disciples were directed by queen Lupa for permission to bury his body (see *A Pilgrims Guide to the Camino Finisterre*).

While the Phoenicians are, perhaps, best known for their syllabic writing which influenced the Aramaic and Greek alphabets developed from their base at Byblos (from which comes our word Bible) they were the great merchant nation of antiquity. They also developed the sea routes to the British Isles to promote the tin trade in particular, helping to develop the Atlantic ports such as Cadiz, Lisbon and Finisterre on the way. In 61 B.C. Julius Caesar became governor of Hispania Ulterior establishing *Olisipo* (modern day Lisbon) as his base from where he conducted naval expeditions along these shores to finally win control of the Atlantic seaboard from the Phoenicians. The most significant Roman remains in Portugal are in Conimbriga which was a major military and trading post on the Via Roman XVI between Olisipo (Lisbon), Cale (Porto) and Bracara Augusta (Braga). The Roman road from Braga to Valença was known as the Via XIX also referred to as the Antonine Itinerary *Itinerario de Antonino*.

• Early Christian Period c. 40 A.D.

While there is little historical evidence to support the view that St. James (The Greater, Son of Zebedee to distinguish him for St. James the Just) came to the Iberian peninsular there is ample anecdotal testimony to that effect. It would appear that he sailed to Padrón and commenced his ministry there. By all accounts his mission was largely unsuccessful and after an apparition by the Virgin Mary in 40 A.D. he returned to Jerusalem where he was decapitated in the year 44 at Herod Agrippa's own hand (and sword). James thus became the first of the apostles to be martyred and his faithful disciples decided to return his body to the place of his earlier ministry at Padrón. On the instructions of the pagan queen Lupa the relics of St. James were taken to Finisterre where permission for burial was refused by the Roman legate. In the famous story of betrayal the disciples managed to escape with their sacred cargo and the body of St. James was finally laid to rest in Libredon (Liberum Donum). These remarkable events then faded from memory until…

• The Middle Ages c. 476 – 1453

The decline and fall of the Roman Empire was hastened in Portugal with the arrival of Visigoth and Suevi tribes from Germany. The Suevi settled further north around the Douro establishing headquarters at the roman port of Portucale (present day Porto and from which we get the name Portugal). The influence of the Visigoths extended further south around the Lisbon (Olisipo) area. It was from their base in Toledo that their incessant internal squabbles resulted in one group seeking support from the Muslim enclave in North Africa – the Moors duly obliged, arriving in 711. Within a decade Islam had effectively conquered the majority of the Iberian peninsular. While we are more familiar, perhaps, with the Arab influence in Spain, they occupied the entire of Portugal where their rule appears to have been much more favourable than life under the Visigoths who initiated the first expulsion of Jews from the peninsular while the Moors allowed freedom of religious expression. The last Islamic stronghold was the coastal area of southern Portugal, which they named al-Gharb (meaning the West) that today we know as the Algarve. Contrary to popular understanding, Mozarabes (Moçárabes) was the name given to freely practising Christians under Moorish rule. It was during this period, in the year 813, that a 'celestial light' led the hermit Pelayo to the Field of Stars *Compo Stellae* and the discovery of the tomb of St. James. This visionary event was immediately endorsed by the bishop of Iria Flavia in whose diocese Libredon was, and the following year King Alfonso II commenced the building of a basilica church.

The discovery of the tomb arrived just in time for St. James to become the figurehead for the Christian re-conquest of the Iberian peninsular from Islam. The night before the battle of Clavijo St. James appeared to the Christian troops as a knight dressed in armour astride a white charger, which was to rally the Christian army that the Arab forces were duly defeated. The re-conquest ebbed and flowed with Almanzor arriving at the door of Santiago cathedral in 997 but the relics of the saint had been removed so the Moors took the bells instead and had them carried by Christian slaves to his base in Córdoba. Al-Mansur provided a further setback in 1190 but Portugal's turning point came

Santiago Matamoros

with Afonso Henriques and the battle of Ourique in 1139 and the taking of Lisbon in 1147. On the strength of these re-conquests he became Dom Afonso I, first King of Portugal. Dom Afonso III (1248-1249) finally providing the *coup de grâce* by winning back the al-Gharb in southern Portugal.

Pilgrimages to Santiago began around the middle of the 10th century, becoming increasingly popular and reaching something of a climax by the middle of the 15th century. While thousands of simple peasants, priests and paupers made the journey, we learn mostly of the exploits of nobility, kings and queens. By this time the main routes via Barcelos, Braga and Viana had become well established. In 915 Dom Ordonho II granted land in Correlhã, near Ponte de Lima, to the city fathers at Santiago de Compostela. This marks the first significant recognition of Santiago as a major pilgrimage destination through Portugal. By coincidence the only chapel dedicated to Santiago (in ruins) on the route in Portugal remains in the townland of Correlhã (see stage 16). D. Henrique and Dna. Teresa ratified the gifting of these lands on their royal pilgrimage to Santiago in 1097. Other monarchs followed with Afonso II in 1219, Dom Sancho II in 1244 and then Queen Isabel (the Saintly) made her first pilgrimage in 1325.

• The Age of Discoveries c. 1500

This period marks Portugal's greatest achievements and the high point in its history. Under the auspices of Manuel I, otherwise known as The Fortunate we see the navigation of the sea routes to India by Vasco da Gama in 1498 and the creation of the first viceroy to India some years later. In 1500 Pedro Alvares discovers Brazil, establishing a link that remains strong to this day. The ensuing foreign trade made Portugal one of the richest countries in the world and saw the flowering of Christianity, art and

Portuguese Caravel *(replica)*

commerce with trade agreements as far flung as China, Persia, India and South America. King Manuel I became a great patron of the arts and this period and its beautiful architectural style is known as *Manueline*. Manuel, a deeply religious man, went on pilgrimage to Santiago in 1502. Amongst other dignitaries who made the pilgrimage through Portugal was Cosme III of the Medicis in 1669. It seems that the famous Italian pilgrim, Doménico Laffi, perhaps inspired by the Medici pilgrimage, made the journey in 1691. The first detailed account of the pilgrimage was by a German traveller, Jeronimo Münzer in 1495. This was followed by the better-known account of Juan Bautista Confalonieri an Italian priest who accompanied Monsignor Fabio Biondo on his pilgrimage in 1592.

• A snapshot of modern Portugal 1807 – 2011

In 1807 Napoleon reached Portugal and the royal family withdrew to Brazil and made their seat of government there. After Napoleon's forces were finally defeated in 1811 unrest within Portugal led to a Constitutional Monarchy in 1820 and an era of relative stability under D. Pedro V and D. Luís I. However civil strife at the turn of the century led to revolution and the establishment of a Republic in 1910 and Manuel José de Arriaga was elected as first president. Political unrest continued through the period of the first World War up to 1926 when an army coup installed General António de Fragoso Carmona to head a new government. He appointed António de Oliveira Salazar as minister of finance. Salazar was deeply religious and set about restoring the power of the church after becoming prime minister and effectively a dictator in 1932.

In 1936 Salazar supported General Francisco Franco during the Spanish civil war and both countries signed a non-aggression pact and declared neutrality during the Second World War. Salazar's rigid regime and economic policies led to low wages with poor labour rights and, inevitably, unrest. The regime resisted all opposition, crushing a revolt in 1947. The 1960's marked another difficult period for Portugal with rebellion in the overseas territories of Goa, Angola, Guinea and Mozambique. Portugal resisted these moves for independence in its African colonies receiving UN condemnation. In 1968 Marcello **Caetano** succeeded Salazar as prime minister. The repressive policies continued at home and in the colonies and Portugal's economic stability was again threatened and this led to a coup by the army in 1974, which installed Gen. António de **Spinola** as president. Spinola oversaw democratic reforms at home and in the African territories and during this period General Francisco da Costa Gomes was elected president. Nationalisation of industry, the banking system and the repossession of many large agricultural estates ensued.

Over the next few decades political unrest between right-wing, communist and socialist factions led to a deepening of the economic and social problems of Portugal and the government has swung from left to right with alarming regularity. Soares (Socialist Party PS) played a prominent role during this period and was re-elected prime minister in 1983 introducing an austerity program that led eventually to Portugal's entry into the European Community in 1986. In 2002 the centre-right coalition elected José Manuel **Barroso** as Prime Minister who resigned in 2004 to head up the European Commission and Santana **Lopes** was sworn in as Prime Minister. The euro crisis saw the Socialist Party (PS) back in power under José **Socrates** but the austerity plans following the EU/IMF bailout agreement in May 2011 led to his resignation. Social Democratic Party (PSD) Prime Minister Pedro Passos Coelho's government took office in June 2011. Since then, the government has been preoccupied with the implementation of broad austerity measures pursuant to the agreement.

• A snapshot of modern Galicia 1975 – 2011

After Franco's death in 1975, King Carlos nominally succeeded and appointed political reformist Adolfo Suárez to form a government. In 1982 the socialist party (PSOE) won a sweeping victory under Felipe **González** who successfully steered Spain into full membership of the EEC in 1986. In 1996 the populace gave the conservative José María **Aznar**, leader of the right wing *Partido Popular* (PP), a narrow mandate but in November 2002 the oil tanker Prestige ran into a storm off Finisterre and the ensuing ecological catastrophe sank not only the livelihood of scores of Galician fisherman but, in due time, the right wing government as well. The disregard for the environment displayed by the President of Galicia and the Spanish environment minister of that time resulted in a popular cry up and down the country of 'never again' *nunca maís*. It only took the government's unpopular support of the invasion of Iraq coupled with the Madrid bombings in March 2004 to put the socialist's back in power under the youthful leadership of José Luis Rodríguez **Zapatero**.

The new government set in motion an immediate change in foreign policy and, more controversially, a sudden but decisive shift from a conservative Catholic to a liberal secular society that led to one newspaper headline declaring, 'Church and State square up in struggle for the spirit of Spain.' The deepening economic crisis led to the election of Mariano **Rajoy** of the centre-right PP in December 2011. And seemingly immune to all these social and political upheavals, the *Camino Portugués* in Galicia goes quietly about her gentle spirit of transformation.

Preparation – A Quick Guide:

[1] Practical Considerations:

• **When?** Spring is often wet and windy but the route is relatively quiet with early flowers appearing. Summer is busy and hot and hostels often full. Autumn often provides the most stable weather with harvesting adding to the colour and celebrations of the countryside. Winter is solitary and cold and many hostels will be closed.

• **How long?** Clear the decks and allow some spaciousness into your life. This entire route is divided into 23 stages so it fits (just) into a 3 week break.

[2] Preparation – Outer: what do I need to take *and* leave behind.

• Buy your boots in time to walk them in before you go.
• Pack a Poncho, Galicia is notorious for its downpours.
• Bring a hat, sunstroke is painful and can be dangerous.
• Look again if your backpack weighs more than 10 kilos.

What *not* to bring:

• Get rid of all books (except this one – all the maps you need are included.)
• Don't take 'extras', Portugal has shops if you need to replace something.
• If you want to deepen your experience, leave behind:
  – your *camera* – you'll be able to live for the moment rather than memories.
  – your *watch* – you'll be surprised how quickly you adapt to a natural clock.
  – your *mobile phone* – break the dependency (excepting solo pilgrims travelling in the winter months when a phone may be useful and a compass necessary to navigate especially in snow when waymarks may become obliterated).

[3] Language learn it now, *before* you go.

[4] Pilgrim Passport, Protocol & Prayer

• Get a *credencial* from your local confraternity – and join it.
• Have consideration for your fellow pilgrims and gratitude for your hosts.
• 'May every step be a prayer for peace and an extension of loving kindness.'

[5] Preparation – Inner: why am I doing this?

Take time to prepare a purpose for this pilgrimage and to complete the self-assessment questionnaire (page 29). Start from the basis that you are essentially a spiritual being on a human journey, not a human being on a spiritual one. We came to learn some lesson and this pilgrimage affords an opportunity to find out what that is. Ask for help and expect it – it's there, now, waiting for you.

Whatever you do – for heaven's sake don't forget to start.

Practical Considerations:

This guidebook provides essential information in a concise format. It is the result of many years of extensive research of the various Ways of St. James in Portugal and provides information on where to eat, sleep and points of interest along the way. The maps have been designed to show relevant information only and accurate distances between points are printed on the map and correspond with the text – they are generally spaced at around 3.5 kilometre intervals which corresponds to around one hour of walking at an average pace. These maps directs you *to* Santiago; if you intend to walk 'in reverse' source different maps.

Each stage begins and ends at a town or village where some suitable accommodation can be found with details and alternatives provided in the text. Interim accommodation is also listed so that you make your own start and finish point depending on variables like weather. Should you become lost use the 'sun compass' for orientation. To those of you who decided to leave your watches behind the sun will also become your natural clock. It is surprising how quickly we get to know the time of day by the length of our shadow. Your body will remind you when you need to eat or drink but my advice is never to pass a drinking font without using it – a minimum of 2 litres a day will help ward off injury and fatigue.

How long will it take? Allow time to complete the journey gracefully. There's already too much pressure in our lives – so clear the decks and allow some spaciousness into your life. Walking pace naturally varies between individuals and when you add in variations in weather, detours (planned and otherwise) and different motivations and time constraints all this results in a heady mix of possibilities. The route has been divided into 23 stages (13 from Lisbon to Porto and 10 from Porto to Santiago). Fit walkers could accomplish the entire route in 3 weeks but this would allow for no rest days, no detours, no injuries and little time for reflection and integration of experiences along the way. A month is ideal and this equates to an average of 25 km per day with 3 rest days, allowing time to explore historic towns such as Tomar, and 2 weekend days to travel to Lisboa and home again from Santiago. (allow 2 weeks Porto to Santiago).

The 'average' pace varies depending on the gradient and contour maps are provided to alert you to strenuous *up*hill stretches. Be mindful, however, that most injuries are sustained while going *down*hill and occur in the early days while pushing the body beyond what it has been conditioned for. It takes the body a few days to adjust to the regular walking with full backpack. Give body, mind and soul time to acclimatise. Don't push yourself at the beginning. It is always advisable to put in some physical training before you go. A full weekend walking with backpack will show up weak spots that can then be worked on to minimise injuries when away and to improve general fitness levels. Walking poles, if used properly, can greatly reduce wear and tear on the body and minimise the likelihood of injury. If you don't have a pair (one in each hand creates better balance and is twice as effective) consider buying a set. They are likely to prove a good investment for this pilgrimage – and future ones!

Remember pace will slow, often considerably, towards the end of a long day's walking. A fit (fast) walker can accomplish up to 35 kilometres in an 8 hour day (4 kph). This drops to 25 km for a more leisurely pace (3 kph). Note that 8 hours daylight would be the maximum in winter. This guide has a daily *average* of 26 km but can (and should) be adjusted to suit individual needs.

Finisterre extension? An additional week will allow time to walk to Finisterre and back to Santiago via Muxía. This waymarked route is still relatively undiscovered and, together with the Camino Portugués, makes one of the most powerful and authentic pilgrim routes available to us today. It is truly 'the path less travelled.' (see *A Pilgrim's Guide to the Camino Finisterre*, Findhorn Press).

When to go? The summer months can be very hot and accommodation, particularly in July and August, in short supply. This problem is aggravated during Holy or Jubilee Years, any year when the feast of St. James (25th July) falls on a Sunday – following the last Holy year in 2010 the next one will not be until 2021. Temperatures as high as 40^C have been recorded in July although the average for the month is 25^C with rainfall of only 20mm. The coast has a moderating influence on temperature but the Atlantic can throw up storms and high winds. Autumn tends to be kinder than spring with an average temperature of 24^C and rainfall of 51mm in September compared to 15^C and 147mm in March.

Full travel (summer) schedules mostly operate from April through September. Outside these months schedules might be more restricted. However, costs are lower and the bulk of tourists have left, so this is a quieter time to travel. Some of the most mystical and transformative trips can be in the depths of winter. There may be fewer flights and ferries and many hotels will be closed, but I have never wanted for a bed to sleep at this time of year. Bring warm waterproof clothes and remember that daylight hours are restricted so that the daily distance that can be covered is reduced.

Travel costs vary widely but national carriers now compete with the budget airlines and the sooner you commit to going the cheaper the ticket but you can sometimes pick up a promotional fare at the last minute. Traffic from the 3 airports at A Corunna, Vigo and Santiago have fallen and a question mark now hangs over whether Galicia can justify 3 airports in such close proximity.

How to get there: In addition to the Portuguese national airline TAP, the following airlines fly into **Lisbon**: BA / EasyJet / bmi baby / Thomsonfly / Aer Lingus / Air France / Ibéria / Vueling / KLM / Lufthansa / Air Berlin / Vueling / Finnair / Egyptair and SATA International: Departure airports in the UK include London, Bristol, Birmingham, Liverpool and Manchester. All major cities throughout Europe are covered in addition to direct flights from Canada and the USA. Recent expansion at **Porto** airport offers a similar spread of opportunities. International rail and bus services into Lisbon and Porto are more limited but there are daily services direct from Paris and Madrid – check with Portuguese rail at *www.cp.pt* with an online booking service in English as does: *www.raileurope. fr/corporate/portugal*. Eurolines, the international arm of National Express has daily services from London to Lisbon via Paris *www.eurolines.com*. Bus and rail within Portugal are efficient and comprehensive

…and back: If you are **returning from Porto or Lisbon** there are 2 daily rail services from Santiago to Porto (Campanha) with frequent onward connections to Lisbon *www.renfe.es*. This is a splendid trip along the Minho river valley and the Portuguese coast that gives a flavour of the Caminho da Costa. You can stop off in

Viana do Castelo and wander the old quarter next to the train station. Alsa **www. alsa.es** have a regular service to Santiago from Porto and Lisbon. Autna **www. autna.com** operate daily direct from Vigo bus station to Porto airport.

•**Air**: •*Ryanair* fly direct to Santiago from London Stansted, Frankfurt, Rome, Madrid, Malaga, Barcelona, Alicante. *Vueling* fly from Paris direct •*Air Berlin* fly from major destinations throughout Europe to Santiago via their hub in La Palma Majorca. •*Aer Lingus* fly Santiago direct from Dublin (summer schedule) and •*BA* and •*Iberia* and other major airlines offer regular services throughout the year via various connecting airports in Spain, mainly Madrid. Check other possibilities from / to nearby airports at La Corunna and Vigo

•**Rail** – you can book online through Spanish rail network RENFE (with an English site) www.renfe.es/horarios/english or Rail Europe at www. raileurope.co.uk/ •**Bus** you can book online with Alsa www.alsa.es (English language option + St. James Way page for route options).

•**Ferry** The advantage of sailing home is that you get a chance to acclimatise slowly – check with Brittany Ferries / Santander - Plymouth 19 hours and Santander - Plymouth 23 hours (twice weekly).

•**Car Hire** If you can find other passengers to share the cost then this is often a relatively cheap and convenient way to travel on to such places as Santander or Bilbao and flying or sailing home from there.

Other Costs: Allow for a basic €25 a day to include €6 euros for overnight stay at a municipal pilgrim hostel (average €10 private) and the remainder for food and drink. Some hostels provide a communal supper on occasions (dependent on the warden *hospitalero*) and most have a basic kitchen *cocina* where a meal can be prepared. Alternatively most locations have one or more restaurants to choose from. If you want to indulge in the wonderful seafood *mariscos* available in Galicia and accompany this with the delightful local *Albariño* wines you can expect to double the basic cost.

Pilgrim hostels *albergues de peregrinos* vary in what they provide but lodging is usually in bunk beds with additional overflow space on mattresses *colchones*. The section from Porto to Santiago has excellent facilities with most hostels offering kitchen and dining / sitting area. The first dedicated pilgrim hostel on the stretch from Lisbon to Porto was opened in 2012 and facilities are improving fast. Opening times vary depending on the time of year but are generally cleaned and open again from early afternoon to welcome pilgrims. You cannot reserve accommodation in advance and phone numbers are provided for emergency calls or to check availability outside the normal seasons (most are open all year but close for holidays or maintenance purposes).

If the hostels are full **alternative accommodation** is generally available in hoteles, moteles, hostales, pensiones *pensãos*, fondas, residenciales or simply camas (literally beds). If locals describe a place as 'bad' *mau/malo* they usually mean it is used as a bordello. In addition Portugal has *quintas* or manor houses converted for tourist accommodation in the luxury bracket (€50 to €90). In Spain a similar standard of accommodation is provided in a type of up-market B&B known as a *casa rural* literally 'rural house' generally built in the traditional Galician style but also relatively expensive (upwards of €40 depending on season). Pilgrim discounts are often available – check before booking).

Bedbugs *chinches* are an increasing source of concern and any accommodation where people sleep in close proximity has added risks. Bedbugs live in mattresses etc. feeding at night, so until the accommodation is treated the problem remains. Carrying a pre-treated pillowcase and bed sheet (e.g. LifeAventure 3X) can be a useful preventative measure. If affected (3 or more bites in a row is a good indication) you need to [1] immediately advise the establishment of the problem and also the next hostel(s) so that they can take preventive measures. [2] wash and/or tumble dry all clothes at highest settings for 2+ hours and [3] Seek medical attention in severe cases (Hydrocortisone). Vinegar is reported to reduce itchiness. Advice is often contradictory so seek help from those who have experience of the problem. The local chemist may be able to help.

Equipment: Light walking boots or shoes are fine for this route. No pack need exceed 10 kilos (22 lbs) in a 55-litre pack. If you are not fluent in Portuguese or Spanish then carry a small phrase book and dictionary. Below is a pilgrim checklist with Spanish and Portuguese translations to help strengthen your vocabulary and assist you to buy or replace items along the way. This is not necessarily a recommended list; this will vary through the seasons. Highlight your essential items and then tick them off as put them into your backpack.

CHECK-LIST:

	Español	*Português*
Clothes:	***Ropas:***	***Roupa:***
hat (sun)	*sombrero*	*chapéu*
sunglasses	*gafas de sol*	*óculos de sol*
shirts [ ]	*camisa*	*camisa*
travel vest	*chaqueta de viaje*	*jaqueta de viagem*
jacket -	*chaqueta -*	*casaco*
… waterproof	*… chubasquero*	*… capa de chuva*
… breathable	*… transpirable*	*… transpirável*
underpants [ ]	*calzoncillos*	*cuecas*
shorts	*pantalones cortos*	*calções / shorts*
trousers	*pantalones largos*	*calças*
handkerchief	*pañuelo*	*lenço*
socks [ ]	*calcetines*	*peúgas*
Shoes:	***Zapatos:***	***Sapatos:***
boots (mountain)	*botas (de montaña)*	*botas (de montanha)*
shoes (walking)	*zapatos (de andar)*	*sapatos (de caminhar)*
sandals (leather)	*sandalias (de piel)*	*sandálias (de couro)*
Size:	***Tamaño:***	***Tamanho:***
larger	*más grande*	*maior*
smaller	*más pequeño*	*menor*
more expensive/cheaper	*más caro / barato*	*mais caro / barato*
model / number	*modelo / número*	*modelo / número*
Essential documents	***Documentos esenciales:***	***Originais essenciais:***
passport	*pasaporte*	*passaporte*
pilgrim record	*credencial de peregrino*	*credencial do peregrino*
wallet/ purse	*monedero / cartera*	*porta-moedas*
cash	*dinero en efectivo*	*dinheiro em efetivo*
credit card	*tarjeta de crédito*	*cartão de crédito*
travel tickets	*pasaje de viaje*	*passagem de viagem*
diary	*diario*	*diário*
emergency addresses	*dirección de emergencia*	*endereço de emergência*
phone numbers	*números de teléfono*	*números de telefone*

Backpack	*Mochila*	*Mochila*
rain cover	*protección de mochila*	*capa para mochila*
sleeping bag	*saco de dormir*	*saco de dormir*
towel	*toalla*	*toalha*
water bottle	*botella de agua*	*garrafa de água*
penknife	*navaja*	*navalha*

Toiletries:	*Artículos de tocador:*	
soap	*jabón*	*sabão*
shampoo	*champú*	*champô*
tooth brush	*cepillo de dientes*	*escova de dentes*
toothpaste	*dentífrico*	*pasta de dentes*
hair brush	*cepillo de pelo*	*escova de cabelo*
comb	*peine*	*pente*
sink stopper / plug	*tapón de fregadero*	*tampa de ralo*
shaving cream	*espuma de afeitar*	*espuma de barbear*
razor (blades)	*cuchilla de afeitar*	*lâminas de barbear*
face cloth	*guante de aseo*	*luva de asseio*
sun cream (lotion)	*crema solar (loción)*	*protector solar*
after sun cream	*leche solar (after sun)*	*loção pós-sol*
moisturiser	*crema hidratante*	*hidratante*
toilet paper	*papel higiénico*	*papel higiênico*
tissues	*pañuelos de papel*	*lenços de papel*
sanitary pads	*salva-slips*	*salva-slips*
tampons	*tampones*	*tampões*

First Aid Kit:	*Botiquín botiquín de primeros auxilios*	*Estojo de primeiro socorros*
painkiller	*analgésico*	*analgésico*
aspirin/ Paracetemol	*aspirina/paracetamol*	*aspirina/paracetamol*
plasters	*esparadrapo*	*penso rápido*
blister pads	*apósito para ampollas*	*penso para bolhas*
compeed-*second skin*	*compeed-segunda piel*	*compeed-band-aid*
antiseptic cream	*crema antiséptica*	*loção anti-séptica*
muscular ache (ointment)	*pomada para dolores musculares*	*pomada para dores musculares*
homeopathic remedies	*remedios homeopáticos*	*remédios homeopáticos*

Medicine (prescription):	*Medicina (prescripción):*	*Medicamentos (receita)*
asthma inhaler	*inhalador para el asma*	*inalador para a asma*
hay fever tablets	*medicina para las alergias*	*remédio para as alergias*
diarrhoea pills	*pastillas para la diarrea*	*pílulas para a diarréia*
other (doctor)	*otros (médico)*	*outros (médico)*

Accessories: (optional)	*Accesorios: (opcional)*	*Acessórios: (opcional)*
monocular	*catalejo*	*luneta*
binocular	*prismáticos*	*binóculos*
camera	*cámara*	*câmara*
torch	*linterna*	*lanterna*
wrist watch	*reloj de pulsera*	*relógio de pulso*
alarm clock	*despertador*	*despertador*
poncho	*poncho*	*poncho*
sleeping mat	*esterilla*	*esteira*
clothes pegs	*pinzas para la ropa*	*molas de roupa*

clothes line (cord)	*cuerda para tender ropa*	*corda para pendurar roupa*
cutlery	*cubiertos*	*talheres*
knife	*cuchillo*	*faca*
fork	*tenedor*	*garfo*
spoon	*cuchara*	*colher*
mug (cup)	*taza / vaso*	*taça / copo*
sandwich box	*fiambrera*	*marmita*

Books: *(limited)*	***Libros: (cupo limitado)***	***Livros: (limitada)***
spiritual texts	*textos espirituales*	*textos espirituais*
inspirational quotations	*citas inspiradoras*	*citações inspiradoras*
poetry	*poesía*	*poesia*
phrase book -	*libro de frases*	*livro de frases*
... (Spanish)	*... (Español)*	*... (Espanhol)*
... (Portuguese)	*... (Portugués)*	*... (Português)*

Credentials *credenciales* **& Certificate of Completion** *compostela*: In order to stay at official pilgrim hostels you need to have a pilgrim passport *credencial* impressed with a rubber stamp (in Spanish: *sello* Portuguese: *carimbo)* at hostels, churches, town halls etc. along the way (2 stamps per day within Galicia). On the Spanish section of the Camino Portugués this is generally done in the official pilgrim hostels *albergues* that are reserved exclusively for pilgrims to Santiago (or Fátima if you are doing the route in reverse). This *credencial* must be presented at the pilgrim office in Santiago in order to receive a Compostela and as proof that you have walked at least the last 100 kilometres (200 if cycling). Those who do not accept a spiritual motivation as part of their reason for making the pilgrimage can obtain a ***certificado*** which is essentially a certificate of completion.

You can obtain one of these 'passports' before travelling from the Confraternity of St. James in London or possibly from a local confraternity in your country of origin (see under *useful addresses).* If all else fails, space has been provided for this purpose at the back of this guide, or you can make up your own. However, there is no guarantee these will be accepted and, in any case, you should make every effort to join and support the work of the confraternities. An official *credencial* can also be obtained from Lisbon, Tui or Porto cathedrals and at the Church of the Martyrs or St. James in Lisbon. Also in several albergues. (see Lisbon city plan p.32).

Take a few moments to familiarise yourself with the symbols used on the maps in this guide (see opposite). Note that in addition to the *actual* distance an *adjusted* distance is also provided based on the cumulative height climbed during each stage. Average pace (1 km in 20 minutes or 3 kph) depends on many factors. End of day pace will produce the biggest variations and you will find your pace slowing considerably and you should allow half the normal pace (double the time) in calculating whether to continue. If you want to follow the *the road less travelled* such as natural pathways and farm tracks then use the 'green' routes when possible.

Decide where to stop according to your individual level of fitness. The maps in this guide are designed for an 'average' pace and based on what fits neatly on one page. Alternatives are limitless by using interim accommodation. e.g.
from **LISBON: Cathedral – Moscavide Youth Hostel 10.0** *km.* **Or take the train to Sacavém and walk to Vilafranca de Xira 26.6 km...**
from **PORTO: Cathedral – Moreira Maia 14.6 km or take the metro to Vilar do Pinheiro and walk to Vilarinho 9.6 km or Rates 21.0 km...**

Map Legend: Symbols used in this guide:

Total km — Total distance for stage map

Adjusted for climb (100m vertical = additional 0.5km)

(850m) **Alto ▲** — Contours / High point of each stage

< 🏠 🏠 > — Intermediate accommodation (*often less busy / quieter*)

◄ 3.5 — Precise distance between points (3.5 km = ± 1 hour)

→ 50m > / ^ / < — Interim distances •50m turn right> / s/o=straight on^ / <left c.=circa (about) / adj.=adjacent / incl.=including

Natural path / forest track or gravel *senda*

Secondary road (*grey*: asphalt) / Roundabout *rotonda*

Main road [N-] *Nacional* (*red*: additional traffic and hazard)

Motorway *autopista* (*blue*: conventional motorway colour)

Railway *ferrocarril* / Station *estación*

Primary Path of pilgrimage; the inner path of Soul

Main physical route (*yellow*: ± 80% of pilgrims)

Alternative Scenic route (*green*: more remote / less pilgrims)

Optional detour *desvío* (*turquoise*)

Alternative road route (*grey*: more asphalt & traffic)

X ? ! — Crossing *cruce* / Option *opción* / Extra care *¡cuidado!*

Windmill / Viewpoint *punto de vista* / Radio mast

National boundary / Provincial boundary *límite provincial*

River *río* / Stream *arroyo*

Sea or lake *Mar o lago* / Woodland *bosques*

Church *iglesia* / Chapel *capilla* / Wayside cross *cruceiro*

Drinking font *fuente* / Café / Shop *minimercado*

menú *V.* — *menú peregrino* 3 course meal + wine / *V. Vegetariano*

Tourist office *turismo* / Manor house *casa señorial* / Picnic

Pharmacy *farmacia* / Hospital / Post office *correos*

Airport / Bus station *estación de autobús* / *gasolinera*

XII — Ancient monument / 12th century

Pilgrim hostel(s) *Albergue Alb.* / Youth hostel *Juventude*

Hotels *H-H****€30-90 / Pension *Q*€20+ / *CR (B&B)* €35+

B.V. — Quinta *Q* €50-90 / Firestation *B.V. Bombeiros* €5-10

(off route accommodation alojamiento fuera de ruta)

[32] — Number of bed spaces (usually bunk beds *literas*)

[÷4]+ — ÷ number of rooms / + additional private rooms €20+

Par. — Parish hostel *Parroquial* donation / €5

Conv. — Convent or monastery hostel *donativo* / €5

Muni. — Municipal hostel €5+

Xunta — Galician government *Xunta* hostel €6

Asoc. — Association hostel €7+

Priv. (*) — Private hostel (network*) €10-15

Average prices (low season) for comparison purposes only
Rest.=Restaurante / Hs.=Hostal / Hr.=Hotel Residencial

Town plan *plan de la ciudad* with page number

(Pop.–Alt. m) — Town population and altitude in metres

City suburbs *suburbios de la ciudad* (*grey*)

Historical centre *centro histórico* (*brown*)

Waymarks: Thanks to the efforts of the various pilgrim associations waymarking is comprehensive and should you lose your way it is more than likely you allowed your thoughts to wander and you lost your focus in the present moment. Consider re-tracing your steps until you pick up the waymarks again. On this route there are relatively few other pilgrims to follow but ideally you will have sufficient *português* and *castellano* (perhaps even some *galego*) to be able to converse with the rural community and understand simple directions etc. Where alternative routes are available your choice is aided by the colour coding in the guidebook (on the ground they will all have the familiar yellow arrow pointing to Santiago). The quieter natural pathways are coloured green I have recommended 'the path less travelled'. My criterion is always to minimise the amount of time spent on asphalt. Finding your way is complicated by the fact that, within Portugal, most people will assume you are heading to Fátima and the route is often waymarked in two directions – to Santiago always with a yellow arrow and to Fátima always with a blue arrow.

A **Sun Compass** is provided on each map as an aid to orientation. Even in poor weather we can generally tell the position of the sun. The route through Portugal is primarily in a northerly direction so the sun will rise to your right in the morning. At midday it will be behind you and by afternoon will appear over your left shoulder.

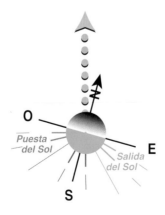

SOUL MAPS AND INNER WAYMARKS

Preparation for the inner journey: *Why am I doing this?*

Take time to prepare a purpose for this pilgrimage. Start from the basis that you are essentially a spiritual being on a human journey, not a human being on a spiritual one. We came here to learn some lesson and this may be your opportunity to find out what it is. While life maybe the classroom, pilgrimage is one way to master the curriculum. It will never be mastered by walking the physical path on its own. You will need help, so ask for it – all the help you need is here, now, awaiting but your asking. We all have a different *Way* and what is right for one may be incomprehensible to another so don't feel pressurised to follow any particular path or opinion. You will know when something rings true for you – trust your resonance. A few suggestions are listed in the bibliography.

When we go on pilgrimage we bring along our individual personality and our physical, mental, emotional and etheric bodies. We may feel a need for healing in one or all of these areas. The impetus to 'take up our bed and walk' is deeply embedded in the human psyche and soul. We do well to remember that the healing power of Love is a two-way flow. We both give and receive healing on the journey. Peter Dawkins of the Gatekeeper Trust, writing in *A Pilgrim's Handbook,* informs us:

> 'As the pilgrim moves through the landscape he or she follows certain paths. These paths become energised beyond the norm by the movement of the loving pilgrim. When Europe was given its name, taken from the myth of Europa and the Bull, it conveyed an important truth about the layout of Europe's inner landscape as a functioning pattern of energy and consciousness... There are many ancient pilgrimage routes which spread out across mainland Europe, all leading to Santiago de Compostela in northern Spain, as if all the energy within Europe is drawn up to the crown and then focused in Santiago.'

This image is mirrored in the camino as the central star route in Europe. In *Paths of the Christian Mysteries, From Compostela to the New World* Virginia Sease and Manfred Schmidt-Brabant write:

> 'Those who travelled along the star route as far as Cape Finisterre had the experience: Here is the end of the sensory world, the abyss! And If I am able to comprehend it, the spiritual world approaches me from the other side. ... Compostela was a final, decisive juncture on an inner spiritual path that was simultaneously a path of nature initiation. ...Rudolf Steiner stated that people have a need to live not only with external history but also with the esoteric, hidden narrative which lies behind it: the history of "the Mysteries."'

These energy lines were well understood in earlier times and it is no coincidence that the Knights Templar set their Portuguese headquarters in Tomar. The power of the location was enhanced by the careful layout of the town and the orientation of its buildings in accordance with geomantic lore. This ancient knowledge would have been well known by St. James and his disciples and it will have been no accident of fate that they chose to enter Europe at its crown – sailing past the Towers of the West *Torres de Oeste* at Catoira to fetch land at Padrón. It is no wonder that the Camino Portugués remains such a powerful route today, its mystical allure still intact and aiding its rediscovery.

The middle path: In *A Course in Miracles* it is written: 'there is a way of living in the world that is not here, although it seems to be. You do not change appearance, though you smile more frequently. To let illusions walk ahead of truth is madness. Many have chosen to renounce the world while still believing its reality. And they have suffered from a sense of loss, and have not been released accordingly. Others have chosen nothing but the world, and they have suffered from a sense of loss still deeper. Between these paths there is another road that leads away from loss of every kind… for this road leads past illusion now. All roads will lead to this one in the end. For sacrifice and deprivation are paths that lead nowhere. Their suffering is but illusion. Yet they need a guide to lead them out of it, for they mistake illusion for the truth. Such is salvation's call. It asks that you accept the truth, and let it go before you, lighting up the path. Walk safely now, yet carefully, because this path is new to you. And you may find that you are tempted still to walk ahead of truth, and let illusions be your guide.

Step back in faith and let truth lead the way. You know not where you go. But One Who knows goes with you. Let Him lead you with the rest. This is our final journey, which we make for everyone. We walk to God. Pause and reflect on this. Could any way be holier, or more deserving of your effort, of your love and of your full intent? Look not to ways that seem to lead you elsewhere.' A.C.I.M. Workbook; lesson 155.

So let us feed the path with our loving intent and make every step a prayer for peace and reconciliation.

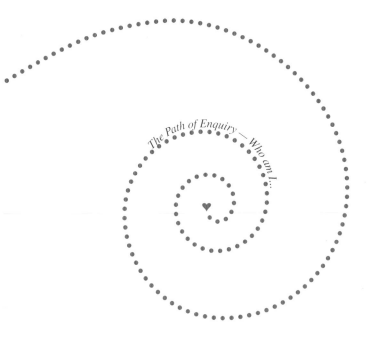

The Path of Enquiry – Who am I…

SELF-ASSESSMENT *INNER WAYMARKS*

This self-assessment questionnaire is designed to encourage you to reflect on your life and its direction. View it as a snapshot of this moment in the ongoing journey of your life. In the busyness that surrounds us we often fail to take stock of where we are headed and our changing roles in the unfolding drama of our life story.

You might find it useful to initially answer these questions in quick succession as this may allow a more intuitive response. Afterwards, you can reflect more deeply and check if your intellectual answers confirm these, change them or bring in other insights. You can download copies of this questionnaire from the *Camino Guides* website – make some extra copies so you can repeat the exercise on your return and again in (say) 3 months time. This way you can compare results and ensure you continue to follow through on any insights that came to you while walking the camino.

❐ How do you differentiate pilgrimage from a long distance walk?
❐ How do you define spirituality – what does it mean to you?
❐ How is your spirituality expressed at home and at work?

❐ What do you see as the primary purpose of your life?
❐ Are you working consciously towards fulfilling that purpose?
❐ How clear are you on your goal and the right direction for you at this time?
❐ How will you recognise resistance to any changes that might be necessary?

❐ When did you first become aware of a desire to take time-out?
❐ What prompted you originally to go on the camino?
❐ Did the prompt come from something that you felt needed changing?
❐ Make a list of what appears to be blocking any change from happening.

❐ What help might you need on a practical, emotional and spiritual level?
❐ How will you recognise the right help or correct answer?
❐ What are the joys and challenges in working towards your unique potential?
❐ What are your next steps towards fulfilling that potential?

How aware are you of the following? Score yourself on a level of 1 – 10 and compare these scores again on your return from the camino.

❐ Awareness of your inner spiritual world.
❐ Clarity on what inspires you and the capacity to live your passion.
❐ Confidence to follow your intuitive sense of the right direction.
❐ Ability to recognise your resistance and patterns of defence.
❐ Ease with asking for and receiving support from others.

OVERVIEW:
        The camino Portugués: is fully waymarked from Lisbon to Santiago. The first 3 stages, as far as Santarém, coincide with the *caminho da Fátima (caminho de Tejo)*. Accordingly this section has many pilgrims. In Santarém the routes separate with the historic Camino de Santiago veering off to the northeast through the Templar town of Tomar and on to Porto and pilgrims become fewer and far between. Facilities along this section have improved in recent years and is now ready to be enjoyed by fit and seasoned pilgrims able to converse in basic Portuguese. The section from Porto to Santiago continues to welcome pilgrims of all abilities. Within Portugal some Fire Brigades *Bomberios Volunatários* may provide basic lodging to pilgrims (bed or floor) and Youth Hostels *Juventude* accept pilgrims with a *credencial*. Telephone prefix for Portugal is +351 and numbers starting with 9 are mobiles. Museums etc generally closed on Monday.
        Lisbon is a wonderful city with an interesting mix of old and new. One of the smallest capital cities in the European Union it is relatively easy to navigate and full of vitality and a sense of pride in its long and fascinating history. Originally known as Olisipo it was a major administrative centre and trading post for the Romans before the Visigoths took over; eventually succumbing to 4 centuries of Arab rule when Afonso Henriques ousted them in 1147. In the 15th century it became the main base for the 'Discoveries' and many of the greatest explorers in history such as Columbus, Cabral, Magellan and Vasco da Gama set sail from here and established Lisbon as one of the great trading capitals of the world. Inevitably, an economy based on colonial spoils (rather than production) began to wane and the financial plight of Portugal took a lurch for the worse at precisely 9:40 a.m on November 1st 1755 when one of the most destructive earthquakes ever recorded hit the city. The Great Lisbon Earthquake and ensuing tsunami destroyed 90% of its finest buildings and killed a quarter of its population. The Marquis of Pombal emerged as the hero of the day and set about reconstruction in the form of the wide boulevards and squares that we see today. The tower of Belém and the adjoining Manueline-style Jerónimos monastery are 2 of the outstanding historic buildings that remain.
        Tourist Offices: ▲ **Airport Arrivals** ℭ 218 450 660 (07:00–24:00). The airport is close to the city centre (20 minutes or 10 minutes to Oriente). Buses leave every 15 minutes. ▲ **Santa Apolónia rail station** ℭ 218 821 606 (08.00-13.00) it's a short walk or taxi ride to the 'lower' area along the river Tagus *rio Tejo* known simply as *Baixa* and forming the heart of the modernized city. On the main square adjoining the river ▲ **Centro Turismo de Lisboa / *Welcome Center*** ℭ 210 312 810 (09.00-20.00) on Praça do Comércio with the *Arco da Rua Augusta* also ▲ **Tourist Kiosk** in Rua Augusta (10:00–18:00 summer).
        Spread out along the grid of streets between *Praça do Comércio* and *Praça Dom Pedro IV* is the main shopping district **Rossio** with its numerous cafés and restaurants spilling out onto the pavements. This is also where you will find many of the city's smaller *pensões* (rooms are often located on the top floor!). The austere building at the far end is the national theatre *Teatro Nacional de Dona Maria* and formerly the site of the Court of the Inquisition in front of which the hanging of heretics and ritual burning of many of Portugal's wise women took place. Just around the corner is the striking neo-Manueline (1886) façade of the old Rossio station and at the bottom end of Avenida da Liberdade is Palacío Foz now the Portuguese *(as opposed to city)* ▲ **Tourist Board** ℭ 213 463 314. And overlooking all this history and activity (to the south) is the *Bairro Alto* which you can access via various antiquated elevators *Elevador San Justa, da Bica* and *da Glória*. This area includes the chic *Chiado* district with its elegant shops and cafés including the famous *A Brasileira*, haunt of many of Lisbon's literary figures (past and present) and the *Basilica dos Mártires* (issues credenciales).

To the north of the city we find the atmospheric *Alfama* quarter that rises to the *Castelo de São Jorge* (photo bottom) passing Lisbon's old cathedral and the church of Santiago *Igreja de S. Tiago* occupying an elevated position above the cathedral on rua Santiago that leads to the castle. The church has a fine statue of Santiago Peregrino (but your only likely sighting will be the photo here as the church is usually closed).

The cathedral *Sé Patriarcal de Lisboa* an austere castellated structure restored after the earthquake (although this Alfama quarter was the least affected part of the city). The original foundations of the cathedral were laid in 1147 just after the town was captured from the Moors and, in a final flourish of triumph, built on the site of the former mosque. Ongoing archeological excavations in the cloister area *claustro* have unearthed structures dating from 4th century B.C.E. The cathedral is open from 09:00 to 19:00 (17:00 Sunday, Monday and holidays). Entrance to the Cathedral is free / €2.50 for the claustro. Pilgrim credencial and stamp available at reception kiosk.

Tram # 28 rattles past the main historic sites including the cathedral and Miradouro S. Luzia directly opposite the Church of Santiago and adjoining a café and public viewing terrace with unrivalled views across the rio Tejo estuary. (see photo right).

The Alfama area also claims one of the best-known fado houses in Lisbon *Parreirinha d'Alfama* adjacent to Largo do Chafariz de Dentro. This mournful music quivers to the Portuguese guitar and the soloist *fadista* sings of the pining for *things that are no more, or will never be* – this is the core of fado with a secondary theme being the pathos of the emigrant and nostalgia for life in general *saudade*. Avoid the tackier tourist venues that are generally overrated and overcharge. The museum *Museu do Fado* in Largo do Chafariz is worth a visit. Open Tues-Sun 10.00-18.00 €5. The camino passes through this area with the first waymark starting at the cathedral entrance.

❏ **Hostales / Pousada de Juventude (YHA)**: Several youth and other hostels from €15-25 in bunk beds - nearest the cathedral: ❶ Amazing Hostels ℂ 218 880 054 Beco do Arco Escuro,6. ❷ Home Lisbon R. de S. Nicolau, 13 ℂ 218 885 312. ❸ Goodnight R. dos Correiros, 113 ℂ 213 430 139. ❹ Yes R. de S. Julião, 148 ℂ 213 427 171. ❺ This is Lisbon Rua Costa do Castelo, 63 ℂ 218 014 549 ❻ Alfama Pátio Hostel Rua das Escolas Gerais, 3. ℂ218 883 127. ❼ Moscavide Parque das Nações (see stage 1 for details). ● Pousada de Juventude de Lisboa city hostel rua Andrade Corvo, 46 ℂ 213 532 696 located in the Saldanha district (top end of Av. Liberdade, East of Parque Eduardo VII). ❏ **Hoteles / Pensões:** *Alfama district* (nearest the cathedral) includes: Pensão São João de Praça €30-45 incl. ℂ 218 862 591 town house adj. the cathedral on rua São João de Praça, 97. *Rossio and Baixa districts* (lower city centre) have a profusion of hotels, pensions and 'rooms'. Above Rossio in Chiado is good value *H****Borges €50+ ℂ 213 461 951 rua Garrett 108 opp. *Basilica dos Mártires* and café *A Brasileira.*

❏ **Pilgrim passports** ✪ *credenciales*: *Via Luistana* ℂ 915 595 213. ✪ *APAAS* Amigos de Apóstolo Santiago ℂ 966 426 851. ✪ *Basílica dos Mártires* Rua Serpa Pinto ℂ 213 462 465 (10:00-17:00). ✪ *Cathedral Sé* (09:30-18:30).

❏ **Historic Buildings and Monuments:** Much of the historic fabric of the city was lost in the 1755 earthquake. Saved were 2 outstanding examples of Manueline architecture: ❶ *Mosteiro dos Jerónimos XVI* Praça do Império (10:00-17:30). Work started in 1502 capturing this illustrious period in Portuguese history. At the entrance is a statue to Henry the Navigator and the interior houses the tombs of Vasco da Gama (below) and the 'Discoveries' poet Luís de Camões. Nearby is the *Torre de Belém XVI* built as part of Lisbon's port defences. Also In this area is the Monument to the Discoveries *Monumento dos Descobrimentos* built to celebrate the 500th anniversary of Henry the Navigator (trams # E15/ E18). ❷ *Basilica dos Mártires* with chapel dedicated to St. James. ❸ **Cathedral** *Sé XII* (# 28E) (09:30-18:30) work commencing in 1150 on Roman foundations to replace the former mosque. 400m above the cathedral ❹ *Igreja de Santiago* rua de Santiago ❺ *Castelo São Jorge XI* (9:00-21:00) Rua de Santa Cruz do Castelo.

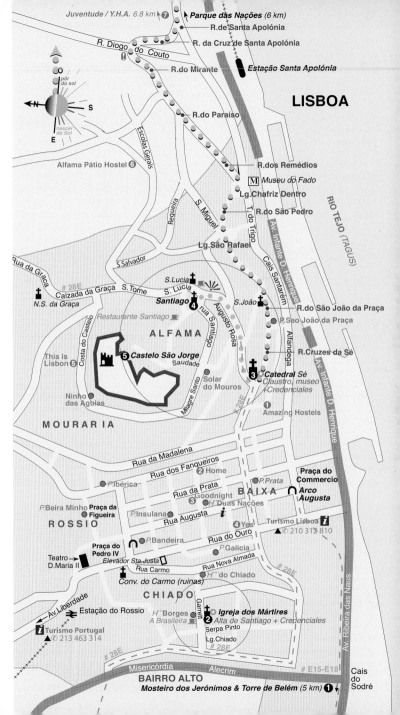

Juventude / Y.H.A. 6.8 km ⑦ **Parque das Nações (6 km)**
R.de Santa Apolónia
R. Diogo do Couto
R. da Cruz de Santa Apolónia
R.do Mirante
Estação Santa Apolónia

LISBOA

R.do Paraíso

Escolas Gerais
Alfama Pátio Hostel ⑥
R.dos Remédios
Ⓜ **Museu do Fado**
Lg.Chafriz Dentro
S. Miguel
Requeira
T. do Trigo
R.do São Pedro
Av. Infante D. Henrique
Lg.São Rafael
Cais Santarém
S.Salvador
Rua da Graça
28E
S.Tomé
Calzada da Graça
S. Lucia
✝ S.Lucia
N.S. da Graça ✝
Santiago ④
rua Santiago
Augusto Rosa
S.João
R.do São João da Praça
P.Sao João da Praça
Restaurante Santiago
ALFAMA
Alfandega
R.Cruzes da Sé
This is ⑤ **Castelo São Jorge**
Lisbon ⑤
Costa do Castelo
Saudade
✝ ③ **Catedral Sé**
Claustro, museo
+Credenciales
Ninho das Aguias
Miragre Santo
Solar do Mouros
28E
① **Amazing Hostels**

MOURARIA

RIO TEJO (TAGUS)

Av. Infante D. Henrique

Rua da Madalena
Rua dos Fanqueiros ② Home
Praça do Commercio
● P.Ibérica
Rua da Prata
BAIXA
③ Goodnight
P.Prata
Arco Augusta
P.Beira Minho **Praça da Figueira**
P.Insulana
H Duas Nações
ROSSIO
Rua Augusta
ⓘ ④ Yes
Turismo Lisboa ⓘ
© 210 312 810
Praça do Pedro IV
P.Bandeira
Rua do Ouro
P.Galicia
Teatro D.Maria II
Elevador Sta.Justa
Rua Nova Almada
28E
Rua Carmo
H do Chiado
✝ *Conv. do Carmo (ruinas)*

CHIADO
Garrett
H Borges
A Brasileira ✝ ② **Igreja dos Mártires**
Turismo Portugal
ⓘ © 213 463 314
Alta de Santiago + Credenciales
Serpa Pinto
Lg.Chiado
28E
Misericórdia
Alecrim
E15-E18
Cais do Sodré
BAIRRO ALTO
Mosteiro dos Jerónimos & Torre de Belém (5 km) ① ↓
Av. Ribeira das Naus

34

❏ **Injustice anywhere, is a threat to justice everywhere.** *Martin Luther King*

01 *614.1 km (381.6 miles) – Santiago*

LISBOA – ALVERCA (Verdelha)

			15.1	--- ---	51%
			4.1	--- ---	14%
			10.3	--- ---	35%
Total km			**29.5** km (18.3 ml)		

29.8 km (+^60 m=0.3 km)
Alto ▲ Alpriarte 50 m (164 ft)
< Ⓐ Ⓗ > Moscavide **9.2** km (+ 800m)
●━┅┅ Oriente / Sacavém / Póvoa

❏ **The Practical Path:** Traversing a city usually presents a challenge. However, navigating your way out of Lisbon is relatively easy as we head down to the mighty estuary of the river Tagus *Rio Tejo* at the Expo'98 Maritime Park *Parque das Nações*. Then we follow the river to its confluence with the modest rio Trancão which we follow inland – leaving it to take a tranquil path up a green valley to the high point of today's stage at a mere 50 m. It's then a gentle descent before entering the busy environs of Povoa de Santa Iria. Here we cross the rail line into an industrial estate to re-emerge just before reaching Alverca do Ribatejo where a short detour brings us to Verdelha de Baixo with a range of accommodation. Amazingly for a city route we find that half is on pathways with the waymarked route now avoiding most of the dangerous N-10.

❏ **The Mystical Path:** The wealth of Portugal was carved out of its colonial past and its seaports were a gateway for the lucrative slave trade from Africa to the Americas. Our affluent Western lifestyle has created enormous injustices in wealth distribution. Chesterton wrote, "There are two ways to get enough; one is to continue to accumulate more and more. The other is to desire less."

❏ **Personal Reflections:** I nearly upset her begging bowl as I stepped over her outstretched legs sprawled across the entrance. I was irritated at her pleading voice and avoided her eyes... inside the church was like a refuge but also a re-minder of my privilege and responsibilities. I sat by the chapel dedicated to St. James and vowed to give a tithe of my en route expenses to those in need. As I left she was no longer to be seen, but other opportunities will arise...

0.0 km Lisboa Cathedral *Sé* The first waymark appears right of the cathedral steps then down into rua São João da Praça, Largo de São Rafael, rua de São Pedro into Largo de Chafariz (Museu do Fado 0.5 km) and ***Option: Estação de Santa Ápolónia*** *with option to take the frequent commuter trains to intermediate stations along the route (see map).* ***Oriente*** *avoids the hard city pavements and starts the camino in the riverside* ***Parque das Nações*** *with 30.4 km to wide range of accommodation in Vila Franca de Xira.* ***Sacavém*** *would reduce this first stage to an easier 26.6 km. The next station directly en route is Santa Iria...*

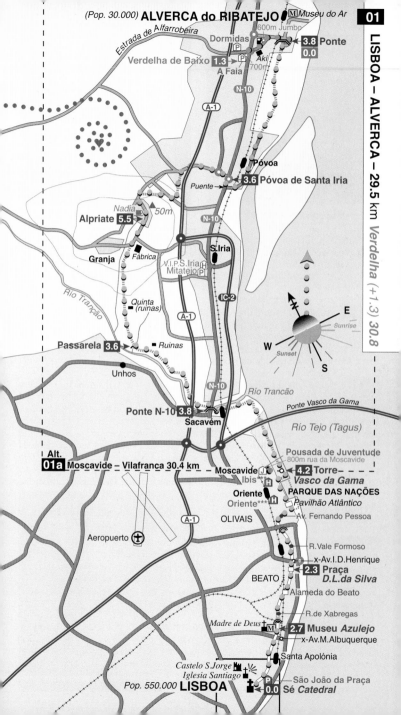

(Pop. 30.000) **ALVERCA do RIBATEJO** M *Museu do Ar*

Estrada de Alfarrobeira

600m Jumbo

Dormidas

P **3.8 Ponte**
0.0

Verdelha de Baixo 1.3 → P *Aki*
A Faia 700m

N-10

A-1

Póvoa

Puente → **3.6 Póvoa de Santa Iria**

Nadia ▲ *50m*

Alpriate 5.5

N-10

S.Iria

Granja ■ *Fábrica*

V.I.P.S.Iria H
Mitatejo P

IC-2

Río Trancão

Quinta (ruinas)

A-1

Passarela 3.6 → ■ *Ruinas*

Unhos

N-10

Río Trancão

Ponte Vasco da Gama

Ponte N-10 3.8 →
Sacavém

Río Tejo (Tagus)

W ← → E
Sunset *Sunrise*
S

Pousada de Juventude
800m rua da Moscavide

Alt.
01a Moscavide – Vilafranca 30.4 km — **Moscavide** J ○ **4.2 Torre**
Ibis **ii** *Vasco da Gama*
PARQUE DAS NAÇÕES
Oriente H
Oriente*** H *Pavilhão Atlântico*

A-1 Av. Fernando Pessoa

OLIVAIS

Aeropuerto ✈

R.Vale Formoso
x-Av.I.D.Henrique
2.3 Praça
D.L.da Silva

BEATO
■ Alameda do Beato

R.de Xabregas
Madre de Deus M **2.7 Museu** *Azulejo*
x-Av.M.Albuquerque

■ Santa Apolónia

Castelo S.Jorge
Iglesia Santiago
Pop. 550.000 **LISBOA** — São João da Praça
0.0 Sé *Catedral*

Museu Nacional do Azulejo

View over the Rio Tejo

For those with the intention to walk the entire route we continue up into rua dos Remédios and s/o via ruas Paraíso, Mirante and cross s/o *over* [!] rua Diogo Couto veering sharp right into rua da Cruz Santa Apolónia, down rua Santa Apolónia up and over Av. Mouzinho de Albuquerque into Calçada da Cruz da Pedra into rua da Madre de Deus to:

2.7 km **Museu Nacional do Azulejo** here we find the splendid museum of Portuguese tiles with delightful courtyard *cafe* and baroque church all housed within a former Manueline convent *Convento da Madre Deus* s/o under rail line into ruas de Xabregas, Grilo and Beato passing the Beato fire station *Bombeiros* and Convento and Alameda do Beato into:

2.3 km **Praça David Leandro da Silva** with public w.c.'s, taxi rank and striking façades of A P da Fonseca & Poço do Bispo. We now cross the wide ring road Av. Infante Dom Henrique into the narrow rua Vale Formoso de Baixo (antigo teatro left) through the underpass (rail line left) and turn right to crossroads and left into Av. Fernando Pessoa down to the roundabout and Expo site and *Parque das Nações*. Our destination is the tower (see photo) reached via Alameda dos Oceanos and Pavilhão de Portugal *or* make your way directly to the Tejo estuary via Jardins da Água (blue waterfall) and Passeio de Ulisses (the start of our own Odyssey). This leads to the seafront past the Oceanário (one of the largest aquariums in the world) and cable car *Teleférico* and along boardwalks over the estuary to Lisbon's emblematic tower:

4.2 km **Torre Vasco da Gama** A variety of bars, restaurants, hotels spill out onto the pavements all developed as part of Expo '98. ❏ *H****IBIS €60 ℂ 210 730 470 Rua do Mar Vermelho. **VIP Arts** €70 ℂ 210 020 400 Av. Dom João II. *H*******TRYP Oriente** €80 ℂ 218 930 000 Av. Dom João II.

Moscavide Detour ● ● ● ● [+0.8km]: Pousada de Juventude €14-20 pilgrim discount ℂ 218 920 890 Rua de Moscavide Lt 47-101. Via Av. da Boa Esperança and Alameda dos Oceanos into rua de Moscavide. We now join the pedestrian walkways

Ponte Vasco Gama — Statue of Catherine of Braganza *(Consort to Charles II)*

through the linear park along the banks of the rio Tejo. Amongst the various sculptures is a handsome bronze statue of Catarina de Bragança who left Lisboa in 1662 to marry Charles II. Her dowry included Bombay and tea! (She and her court introduced tea and 'tea time' to England). Continue under the magnificent 17 km-long Ponte Vasco da Gama bridge following the Tejo until it meets a small tributary **Foz del rio Trancão**. This is a good place to rest and view the route north up along the Tejo. There are bench seats and shade and the first concrete bollard marking the Caminho de Fátima (blue arrows to Fátima, yellow to Santiago (see photo previous page). We now follow the modest Trancão inland passing under the ring road (IC-2) and rail line at Sacavém. Shortly afterwards we pass restaurant *O Siphão* to meet up with the old N-10 (*café / bars* in the vicinity).

3.8 km **N-10 Ponte Sacavém** turn right over the bridge and immediately left over the N-10 [!] onto path out under the A-1 viaduct and along a raised bank by the river passing ruins (right) before leaving the rio Trancão over a small stream.

3.6 km **Pasarela** footbridge aross small stream and take the wide farm track up along a green valley where time seems to have stopped (except for the aircraft from Lisbon airport). Various Quintas lie abandoned in ruins and lead us to the high point of today at 50m. An enterprising family are slowly bringing life back to the Quinta del Brasileiro *[opposite which is as a small bridge leading to **Granja** a short (200m) detour ● ● ● ● to village with café and restaurant]*. Continue s/o past factories (right) and continue s/o at the roundabout to the small village of:

5.5 km **Alpriarte** *[F.]* with welcoming *bar restaurante* operated by the helpful Nadia (50 m off route left). Rejoin a path through fields over asphalt road and continue on path alongside A-1 to cross back *under* motorway and down past the Olival Parque roundabout and down again to the 2nd roundabout on the N-10:

3.6 km **N-10 Póvoa de Santa Iria** busy dormitory town. Waymarks here can be confusing as we turn *back* [!] towards Lisbon along the N-10 for 200m *[H***Vip Santa Iria €40 © 210 032 300 + 1.8 km on N-10 + Hs Miratejo €30 © 219 591 216 (EN 10 - Galp)]* cross over the railway and <left through industrial park onto a path at the far end that winds its way through rough vegetation up to the next road bridge back <left over the railway line.

3.8 km **Ponte Option:** Road bridge on the outskirts of Alverca do Ribatejo. Proceed s/o to the railway station and next stage *or* take the detour to:

Detour *off* **route:** ● ● ● ● Note that currently (2015) there is no accommodation en route in Alverca itself (an albergue is planned). To stay the night in the area you need to leave the waymarked route at this point and make your way towards the **N-10** and turn <left at the petrol station **Jumbo [400m]** and continue past the major **AKÍ** store to the 2nd roundabout and cross over [!] to the start of Estrada de Alfarrobeira in.

1.3 km Verdelha de Baixo *(Total distance from Lisboa cathedral – 31.1 km).* Here at a major intersection of roads we find a variety of rooms and restaurants serving the workers from the adjacent industrial parks (busy during week days). They provide an inexpensive opportunity to find a bed for the night. Best bet is to try the first one on the corner: **Restaurante A Faia** *Dormidas* €20-30 ℭ 219 574 103 and then work your way up the road to **Alojamentos Particulares** €16-26 Estrada de Alfarrobeira Nº 10 ℭ 219 580 475 and at Nº 17 **Restaurante A Lanterna** *Dormidas* €15-30 ℭ 219 576 488. Several other private houses along Estrada de Alfarrobeira may offer rooms.

A Faia – Quartos

Alojamentos Particulares

Other (temporary) alternatives in Alverca do Ribatejo as follows: *Alb.* **Fundação CEBI** €5 ℭ 219 589 130 (phone in advance) rua Eduarda Maria Segura de Faria (+ 0.8 km *off* route. Directions: from rail station continue up Av. Infante Dom Pedro and cross over N-10 and turn left by park past Lidl). Also **Vivenda Lurdes** €-donativo ℭ 938 604 347 Estrada da Arruda 31-33 (+ 1.5 km *off* route) on the eastern suburbs of Arcena on the far side of the N-10. (see next stage for approximate location). Phone Dª Lurdes Inácio to check availability and for directions (Portuguese only spoken). This is a termporary solution pending the building of a pilgrim albergue en route.

If you don't wish to detour for accommodation you can take the rail to *Moscavide* then join the waymarked route to *Vila Franca de Xira* (see page 43 for list of hotels) a total distance of 31.2 km (instead of 31.1 km as described above) or commence in *Sacavém* or any of the frequent interim rail stations along the route.

REFLECTIONS:

_____
_____
_____
_____
_____
_____
_____
_____
_____
_____
_____
_____
_____
_____
_____
_____
_____
_____
_____
_____

Santiago Peregrino – rose window Lisbon cathedral.

❏ **It is more blessed to give than to receive** – *Acts 20:35*

02 *584.6 km (363.3 miles) – Santiago*

ALVERCA (Verdelha) – AZAMBUJA

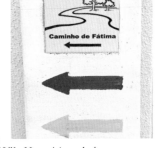

⦙⦙⦙⦙⦙⦙⦙⦙⦙	--- ---	8.3	--- --- 29%
▬▬▬▬	--- ---	12.6	--- --- 44%
▬▬▬▬	--- ---	<u>7.7</u>	--- --- 27%
Total km		**28.6** km (17.8 ml)	

▲ --- --- 28.9 km (+^ 50 m = 0.3 km)
Alto ▲ Vila Nova da Rainha 30 m (98 ft)
< 🅐 🏠 > Alhandra **6.2** km – V.F Xira **10.1** km
━● ···· Alhandra / Castanheira / Carregado / Vila Nova / Azambuja

```
100m -------------------------------------------------------
ALVERCA      V.N. de Xira🏠         V.N. da Rainha ▲30m   AZAMBUJA
   Río Tejo          Río Tejo
0 km      5 km      10 km   15 km      20 km      25 km      30
```

❏ **Practical Path:** A level day's walk much of it parallel to the busy N-10 that we have to join at several stages so the majority of our journey is on asphalt much of it through built-up industrial areas and 27% along the N-10. Alternatives are constantly under review but the grassland fronting the estuary has deep dykes that prevent passage of pilgrims and the wild bulls that graze the area awaiting the bullfight! However, a lovely interim 8 km stretch has recently been opened allowing safe passage between Alhandra and Castanheira. Note the first 3 days out of Lisbon (as far as Santarém) coincides with the route to Fátima known as the *Caminho do Tejo* (blue arrows to Fátima / yellow to Santiago).

❏ **The Mystical Path:** Giving and receiving are two sides of the same coin Accumulating for oneself alone is Self defeating. "It will be given you to see your brother's worth when all you seek for him is peace. And what you want for him *you* will receive." ACIM

❏ **Personal Reflections:** My roommate was French with penetrating eyes and dark beard. He told me he was anxious to get back to Toulouse but his bank had failed to transfer funds – he was short €20 for his fare. I judged him dishonest and chose not to help. It was only after we parted I realised my tithing commitment from yesterday was €20 – its distribution proving oddly difficult – my mistrust and prejudice were deeper than I realised. Christ appears in many guises.

0.0 km Verdelha de Baixo If you stayed in Verdelha de Baixo return to the waymarked camino by the bridge over the railway.

1.3 km Ponte **0.0 km** Ponte continue into **Alverca do Ribatejo** rail station and air museum *museo do Ar.* Cross the railway *Café* and veer right into rua Infante D. Pedro to skirt the town out past the playing fields onto pathway and up through an industrial area back to the N-10.

3.2 km N-10 [!] This is a busy junction and we have to cross over the N-10. Having made it to the far side we then continue alongside it for 2 kilometres passing under 2 grain chutes before re-crossing the N-10 [!] and taking the steps

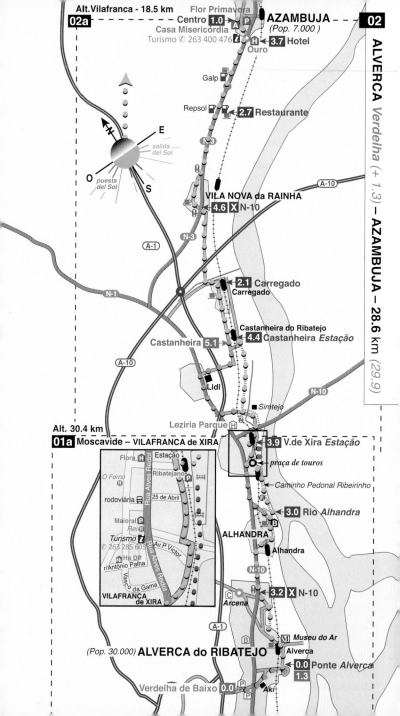

02a Alt. Vilafranca – 18.5 km

Flor Primavera

02 AZAMBUJA (Pop. 7.000)

Centro **1.0** Casa Misericórdia
Turismo ℃ 263 400 476

3.7 Hotel
Ouro

Galp

Repsol **2.7** Restaurante

VILA NOVA da RAINHA
4.6 X N-10

A-10

2.1 Carregado
Carregado

Castanheira do Ribatejo
4.4 Castanheira *Estação*

Castanheira **5.1**

Lidl

N-10

Simtejo

Leziria Parque

3.9 V. de Xira *Estação*

praça de touros

01a Moscavide – VILAFRANCA de XIRA
Alt. 30.4 km

← Caminho Pedonal Ribeirinho

3.0 Rio *Alhandra*

Flora
Estação
O Forno
Ribatejano
rodoviária
25 de Abril
Maioral
Rei
Turismo **7**
℃ 263 285 605
Hs DP
r/António Palha
Vasco da Gama
VILAFRANCA de XIRA

ALHANDRA

Alhandra

3.2 X N-10

Arcena

Museu do Ar

(Pop. 30.000) **ALVERCA do RIBATEJO**

Alverca

0.0 Ponte *Alverca*
1.3

Verdelha de Baixo **0.0**

Aki

down from the bridge to **Alhanda** rail station *estação Praça 8 de Maio Café* from here we make our way *towards* the town centre. Like Alverca there is no lodging (apart from the fire station) in this sizable town but there are a variety of bars and shops). The new riverside route no longer goes through the town centre but veers right> into ruas 20 de Maio and Catarina Eufémia to pass Bombeiros Voluntários (no longer receiving pilgrims) at the end of Rua Vasco da Gama by the river.

> ***Note:*** *Be careful not to follow the original waymarking which is still in place and heads through the town centre and out past the municipal swimming (right) pool and over a pedestrian bridge to rejoin the busy N-10 again.*

3.0 km Alhandra *Marina* we now follow past the marina, museum, boat club *Vela* (with pilgrim stamp!*)* the municipal swimming pool (left). There are several water fonts and a w.c. along this delightful new riverside path *passeio ribeirinho pedonal (see photo).* The waymarked route takes us over the rail to pass the impressive bullring *Plaza de Toros.*
(An alternative is to continue along the river front and pick up the waymarked route at the station. This avoids having to cross the railway – twice!). From the bullring the original road route joins from the left and we follow the road into town to the central railway station at:

3.9 km **Vilafranca de Xira** Rail station *Estação.* ***Posto de Turismo*** *(summer only)* at *Câmara Municipal* © 263 285 605 Praça Afonso de Albuquerque. An attractive town with wide range of *cafés e restaurantes* and lodging including: *Hs* **Vilatejo** *(Ribatejana)* €10-25 © 263 272 991 m: 925 912 679 (Mariano) rua da Praia, 2. *Hs* **DP** €12-25 © 263 288 012 m: 926 070 650 (Fernando e Carolina) Rua António Palha, 2. *Hs café* **Maioral** €27-€37 © 263 274 370 travessa do Terreirinho, 2. *H* **Flora** €35 rua Noel Perdigão, 12. © 263 271 272 and on the outskirts **Camping** © 263 276 031 (summer only) further out on the EN-1 is the upmarket *H* **Lezíra Parque** €75+ © 263 276 670.

This busy town had links with the English crusaders *[they came this way en route to the Holy Land and named it Cornogoa (after Cornwall]*. It stands at the edge of Portugal's main wetland reserve *Reserva Natural do Estuario do Tejo* home to large numbers of migrating (and domestic) wildfowl. Today it is better known for the breeding of fighting bulls and its popular 'running the bulls' that takes place during the 'Fiesta Red Waistcoat' *Festa do Colete Encarnado* that takes place during the first 2 weeks in July and again in October *Feira de Outubro* when accommodation is all but impossible to find.

Take the overpass in the rail station out along an attractive riverside park under the N-10 (which goes over the Tejo at this point). A rough path runs parallel to the road and turns right after the Simtejo factory. ❖ *[Note the original route went s/o over the bridge ahead and arrows still may point in that direction. The former route is dangerous and not advisable]*. ❖ Veer right along gravel track to cross back over the railway line at:

4.4 km **Castanheira do Ribatejo.** This is the point where the original road route joins from the left. Continue parallel to the railway line to:

2.1 km **Carregado** *Alenquer* several *cafés.* We now turn inland along a dyke and turn right> by *café/bar* over bridge past the power station *termoeléctica.* The route continues under the A-10 and over the N-3 into the village of.

4.6 km **Vila Nova da Rainha** *café e restaurantes.* Continues through the village and rejoin the N-3 for a 6 km slog! into Azambuja relieved only by a surprisingly good fish *restaurante* (right) tucked behind a Repsol garage.

2.7 km **Restaurante** *Mercearia do Peixe.* Continue over roundabout past Galp *café* (left) to the outskirts of Azambuja:

3.7 km **Azambuja** Hotel *H Ouro (Garibéu)* Ⓒ 263 406 530 N-3, Km 10 at roundabout at entrance to the town. *Café* Aldi *supermercado* and bullring *plaza de Toros* (left). Continue s/o over roundabout past *Páteo Valverde* with **Turismo** to the rear of the courtyard (left). Continue past the Bombeiros Voluntários on rua José Ramos Vides (longer accepting pilgrims at this time) up to the town centre.

1.0 km **Azambuja** *Centro* pleasant town (population 7,000) with good facilities and popular fiesta during the last week in May *Feira do Maio* with its own 'running of the bulls.' The area is also known for its robust red wines coaxed from the Periquita grapes. The town has a good range of *cafés bars & restaurantes.*

AZAMBUJA: Accommodation: A pilgrim hostel has now opened on the lovely main square Praça do Município. Operated by the local Casa de Misericórdia who have plans to open a permanent shelter adjoining the historic Casa de Misericórdia chapel in rua Vítor Cordon. *Alb.* **do Peregrino** *Asoc.[24÷1]* €-donativo Ⓒ 917 038 116 (meu-supermercado hold the key). *Hs* **Flor da Primavera** €30 Ⓒ 263 402 545 rua Conselheiro Francisco Arouca, 19. *P* **Jacinto** Ⓒ 263 402 504 rua dos Campinos 3c (tr. Da Misericordia) and back at the roundabout the hotel **Ouro**.

Páteo Valverde also has a museum and cultural centre. Here we find portraits of local bullfighters and one of the most feted female matadors in Portugal, Ana Maria (see photo below). The Centro Comercial Atrium on rua Eng. Moniz da Maia has free internet access.

REFLECTIONS:

❏ *Do one thing in this life – eradicate prejudice.* Peter Ustinov.

03 *556.0 km (345.5 miles) – Santiago*

AZAMBUJA – SANTARÉM

....	--- ---	18.7	--- ---	58%
━━━	--- ---	13.6	--- ---	42%
▬▬▬	--- ---	0.0	--- ---	0%
Total km	--- ---	**32.3 km** (20.1 ml)		

▲ 33.0 km (+^ 140 m = 0.7 km)
Alto ▲ Santarém 135 m (443 ft)
< 🅰 🏠 > Valada **12.8** km – Porto de Muge **16.4** km
⬤━━┅┅┅ Reguengo / Cataxo / Vale de Santarém / Santarém

```
100m                                              Alto 135m
                                              SANTARÉM ▲
AZAMBUJA        Valada⬛Ⓒ  Ⓒ⬛Port de Muge
   río Tejo                          río Tejo
0      5 km    10 km    15 km    20 km    25 km    30 km
```

❏ **The Practical Path:** Today we traverse the flood plains *lezíria* – half the route is via delightful farm tracks through this agricultural area with its cropfields, fruit and vegetable production (tomatoes) and vineyards. This is the market garden of Portugal covered with the rich alluvial soil of the Tejo which has now narrowed to a more intimate river as distinct from its estuarine form but all the more hazardous for that as it can (and does) rise and flood this totally flat terrain – a rise of 8 meters has been recorded! The only climb today is up to Santarém at 110m. Facilities are limited so carry some food and water. The only shade is occasional stands of poplar so take precautions against the sun.

❏ **The Mystical Path:** Everyone, without exception, is a child of the One God and to look on another with the vision of Christ is to recognise one's true Self in reflection. *The eye with which I see God, is the same eye with which God sees me.* Meister Eckhart.

❏ **Personal Reflections:** I looked out dreamily across the Tejo, contemplating the journey ahead and suddenly realised my camera was being lifted from my pocket. I lashed out in anger and recognised the young gypsy from an earlier confrontation. The strength of my reaction alarmed me. I write these notes in the calm of the evening and re-dedicate this journey to eliminating prejudice from my heart and to making every step a prayer for peace and understanding... *He who angers you, conquers you.* Elizabeth Kenny.

0.0 km **Azambuja.** From the central square follow the waymarks that lead down rua Conselheiro Federico Arouca directly to the railway station up the metal staircase and over the N-3 and rail line to follow a quiet tree-lined road on the far side to a bridge.

1.8 km **Ponte.** Immediately over the bridge turn down sharp <left (waymark below road) and make your way along a quiet riverside path crossing over a side canal to skirt the quinta ahead and pick up wide farm tracks that wind their way to an asphalt road at:

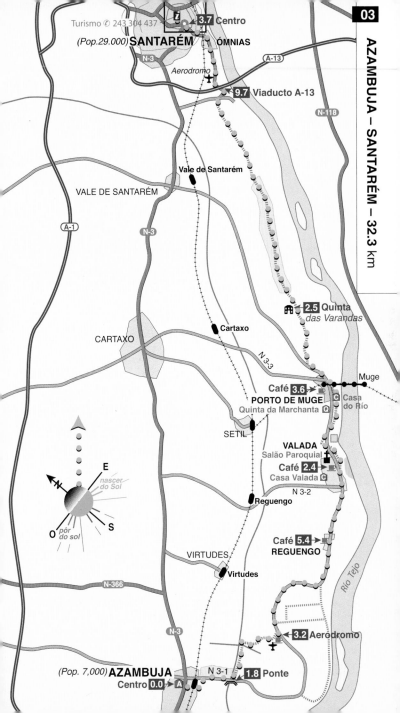

Turismo ℡ 243 304 437

(Pop.29.000) **SANTARÉM**

3.7 Centro

ÓMNIAS

A-13

Aerodromo

9.7 Viaducto A-13

N-118

Vale de Santarém

VALE DE SANTARÉM

A-1

N-3

2.5 Quinta
das Varandas

Cartaxo

CARTAXO

N 3-3

Muge

Café **3.6**

PORTO DE MUGE

Casa
do Río

Quinta da Marchanta

SETIL

VALADA

Salão Paroquial

Café **2.4**

Casa Valada

N 3-2

Reguengo

Café **5.4**

REGUENGO

Rio Tejo

VIRTUDES

Virtudes

N-366

E
*nascer
do Sol*

O
*pôr
do sol*

S

N-3

3.2 Aeródromo

(Pop. 7,000) **AZAMBUJA**

N 3-1

1.8 Ponte

Centro **0.0** A

3.2 km **Aerodromo** *café* serving the pilots but welcomes pilgrims if flying is in progress. We now turn <left along the road to make out way back to the river. *[Note: after 400m old waymarks point right off the road but then evaporate in a maze of farm tracks through crop fields which require you to make your way east as best you can to rejoin the road]* or simply stay on the asphalt road that bends first right and then left with the Tejo lying 'hidden' behind the high flood barrier that follows the river at this point passing a welcome sign as we enter:

5.4 km **Reguengo** welcome riverside village with *café*:

2.4 km **Valada** *Cafés*. **Casa Velha de Santo António** €10-25 ℰ 919 268 039 (Helena Almeida - see Casa do Rio below) Rua Santo António 27. **Salão Paroquial de Valada** €2 ℰ 243 749 277 (Dᵃ Rosa Fernanda) Largo da Igreja *(floor only, sleeping mat essential)*. A flood bank separates the village from a sandy beach and a stone marks the flood level in 1979 when it rose to the top. Igreja de N.Sᵃ do Ó dates from 12ᵗʰc.
We continue past water treatment plant through Casal Fidalgo. An overgrown path runs along *part* of the flood wall and on the outskirts of the next village:

3.6 km **Porto de Muge** *Morgado Café*. **Quinta da Marchanta** €20-€70 ℰ 910 967 415 (Dᵃ Graça) m: 243 749 279 rua do Maltratado (blue and while quinta left). **Casa do Rio** €10-25 ℰ 919 268 039 (Helena Almeida pre-phone) rua do Morgado,2 (first house right on top of bank with garden backing onto the river). We now enter delightful sandy tracks that meander for 9 km through this rich agricultural area *Lezíria* with variety of crops, especially tomato.

2.5 km **Quinta** *das Varandas* One of the few signs of habitation is after which the first views of Santarém open up on the horizon ahead. Join asphalt road to:

9.7 km **Viaducto A-13** pass under the motorway by a local aero club and under the railway in **Ómnias** for the final steep ascent up into:

3.7 km **Santarém Centro** Main roundabout *Largo Cândido dos Reis* with Hospital de Jesus Cristo church and adjoining Santa Casa da Misericórdia. Santarém, a charming historic city, straddles a fortified hilltop well out of reach of the floodwaters of the Tejo. Its commanding position affords wonderful views of the river especially from the viewpoint *miradouro* also called Gates of the Sun *Portas do Sol* where extensive gardens form a viewing platform on what was formerly the Moorish citadel. The town provided a major stronghold for the Romans and Julius Caesar chose it as the administrative centre *conventus* for the region. When the Moors arrived it became a stronghold for Islam and was considered to be unassailable until the first king of Portugal *Dom Afonso Henriques* recaptured it in 1149 and returned the town to the Portuguese who have occupied it happily ever since. *Note: for detour to Fátima see page 10.*

REFLECTIONS:

Rio Tejo from Santarém

PORTAS DO SOL

❏ **Historic Buildings and Monuments:** At the entrance to the town ➊ *Igreja do Hospital de Jesus Cristo* XV[th]c (adjoining the Santa Casa da Misericórdia). ➋ *Praça Sá da Bandeira* this exquisite square includes a flight of steps up to *Igreja N.Sra. da Conceição e Seminário* XVII[th]c which dovetails as the cathedral and on the opposite side is *Igreja N.Sra da Piedade*. Next on the circuit is the Manueline gem ➌ *Igreja de Marvila* with its wonderful display of ceramic tiles *azulejos* dating from XVII[th]c although the original site was donated by D. Afonso Henriques to the Knights Templars in the XII[th]c. ➍ *Igreja da Graça* XV[th]c with its fine rose window and which houses the tombs of Pedro Alvares Cabral (after whom the square is named) the 'discoverer' of Brazil whose simple stone slab is outdone by the ornate sarcophagus of Pedro de Menezes the first governor of Ceuta (Morocco). ➎ *Portas do Sol* 'Gate of the Sun' is a wonderful viewpoint *miradouro* occupying the site of the original Roman forum and the Moorish citadel. ➏ *Porta de Santiago* medieval pilgrims gateway. There is an alternative waymarked route around town (grey on plan).

❏ **Turismo** ✆ 243 304 437 rua Capelo e Ivens, 63. *Albergue* ➊ Hs **Santarém** *Priv. [24÷2]+* €15–€30/£40 ✆ 243 322 256 m: 965 832 702 *(Mário)* welcoming hostel with outdoor patio in central location near the tourist office Rua Eng. António Antunes Júnior, 26. ➋ **Seminário** *Conv.[96÷24] (grupos 10+)* €10+ ✆ *913 023 728 (Sra. Aida)* Praça Sá da Bandeira *(museo €4)*. ➌ **Casa da Misericórdia** *Conv. [6÷1]* €5 ✆ 243 305 260 Largo Cândido dos Reis. **N1 Hostel Apartments and Suites** €15 ✆ 243 350 140 Av. dos Combatentes, 80 *(+ 0.5km). CH* **Casa Flores** Rua Pedro Canavarro, 9 ✆ 965 612 001 (duplex sleeps 4 €50+). *P* **Arminda** ✆ 243-110 079 Trav. Do Frois,14. *H***¨ Vitória** ✆ 243-309 130 rua Visconde de Santarém, 21. **Residências do Valle** Av. António dos Santos, 36 ✆ 243 377 800. *Hr* **Beirante** ✆ 243-322 547 rua Alexandre Herculano (opp. Câmara Municipal). *H*¨¨¨ **Umu** ✆ 243 377 240 Av. Bernardo Santareno 38 *(+1.5 km down in modern suburbs adj. Hospital)*. Also in this area **BV** *Muni.[4÷1]* €10 ✆ 243 377 900 Rua Brigadeiro Lino Dias Valente. *H*¨¨¨¨**Corinthia Santarém** ✆ 243-309 500 Av. Afonso Henriques, 19 *(+1.3 km)*. On the way out in Portas do Sol is the luxurious *Q* **Casa da Alcáçova** €90+ ✆ 243 304 030 Largo do Alcáçova 3 and down market down in Ribeira de Santarém *(+1.1 km)* **Café Inácio** €15 ✆ 243 322 549. ❏ **Fátima** *ônibus* €9: Santarém 10:45–Fátima 11:30 / Fátima 17.45–Santarém 18:30. *Info:* Hostel Pereira Fátima ✆ *960 330 636 (Armando Pereira)* www.hostelpereira.com

Praça Sá da Bandeira

Igreja da Graça

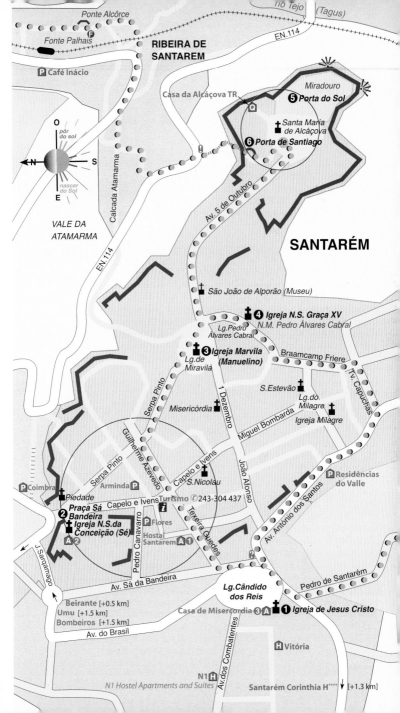

❏ The possibility of the impossible is the subject of my novels. *José Saramago*

04 *523.7 km (325.4 miles) – Santiago*

SANTARÉM – GOLEGÃ

▫▫▫▫▫▫	--- --- 16.6	--- ---	52%
▬▬▬▬	--- --- 14.6	--- ---	48%
▬▬▬▬	--- --- 0.0	--- ---	0%
Total km	**31.2 km** (19.4 ml)		

▲▲▲ 31.3 km (+^20m=0.1 km)
Alto ▲ Santarém 135 m (443 ft)
< 🅐 🅗 > Azinhaga **24.3** km.
⬤▬▬ ····· **Santarém / Vale de Figueira / Mato de Miranda**

▲135m
■SANTARÉM 100m
Vale de Figueira ▪   Azinhaga ⌂   **GOLEGÃ** ■
rio Tejo   Alviela   Almonda
0 km   **5** km   **10** km   **15** km   **20** km   **25** km   **30**

Practical Path: Another pleasant day walking split between quiet country lanes and farm tracks running parallel to the river Tejo. The historic camino now leaves behind the blue arrows that pointed to Fátima to follow the more modest yellow arrows as we head down onto the flat alluvial soils of the Tejo towards Santiago. Flooding in recent years has necessitated re-routing of the path into Golegã The original route via Azinhaga is now shown as an alternative *(green)*. Facilities along this stage are limited so stock up with water and food before leaving Santarém.

❏ **Mystical Path:** Let me live in my house by the side of the road, where the race of men go by; they are good, they are bad; they are weak, they are strong, wise, foolish – so am I; then why should I sit in the scorner's seat, Or hurl the cynic's ban? Let me live in my house by the side of the road, and be a friend to man.
Sam Walter Foss

❏ **Personal Reflections:** I was cold and wet and the batteries in my GPS suddenly went flat. I wearily retraced my steps and met her locking up the office by the side of the road. She knew of a place to sleep and, perchance, it was her birthday so she would be delighted to celebrate and share a meal with me. As I luxuriated in a hot bath it was not only the batteries that were being recharged – my heart was being filled with gratitude for unexpected friendship and trust offered to a total stranger by a lady at the side of the road in Azinhaga.

0.0 km Centro The route now takes the pedestrian Serpa Pinto to **Porta do Sol** **[1.0]** out through St. James Gate *Puerta de São Tiago* to head down steeply [!] on woodland paths <left across the EN-114 [!] and Igreja Santa Cruz down to the rail line at **Ribeira de Santarém [1.1]** Casa Café Inácio Ⓒ 243 322 549 *(500m left)* beds from €10. Pass fonte de Palhais and medieval bridge turn right> over rio Alcorce onto quiet country road to farmhouse and path **[1.1]**:

3.2 km Camino turn <left by house onto path that now veers right> through crop fields running parallel to the road which we cross at:

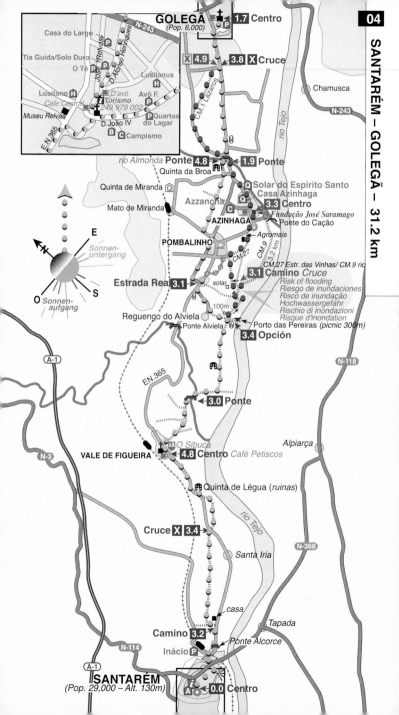

GOLEGÃ
(Pop. 6,000) 🅿 1.7 Centro

X 4.9 3.8 X Cruce

Chamusca

N-243

rio Tejo

Casa do Largo

Tia Guída/Solo Duro
O Té

Lusitanus

Lusitano 🅷
Café Central

Museu Relvas

D'avó
i Turismo
249 979 002

Avó F.

🅷

D.João IV

Quartos
do Lagar

E.N.365

🅱 🅲 Campismo

rio Almonda **Ponte** 4.8 1.9 **Ponte**

Quinta da Broa

Quinta de Miranda 🏛

Mato de Miranda

Azzancha

Q **Solar do Espírito Santo
Casa Azinhaga**

Q

🅲 3.3 **Centro**

AZINHAGA

Fundação José Saramago
Ponte do Cação

POMBALINHO

Agromais

CM.27

CM.9
3.2 km

CM.27 Estr. das Vinhas/ CM.9 rio

Estrada Real 3.1

3.1 **Camino** *Cruce*

solar

Risk of flooding
Riesgo de inundaciones
Risco de inundação
Hochwassergefahr
Rischio di inondazioni
Risque d'inondation

100m

Reguengo do Alviela

Ponte Alviela

Porto das Pereiras *(picnic 300m)*

3.4 **Opción**

EN.365

3.0 **Ponte**

Alpiarça

N-118

A-1

N-3

VALE DE FIGUEIRA

🆁 O Sibuca
4.8 **Centro** *Café Petiscos*

🏛 Quinta de Légua *(ruins)*

rio Tejo

N-368

Cruce X 3.4

Santa Iria

casa

Tapada

Camino 3.2

Inácio 🅿

Ponte Alcorce

A-1

N-114

SANTARÉM
(Pop. 29,000 – Alt. 130m)

🅰 i 0.0 **Centro**

Sonnen-
untergang

E

N

O Sonnen-
aufgang

S

3.4 km [X] **Cruce** continue s/o along path to rejoin road by Quinta Cruz da Légua (ruins) past Quinta Boavista into a village typical of the *lezíria*:

4.8 km **Vale da Figueira** *Centro café* / church. Continue s/o to next •*café* [0.2 km] turn right> onto track veering <left at fork in cork tree plantation and right> at T-junction [1.2 km] turn right> past ruin (right) continue to **bridge** [1.7 km].

3.0 km **Ponte** rio Alviela (tributary of the Tejo) the route now alternates between country lanes and farm tracks through crop fields, mostly corn *maizales* past farmyard and Quinta to T-Junction and option point:

3.4 km [X] **Opción** ▲ Flooding in 2012 necessitated finding an alternative route away from the river. The Município de Golegã decided to waymark along the Estrada Real north of Pombalinho. It is the same distance as the original route but misses the delightful village of Azinhaga which is now shown as an alternative preferred 'green' route in dry weather as follows: *Note: At this point a track (right 300m) to Porto das Pereiras picnic spot on the rio Tejo (no facilities).*

Option [1] Turn <left and imm. right> [0.1 km] [!] onto rough track. Turn <left [1.5 km] (opp. woodland) right> [0.4 km] (not path s/o) to T-junction [1.1 km].

3.1 km **Cruce** *[A variant 1a veers right> on CM27–CM9 on original route (fading waymarks) into Azinhaga via sandpits and water treatment plant to Ponte do Cação].* Waymarked route turn <left past **solar panels** [0.3 km] to **cross-tracks** [0.5 km] (s/o Pombalinho ½ km) turn right> along track past **Agromais silos** [1.4 km] right> on main road [0.3 km] s/o at roundabout past ruinas S. Sebastian *XVI* and *Café Taberna do Maltez* [0.3 km] veer right> at Blacksmith statue *Tributo ao Ferrador* [0.1 km] into the **town centre** [0.4 km]:

3.3 km **Azinhaga** *Centro* Turn right> in Largo da Praça by Foundation offices dedicated to the works of Nobel Laureate José Saramago who was born in the village in 1922 and died in 2010. He became the first Portuguese writer to win the Nobel Prize for literature in 1998 and his works have been published in over 30 languages. His social beliefs were clear: *"As citizens, we all have an obligation to intervene and become involved – it's the citizen who changes things."* Azinhaga is an attractive town with a resident population of 2,000 supporting a variety of *café-bars* and connections to the original medieval pilgrim route.

In rua da Misericordia we pass an ancient pilgrim hospital adj. the Capilla del Espíritu Santo *XIV* and the ivy-clad *VIII*th c **Quinta** [0.1 km] Casa da Azinhaga *Ⓒ* 249 957 146 rooms from €70 and [0.2 km] further on Solar do Espirito Santo *Ⓒ* 249 957 252 equestrian centre with rooms from €65. At the 'back end' of town is *CR* Casa de Azzancha €20 incl. *Ⓒ* 249 957 253 m: 919 187 773 (Dª Helena Santos) Rua dos Altos Montijos, 68. Private house at the edge of town [+1.0 km]. Continue out along the main to **rotunda** [0.4 km] *Estátua do Campino* s/o past Capela Sao Joao Ventosa road to *XV* (ruins – right) to **Quinta** [1.2 km]:

1.9 km **Quinta da Brôa** where the new route joins from the left.

▲ To continue from original option turn <left at T-junction (past track 100m) and turn right> [1.3 km] skirting village of **Reguengo do Alviela** *(left – no facilities)* to main road [!] [0.9 km] turn right> to wetland area and another option point.

3.1 km **Estrada Real.** Camino information board and 2nd option to Azinhaga.

Azinhaga **Option [2]** (not waymarked) continue s/o and veer **right> [0.2 km]** to **T-junction [1.0 km]**. Turn right> (Pombalinho centre with cafés 300m left) to re-join **option [1]** at **Cross-tracks [0.4 km]**.

For the new waymarked route turn sharp <left onto **Estrada Real** (CM.7) and s/o at crossroads **[0.7 km]** (Pombalinho right) to next junction **Casal Centeio [1.1 km]** turn <left and then right> [!] **[0.4 km]** onto track s/o at track crossing (Quinta da Cholda/Azinhaga sign 0.8 km but 1.5 km to centre!) back onto asphalt at sign for Mato de Miranda *[also Quinta de Miranda © 249 957 115 Pilgrim price from €55 – 4.5 km off route]* continue s/o to:

1.9 km **Quinta de Brôa** and bridge over rio Almonda. From here the 'official' route is along the dangerous main road (with no margin) all the way into Golegã.

For alternative route (not waymarked) 1.9 km longer but avoiding 3.8 km of main road: Turn <left onto CM.1 Estrada Lázaros **[0.2 km]** veer right> onto farm track **[3.1 km]** right at T-junction **[1.4 km]** to crossroads **[0.2 km]** total 4.9 km.

3.8 km **Cruce X** (alt. route joins from left). Continue s/o past lake (right) and at the end of the tree-lined park turn right and up into the main square:

1.7 km **Golegã** *Centro* The central square has popular cafés and tourist office (summer only) and the 14[th]c parish church *Igreja Matriz N.Sra. da Conceiçao* with beautiful Manueline door. The other area of activity is around the large main square *Largo do Marquês de Pombal* (equestrian arena). Golegã is a lively town with 6,000) residents whose roots go back to the 12[th]c when a Galician woman (from "Galego" *Golegã*) set up an inn for travellers and pilgrims on the Royal Way *Estrada Real* from Lisboa to Porto.

      Golegã is now better known as the 'horse capital of Portugal' famous for its national (and international) horse fair *Feira Nacional do Cavalo* held during the first 2 weeks in November (St. Martin's Day) when accommodation for miles around is booked out a year in advance! Apart from the equestrian events there is also the 'running of the bulls' and bullfighting *a la Portugués*. Towards the top of rua José Relvas (on the direct route into town) is *Casa-Museu de Fotografia Carlos Relvas* with the ornate house in which his early photographic material is displayed.

❏ **Accommodation:** *Posto de Turismo* © (351) 249 979 002 centrally situated in Largo Imaculada Conceição. **Calvo Branco** © 249 979 003 bungalow rooms from €29 (3 beds) part of the **Parque Campismo** © 249 979 003 (tents available to rent). Located off rua D. Joao IV as you enter the town adjacent to **Bombeiros Voluntários** © 249 979 070 with possibility of floor in its large hall *salão* (you can shower in the adj. campsite for a small fee). *Albergue* **Solo Duro** *Priv.[10÷2]*+ €10 incl. © 249 976 802 m: 935 640 550 rua José Relvas, 84 + the adj. **CR Casa da Tia Guida** €30 (same owners). Opposite *Hs* **O Té** €10-30 © 249 976 404 rua José Relvas, 119 with restaurant. Directly on the waymarked camino: **Quartos do Lagar** €15+ © 917 591 833 (Josefino) rua D. João IV, 136. Opp: **Pátio da Avó Faustina** €65 © 935 640 545 rua D. João IV, 141. **Casa do Largo** €55+ © 249 104 850 Largo 5 de Outubro. **Lusitanus** *A.N.T.E. part of the equestrian centre* Largo Marquês de Pombal © 249 976 933. *H****Lusitano* €100+ © 249 979 170 rua Gil Vicente. Municipal •**Sporthotel** *equuspolis* © 249 979 000 available for groups on Largo D. Manuel I. *See next stage for:* **Albergue** Sao Caetano 5.9 km

❏ **Practise random acts of loving kindness and senseless acts of beauty.**

---

05 *492.5 km (306.0 miles) – Santiago*

GOLEGÃ – TOMAR

ᴵᴵᴵᴵᴵᴵᴵᴵᴵᴵᴵᴵ	--- --- 12.3	--- ---	*41%*
▬▬▬▬▬	--- --- 12.2	--- ---	*41%*
▬▬▬▬	--- --- 5.2	--- ---	*18%*
Total km	**29.7 km** (18.5 ml)		

◣▬ 31.3 km (+^ 320 m = 1.6 km)
Alto(*m*)▲ Grou 145 m (475 ft)
< 🅰 🅷 > S. Caetano **5.6** km / *V.N. da Barquinha 8.7 (+1.1)* – Atalaia **10.9** km.

Practical Path: We set out today towards one of Portugal's most notable manor houses *Quinta da Cardiga*. The first half is along quiet country lanes relieved with the occasional farm track as we head back towards the Tejo where it takes a pronounced bend away from our path at Vila Nova da Barquinha and we leave it for the last time. This is the point where we also leave the flat alluvial plains and head into more interesting countryside with gentle rolling hills covered in woodland offering us shade. We also encounter villages at regular intervals with the possibility of refreshments and we end this stage in the historic Templar town of Tomar, the quintessential pilgrim halt, where the welcome felt by the medieval pilgrim is extended to those of us who follow in their footsteps.

❏ **Mystical Path:** Love simply *is* and needs no defence. It is the desire for love that makes it manifest and dissolves the barriers erected in a vain attempt to keep it hidden. Camões says it thus:

> *The lover becomes the thing he loves*
> *By virtue of much imagining;*
> *Since what I long for is already in me,*
> *The act of longing should be enough.*

❏ **Personal Reflections:** I arrived in the heat of the afternoon and rested by the gate – I didn't have long to wait and was treated like an old friend with love and kindness. I merely mentioned an interest in visiting the castle at Almourol and was driven there without a moments hesitation along with a visit to Constância beautifully located at the confluence of the Tejo and Zezere. It was here, in the 16th c, that Portuguese poet Luís Vaz de Camões was forced into exile and wrote some of his masterful verse, oft compared to that of Shakespeare.

0.0 km Golegã *Centro* despite its compact size it is easy to get lost in the maze of streets; use the sun for orientation (if you stayed here last night head east towards the rising sun). *[For an alternative route (fading waymarks) head up the main shopping street Afonso Henriques and s/o over the bypass N-243 [0.9 km] onto track to intersection with road and **main route [2.0 km]**: Total 2.9 km.]*

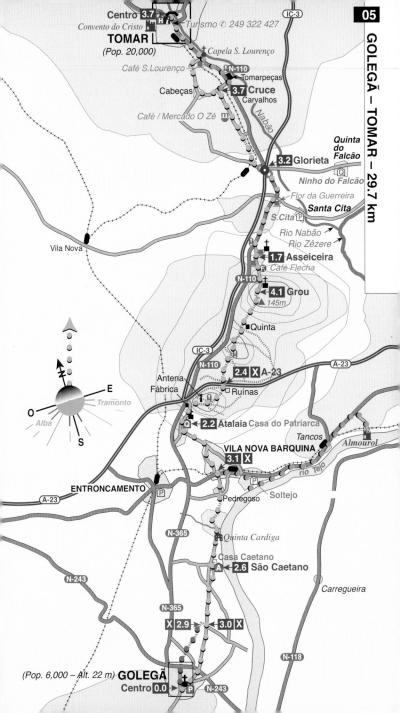

Main route via rua D. Joao IV past Quartos do Lagar (right) Capela S. Joao (left) veer right at A1 sign **[0.9 km]** and s/o at N-243 **[0.5 km]** to junction **[1.6 km].**

3.0 km **Cruce** Here the alternative route joins from the left and we continue s/o by road passing Quinta do Matinho into the Land of the Templars *Terra de Templários* with Templar cross in the peaceful hamlet of:

2.6 km **São Caetano** welcoming albergue *Alb.* **Casa São Caetano** *Priv.[10÷5]* €20 incl. ✆ 914 951 076 . Continue to **Quinta Cardiga [0.7 km]** *take a rest in the shade and soak up the peaceful atmosphere with its images of old and new world wealth and privilege. A leisurely stroll down the tree-lined avenue is to take a trip down memory lane with old retainers trying to maintain some order out of the fading opulence. Strategically located on the banks of the Tejo it started life as a castle given by D. Afonso Henriques into the care of the Templars which, along with Almourol (see below) formed part of the defensive system against both Spanish and Arab invasion. From castle it became royal palace, home to religious orders, hospital for pilgrims, home to nobility passing into... history?*

Continue over the stone bridge *Ribeira da Ponte da Pedra* over a stream that enters the Tejo immediately to our right (the gardens of the quinta front the river). The route now wends its way past Pedregoso passing sign for V. N. Barquina and across the main road (EN-3) and **railway line [2.4 km]**.

3.1 km **V. N. da Barquinha** *Options:* [?] We now have several options.

Detour [1] ● ● ● ● Vila Nova da Barquinha ½ km detour to the attractive and historic town centre beautifully preserved with all facilities including a riverside park and *Hs* **Soltejo** ✆ 249 720 150 on the N-3 and **Bombeiros Voluntários**.

Detour [2] ● ● ● ● If time and energy allow then a further excursion of 4 km along the banks of the Tejo to ***Almourol castle*** is worth considering but would require spending the night in Atalaia, Barquina, Tancos or Entroncamento. In the summer a boat trip also runs from the town of Tancos which can be accessed either by riverside walk, rail or taxi. This magnificent stronghold of the Templar knights stands on a tiny rocky island just off the northern bank of the river.

Continue over rail in V. N. Barquinha up through the residential suburbs of V. N. Barquina that merge into Atalaia via ruas de São Matias and Patriarca D. José to:

2.2 km **Atalaia** *CR* **Casa do Patriarca** €40+ ✆ 249 710 581 m: 962 818 115 (Dª Luisa Oliveira) rua Patriarca Dom José 134. Welcoming manor house with shaded gardens (right) directly on the camino with restaurant nearby. Continue up to the well preserved 16thc Parish church (National monument) with beautiful Manueline porch **[0.2 km]**. We now head down towards the N-110 and

turn right> onto track **[0.5 km]** immediately *after* the sign for leaving Atalaia, opposite industrial building *(not the first track with dog kennels).*

[!] *Extra vigilance is needed through this section (to Grou) as clear-felling of trees in the area and a recent forest fire have removed waymarks so look carefully for signs on pylons and rocks. If new waymarks are clear then follow them otherwise follow the original route as follows:* Keep to the main track through woodland up to a central clearing and intersection of forest tracks **[1.1 km]** (pylon to the right). Veer <left and then immediately right> *(the main track continues up left to a radio mast and eventually meets the A-23 before reconnecting to the original waymarked route described next).* There are several indistinct paths that now head over to our left parallel to pylons towards a small derelict building *ruinas* on the horizon beside a bridge *ponte* **[0.6 km]** over the A-23 motorway 'hidden' in a cutting in the landscape at this point (see photo below).

2.4 km **Ponte A-23** cross the bridge and turn <left back above the A-23 before turning up right> **[0.3 km]** on a steep path through the trees up to a clearing where overhead cables cross and several paths branch off **[0.9 km]**. Take the central path s/o to next intersection and turn <left **[0.3 km]** and immediately right> down into the valley ahead (see 2nd photo) and at the bottom turn <left (quinta straight ahead through trees) and right> over river-bed **[1.2 km]** and up steeply where the forest track yields finally to an asphalt road into Grou **[1.4 km]**

4.1 km **Grou** views towards Tomar *Café Palmeira Alto* (often closed and *[F]* maybe dry!). Continue along asphalt road passing modern church (up to our right) down to the valley floor with *[F]* **[1.3 km]** and up again into the village of Asseiceira with several cafes to the centre **[0.4 km]**.

1.7 km **Asseiceira** *Café O Flecha*. Proceed down to the **N-110** **[1.0 km]** turn right> along main road into **Guerreira** **[1.2 km]** *Café Flor da Guerreira. They also own the pension: [❖ Detour: Santa Cita (+ 0.9 km)* ● ● ● *P** Residencial Santa Cita* ℂ 964 682 805 Largo da Igreja]. Continue by main road over *Ribeira da Bezelga* to major **roundabout [1.0 km]**:

3.2 km **Rotunda A-23 / IC-3 / N-110** [!] Restaurante (right). [❖*Detour right to* **Quinta do Falcão** *(+ 1.1 km):* *P** Ninho do Falcão* €35+ ℂ 249 380 070 Estrada do Castelo Bode, 24. **Pause** [!] We now head *under* the flyover (the new bypass around Tomar) following signs to Zona Industrial / Leiria *around* the next roundabout and *over* rail bridge **[0.4 km]** and immediately turn down right> onto path alongside railway keeping s/o at level crossing and up onto asphalt road **[2.0 km]** (rua Casal Marmelo) to top of rise passing *Cafe O Zé* and mini mercado *[F]* to T-Junction and **option [1.3 km]**.

3.7 km **Cruce/Opción** A new route <left avoids some of the busy N-110. *[For the original road route turn down right> over railway to the main road at Tomarpeças. Turn <left along N-110 into São Lourenço to rejoin route below].* For new route turn <left at T-junction and right> in **Cabeças [0.7 km]** turn right> **[1.0 km]** down *under* rail into rua Nova S. Lourenço and N-110 **[0.4 km]**.

Restaurante S. Lourenço. The tiny chapel XVIth opp. was built in the maneuline style to commemorate the spot where, in 1385, the troops of D. Joao I joined with those of D. Nuno Álvares Pereira prior to the epic battle of Aljubarrota resulting in the defeat of the Spanish and establishing the independence of Portugal under Dom Joao I (king John 1st). This decisive victory led to the construction of the monastery of Santa Maria da Vitória na Batalha (battle) now a UNESCO World Heritage Site where the king along with his English born wife, Philippa of Lancaster lie buried. The blue and while tiles azulejos depict this famous meeting. Behind the chapel is a memorial column O Padrao de D. Joao II.

The route now follows the narrow N-110 [!] parallel to the river Nabão into Tomar suburbs past rail station (left) up the commercial rua António Joaquim de Araújo past *Trovador* and access to bus station (left) to **roundabout [1.4 km].**

[Alt. route <left enters the old town via rua Infantaria into the main square Praça da República with statue of the founder of Tomar and Grand Master of the Knights Templar Dom Pais who overlooks the beautiful Manueline church of S. João Baptista (see photos below). The camino continues down the pedestrian street rua Serpa Pinto (Corredoura) to join the shorter route at the bridge].

3.7 km **Tomar** *Centro histórico da cidade* Praca da Republica:

Praca da Republica

São João Baptista

REFLECTIONS:

_____

_____

_____

_____

_____

_____

_____

_____

_____

_____

_____

Convento do Cristo *(above)* Quinta da Cardiga *(below)*

Tomar is *the* quintessential medieval pilgrim town and the most perfect example of Templar layout and architecture to survive to this day. The main sites of historic interest are shown on the town plan opposite (described overleaf) numbered ❶ – ❻. The Templar castle (picture previous page), Convent of Christ and the incomparable *Charola* occupy a commanding location overlooking the town and have been declared a World Heritage Site. Successive Grand Masters including King Henry 'The Navigator' helped to plan the Great Discoveries from here. Gualdim Pais, founder of Tomar is buried in the Templar Mother church on the far side of the river. This historic town has a population of 21,000 and excellent facilities with a good range of accommodation in all price brackets. The helpful regional tourist office is prominently located opposite the old bridge *Ponte Velha* at the start of the main pedestrian street – rua Serpa Pinto (locally referred to as Corredoura) and is a good place to start a tour of the town. Consider spending a rest day here to explore its Templar past and to soak up the peaceful atmosphere that pervades the old town.

❏ *Turismo* 09:00-12:30 / 14:00-17:30 ✆ 249 329 800 Praça da República. ❏ *Hostales Central:* *rua Serpa Pinto @Nº43* albergue run by Sónia Pais *Alb/Hs* Thomar 2300 €15 incl. ✆ 965 515 100. @Nº94 *P*º União €28 ✆ 249 323 161. @Nº144 *P*º Luz ✆ 249 312 317. *H*ººCavaleiros de Cristo €25 ✆ 249 321 203 rua Alexandre Herculano,7. *Hs* Sinagoga €30 ✆ 249 323 083 rua Gil Avo,31. *Hs* Luanda ✆ 249 323 200 Av. Marques de Tomar, 15, above the restaurant overlooking the river. Directly opposite (far side of the rio Nabão) is the old fashioned Estalagem de Santa Iria €45 ✆ 249 313 326 Parque do Mouchão (rio Nabão). Also on the river (further out of town) *H*ºººº dos Templarios €70 ✆ 249 310 100 Largo Cândido dos Reis. *R* Trovador €30 ✆ 249 322 567 rua 10 de Agosto de 1385, 22 (near bus station). **Bombeiros Municipais** ✆ 249 329 140 rua de Santa Iria. **Casa de Dormidas Convento** ✆ 249 311 903 Av. Cândido Madureira,18.

❏ Restaurants and cafés aplenty: Taverna Antiqua Av. D.Vieira Guimarães, 3 (adj. Praça da República) has a good value *menú peregrino.*

Town Centre & Templar castle *above*

Convento de Cristo *Chapter window*

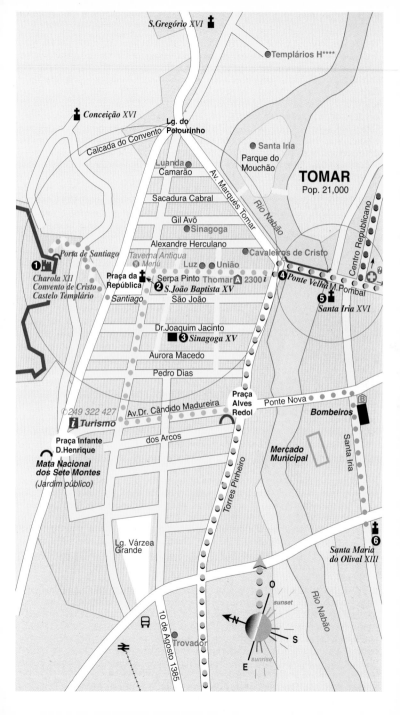

Tomar was founded in the 12thc by Gualdim Pais, first Grand Master of the Knights Templar, who established Tomar as the headquarters of the Order in Portugal. A statue of Pais takes centre stage in the beautiful *Praça do República* at the top end of the main pedestrian street where we also find the impressive ❷ *São João Baptista* built in the Manueline style with octagonal bell tower, opposite is the graceful 17thc town hall and rising above it all is the incomparable beauty and mystery of the Convent of the Knights Templar (transferred to the Knights of the Order of Christ in 1344) ❶ *Convento de Cristo* which forms the backdrop of the whole town. It is a pleasant 15-minute walk but allow a few hours to explore its dramatic buildings and beautifully maintained gardens. The entire complex forms the cradle of the Templar Order in Portugal and was inscribed by UNESCO as a World Heritage site *Patrimônio Mundial* in 1983.

Convento do Cristo – Charola

Gualdim Pais was a crusader knight who spent many years in the Holy Land and returned to supervise the building of the fortress and the *Convento de Cristo* with its fascinating chapel *Charola* based on the octagonal shape of the Temple Mount in Jerusalem (alluding to the wisdom within Solomon's Temple). This became a hallmark of the Order whose roots were directly connected to the Temple where the original knights were based and from which grew its phenomenal power base and esoteric traditions. The chapel's double octagonal form gives the impression of a round building – indeed it was known as the Rotunda. Its richly embellished interior is full of mystery and occult symbols and the layout was reputedly designed to allow the knights to attend mass on horseback. The high altar and surrounding alcoves were subsequently decorated with monumental paintings and murals (a major restoration program of the Charola area commenced in 2008 and is ongoing).

When the Templar Order was outlawed by king Philip of France and suppressed by the papacy in 1312 the surviving knights fled to Portugal where Dom Dinis gave them sanctuary and in a stroke of genius re-branded the knights under the title the Order of Christ redesigning the famous insignia by placing the red cross on a white band symbolizing that the old order was now 'purified' which satisfied the Vatican and the vast Templar property including the Tomar headquarters now passed to the new order under the patronage of the Portuguese throne. Prince Henry 'the Navigator' became Grand Master between 1417 and 1460 and established his court here. Dom Manuel succeeded as Grand Master in 1492 (becoming King a few years later) and Columbus, Vasco da Gama and other 'discoverers' were almost certainly received in these buildings as Dom Manuel and the Order became intricately involved in the financing and planning of the expeditions to the 'New World'. João III succeeded to the throne in 1521 and under his stewardship the Order became more religiously orientated and its hitherto political power base began to wane. It now became a more identified with monastic discipline and rule. The Great Cloister adjoining the chapter house was commenced at this time and marks the arrival of the Renaissance classical style in Portugal. The interconnecting courtyards (7 in all) and extensive halls and dormitories which welcomed pilgrims en route to Santiago give some impression of the grand scale of the whole complex and the beauty and diversity of its architectural forms which represent some of the finest examples of Romanesque, Mozarabic, Manueline and Portuguese Renaissance periods. Of particular note is the exquisite Chapter Window (see photo previous page) with its intricate sculptured maritime elements and topped by the cross of the Order of Christ.

The complex was allegedly connected by secret tunnels to the town below and to the Templar mother church St. Mary of the Groves ❻ *Santa Maria dos Olivais.* A drinking well to the right of the church was reputedly disguised as an aerating shaft as the tunnel itself was kept sealed. The church was the resting place of over 20 Templar knights and several Grand Masters including that of the town's founding father Gualdim Pais. In one of the many atrocities perpetrated against the Order the bodies were disinterred but fear of a political backlash convinced the Establishment to re-inter the body of Pais. In a further act of cultural and historical sacrilege a new bypass was recently constructed through this ancient historical site – the modern power base may have shifted to

Santa Maria dos Olivais

the motoring lobby but the custodianship of the church still resides in the loving care of António who provides a rich source of information. The simple layout of the church contains many hidden symbols of the Order.

Tomar has other sites to enthral the visitor and these include the 16[th]c chapel to the patron saint of Tomar ❺ *Capela de Santa Iria* which adjoins the lovely stone bridge over the river Nabão ❹ *Ponte Velha.* Near Praça República is the well-preserved ❸ *Sinagoga e Museo Luso-Hebraico Abraham Zacuto* in rua Joaquim Jacinto, 73. 15[th]c synagogue named after the astronomer who made the navigational equipment for Vasco da Gama's discovery of the Americas. The town also hosts the famous Festival of the Trays *Festa dos Tabuleiros* with obscure origins dating back to the 16[th]c and generally considered to be related to

the cult of the Holy Spirit. It is held in July every 4 years with the next one in 2011 (the last one in 2007 attracted over 600,000 visitors). The procession of the trays consists of around four hundred young women each carrying on her head a tray with loaves of bread and crowned with a white dove – the symbol of the Holy Spirit. The headdress weighs in the region of 15 kg so young men assist in the procession by escorting each maiden *(see right hand side of tile photo>)*

IGREJA Sᵗᵃ MARIA DOS OLIVAIS

❏ **Non nobis, Domine, sed nomini tuo da gloriam!** *Psalm 113*

06 *462.8 km (287.6 miles) – Santiago*

TOMAR – ALVAIÁZERE

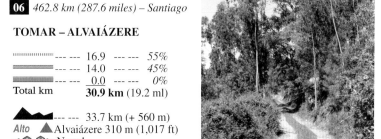

⋅⋅⋅⋅⋅⋅⋅⋅	--- ---	16.9	--- ---	55%	
▬▬▬	--- ---	14.0	--- ---	45%	
▬▬▬	--- ---	0.0	--- ---	0%	
Total km		**30.9 km (19.2 ml)**			

▰▱ --- --- 33.7 km (+ 560 m)
Alto ▲ Alvaiázere 310 m (1,017 ft)
< Ⓐ Ⓗ > None!

Physical Path: A day of varied terrain as we climb out of the flat plains of the Ribatejo into the central province of Beira Litoral over several hills *serras* to the high point today which is Alvaiázere itself at 310m. The surface underfoot likewise changes from town pavements into earth farm tracks, roman roads, woodland paths and quiet country lanes. Few of the tiny hamlets we pass through have facilities so stock up on water and some food before leaving Tomar.

❏ **Mystical Path:** *Not unto us, o Lord, but unto your name grant glory!* The words of this psalm were chosen by the Templar Knights as their Motto and serve us well today; self-glorification is a condition of our ego-orientated world and has made us blind to the Source of our true Self identity.

❏ **Personal Reflections:** He was a mine of information but responded only to what was asked – humbleness exemplified. He indicated the general direction of the secret symbol but invited me to feel its power rather than observe its form. The Holy Grail is an inward understanding not a physical object. We have been looking in the wrong direction and found only emptiness in our blindness.

0.0 km Tomar *Ponte Velha* We leave town over rio Nabão *old bridge* to chemist *Farmácia Central* **option ❶ [0.1 km]** *[the original route continues s/o along rua Marqués de Pombal and veers at roundabout]*. At the Chemist turn <left into rua Centro Republicano to **option ❷ [0.4 km]** *[The new summer river route ❸ s/o is described on the next page]*. For the main route turn up right into Av. Dr. Egas Moniz and veer <left at **bullring [0.4 km]** diagonally into rua Antonio Duarte Faustino into Rua Principal da Choromela s/o at crossroads *Café Choromela* up steeply into rua Vincennes past military barracks (right) to high point of this stage 105m **alto [1.0 km]** at new city heights *Café Cidade Nova* before finally dropping down to turn <left into rua Ponte Peniche onto wide track through olive orchards. River route joins (left) to the medieval stone bridge **[1.1 km]**.

3.0 km Ponte de Peniche Here all routes converge to pass under the IC-9.

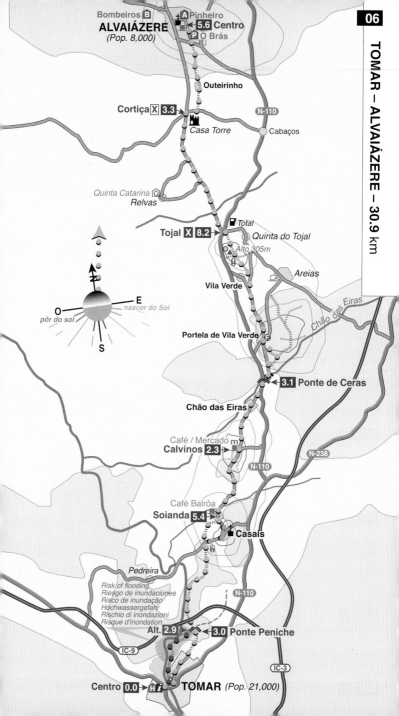

Bombeiros **B**
ALVAIÁZERE
(Pop. 8,000)
A Pinheiro
5.6 Centro
P O Brás

Outeirinho

Cortiça **X** **3.3**
Casa Torre
Cabaços
N-110

Quinta Catarina
Relvas

Total
Tojal **X** **8.2**
Quinta do Tojal
Alto 305m
Areias

Vila Verde

Chão das Eiras
Portela de Vila Verde

3.1 Ponte de Ceras

Chão das Eiras

Café / Mercado
Calvinos **2.3**

N-110
N-238

Café Balrôa
Soianda **5.4**
Casais

Pedreira

Risk of flooding
Riesgo de inundaciones
Risco de inundação
Hochwassergefahr
Rischio di inondazioni
Risque d'inondation

N-110

Alt. **2.9**
3.0 Ponte Peniche

IC-9
IC-3

Centro **0.0**
H **i**
TOMAR *(Pop. 21,000)*

E
nascer do Sol
O
pôr do sol
S

❖ **Option ❸** offers a delightful riverside path in dry weather. The path is low-lying and floods in wet weather when the river is high. In good weather continue s/o into Rua Ponte da Vala alongside disused canal and factory (left). The asphalt eventually gives way and we cross onto a path up past Tágusgás depot and down to the majestic **rio Nabão** [**1.9** km] (from the start at ponte velha). Continue alongside river passing weir and canal entrance (disused) past series of water wells to join the main route on wide earth track [**0.8** km]. Turn <left to bridge [**0.2** km] :

2.9 km Ponte de Peniche. Medieval bridge over tributary of río Nabão.

The route now continue on a delightful earth track through pine and eucalyptus forest under the motorway IC-9 [**0.3** km] to pick up the path again down to the rio Nabão where we turn right> along the river bank past a weir before turning up right> [**0.8** km] onto a steep path that cuts its way through the rock under power lines to take a track along to the asphalt road and option [**2.2** km].

3.3 km Option A new (recommended) route now bypasses the village of Casais *[still waymarked down to the right; all by asphalt road with a steep climb to top].* For new route continues s/o over road onto earth track through scrubland following old red / white GR signs. The track continues down s/o right ½ km and imm. s/o left up into woodland that winds its way back to the road in Soianda.

2.1 km Soianda *Café Balrôa* (photo) Continue s/o over **stream** [**1.5** km] into crossroad village of **Calvinos** [**0.8** km].

2.3 km Calvinos *Café Cabeleira & mini-mercado (the last opportunity to buy refreshments before reaching Alvaiãzere).* Turn <left (direction Chão das Eiras) to join the N-110 for a short stretch to the bridge in Ceras.

3.1 km Ponte Ceras. Do not cross the main bridge but take the side road *rua lagar do Boucha* (s/o right) to cross the **Ribeira do Chão das Eiras** [**0.1** km]onto the Estrada Romana. The road now turns right> uphill along rua das Azenhas before turning up sharp <left [**0.5** km]. *[An alternative track **not** waymarked continues s/o and winds it way into Areias to rejoin the main route in Tojal].* The steep rough track continues sharply up left onto a delightful forest path leading into and through the straggling hamlet of [**1.4** km].

2.0 km Portela de Vila Verde with fine views over the countryside. No facilities excepting a water tap *[F]* at the far end of the hamlet. [!] While the route is generally well waymarked it now crisscrosses a maze of small country lanes through tiny hamlets – stay focused. The path maintains the high ridge past Vila Verde to turn off <left onto a forest path.

3.2 km Camino through mixed woodland (eucalyptus / pine) where waymarks are less obvious but generally maintain the contour line and s/o at cross of woodland tracks **[1.5 km]** past water tower **[0.1 km]** (white building off the path left, which marks the high point of this stage at 305m). Continue down passing specimen cork tree and continue s/o on over crossroads **[1.4 km].**

3.0 km Cruce *Tojal* direction Alvaiãzere Sul. *[Detour: If you need refreshment there is a filling station and cafe/restaurant Salimar off route 200m right]*. We now have a long stretch of asphalt road passing sign for Relvas TR **[1.8 km]** *(Quinta Catarina 1½ km detour but invariably closed)*. Continue s/o to Casa Torre at Cortica **[1.5 km]:**

3.3 km Cruce *Cortiça* turn right at crossroads and left (800m) onto a series of cobbled lanes through the straggling hamlets of Outeirinho and Feteiras up into the southern suburbs of Alvaiãzere (top end of town). Here a new bypass has cut off the original road into town. If you can scramble down the bank it saves a very long loop down and up again to this point. Continue into Rua José Augusto Martins Rangel passing restaurante and pensão **Residencial O Brás** €20-35 *Ⓒ* 236 655 405 m: 966 495 337 + *menú* €10.

5.6 km Alvaiãzere *Centro* **Albergaria Pinheiro** €10+ *Ⓒ* 915 440 196 / 925 850 756 (Carlos) rua Doutor Acúrcio Lopes /Plaza Mayor where the delightful Dᵃ Irene Pinheiro has a launderette underneath. Several pleasant cafés and shops around the central square and church and takeaway cafe 200m. **Bombeiros Voluntários** *Ⓒ* 236 650 510 welcome pilgrims ½ km further out of town in Rua dos Bombeiros Voluntários – just below the municipal gardens *jardim municipal*. The town has a population of 8,000 and the name Alvaiãzere *(pron: Al-Vy-Ah-zay)* comes from the Arabic *Al-Baiaz* 'land of the Falconer.' It is linked with the Knights Templar.

Theirs is an endless road, a hopeless maze, who seek for goods before they seek for God. *Bernard of Clairvaux*

07 *431.5 km (268.1 miles) – Santiago*

ALVAIÁZERE – RABAÇAL

⸬⸬⸬⸬⸬⸬	--- ---	14.3	--- ---	44%
▬▬▬▬	--- ---	18.2	--- ---	56%
▨▨▨▨	--- ---	0.0	--- ---	0%
Total km		**32.5** km (20.2 ml)		

◢◣ 35.1 km (+^ 520 m = 2.6 km)
Alto(m)▲ Vendas 470 m (1,542 ft)
< Ⓐ Ⓗ > Ansião **14.5** km – Alvorge **23.9**

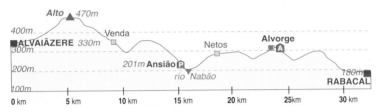

Physical Path: Another delightful day of undulating terrain through afforested valleys interspersed with olive groves and small crop fields that brings us into Ansião, conveniently located around ½ way – a good place to take a midday break or possible stopover for the night. Note an alternative route to and from Fátima connects at Ansião so be careful not to follow any blue arrows!

❏ **Mystical Path:** There are many paths back to our divine origins but many that lead us in the opposite direction. We do well to remember that... *money will buy a bed but not sleep, books but not brains, food but not appetite, finery but not beauty, medicine but not health, luxury but not culture, amusement but not happiness, a crucifix but not a Saviour, a temple of religion but not heaven.*

❏ **Personal Reflections:** She gave me a smile of such penetrating love that I was momentarily stilled, like one of her flock of peacefully grazing sheep and goats... And now I sit in this welcoming hostelry and eat the famous Rabaçal cheese, a mixture of local sheep and goat milk with the unique flavour of the pasture of this peaceful landscape... and the love of the shepherdess. I feel blessed and satiated.

0.0 km **Alvaiázere** From the town centre head down to the main street turning right> to main crossroads and municipal gardens where we veer up right and then <left (signposted Laranjeiras) and follow the road up into:

3.3 km **Laranjeiras** *Vendas mini-mercado* in house (right). Continue up steeply up through the Serra dos Ariques attentive for the waymarks as we twist and turn into **Venda** [F] **[1.2 km]** s/o to high point of this stage at 470m after which we turn right onto track **[1.9 km]** (GR 26) to the pretty chapel **[1.0 km]** in:

4.1 km **Venda do Negra** *ermita*. The route to Ansião now passes through a series of straggling hamlets (no facilities) along alternating surfaces of asphalt,

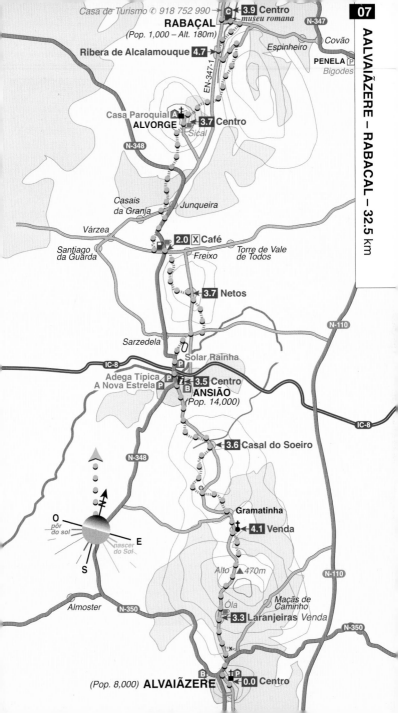

Casa de Turismo © 918 752 990

3.9 Centro
RABAÇAL
museu romana
(Pop. 1,000 – Alt. 180m)

N-347

Espinheiro

Covão

PENELA P
Bigodes

Ribera de Alcalamouque 4.7

EN-347-1

Casa Paroquial ✝
ALVORGE
3.7 Centro
Sical

N-348

Casais da Granja

Junqueira

Várzea

Santiago da Guarda

2.0 X Café

Freixo

Torre de Vale de Todos

3.7 Netos

N-110

Sarzedela

IC-8

P

Solar Rainha

P

Adega Típica
A Nova Estrela P

3.5 Centro
ANSIÃO
(Pop. 14,000)

IC-8

3.6 Casal do Soeiro

N-348

Gramatinha
✝
4.1 Venda

O
pôr do sol

E
nascer do Sol

S

Alto ▲*470m*

N-110

Almoster

N-350

Óla

Maçãs de Caminho

3.3 Laranjeiras *Venda*

N-350

(Pop. 8,000) **ALVAIÃZERE**

B
✝P **0.0 Centro**

earthen tracks (several local red/yellow path signage), cobblestone lane-ways and woodland paths. We pass first through **Gramatinha** and **Casais Maduros** and continue upwards into Casal do Soeiro where turn off <left onto path:

3.6 km **Casal do Soeiro** *camino* we now branch <left onto a woodland track (also local walking trails *Empeados de Cima* & wayside shrines *alminhas*) down to the asphalt road s/o over roundabout into the bustling market town of Ansião arriving at the main square with parish church (right). Proceed down the main street to the centre with tourist office, adj. Council office *Junta de Freguesia* opp. Adega Típica.

3.5 km **Ansião** *Centro*. The town is one of the larger municipalities we pass through with a population of 13,000 and source *nascente* of the river Nabão. *[Note: Ansião offers a main detour to Fátima indicated with blue arrows].* It is has a good range of facilities and a choice of accommodation which includes: **Residencial Adega Típica** ℭ 236 677 364 where Carlos (speaks English) and his brother João run this popular establishment (traditional Portuguese cooking) in rua Combatentes

da Grande Guerra (see photo above with council offices and jurisdictional pillar *picota*). **Nova Estrela** ℭ 236 677 415 Av. Dr. Victor Faveiro which also has a welcoming restaurant. **Pensão Larsol** *Avelar* ℭ 236 621 287 rua Nova, Avelar. At the other end of the bridge (on the way out) **Solar da Rainha** ℭ 236 676 204 Alto dos Pinheiras just beyond the IC-8 overpass, 14 rooms and restaurant. **Bombeiros Voluntários** ℭ 236 670 600 Av. Dr. Vitor Faveiro. Tourist office in the centre of town (often closed). Free internet available in the modern municipal library.

Leave Ansião over the 17[th]c bridge *Ponte da Cal* under the IC-8 up past Solar da Rainha, around a new sports ground onto short path around Bate Água/Além da Ponte and up steeply through woodland onto asphalt road into Netos:

3.7 km **Netos** *Camino* turn right at the end of the village and <left onto a forest track that undulates sharply through pine forest where sap is still collected in funnel shaped receptors (see photo right). The woodland is interspersed with olive groves and we suddenly emerge at a major crossroads with petrol station by Freixo:

2.0 km **Freixo** *Cruce* Petrol station *café/snack bar* at major cross of 5 roads *[Detour* ● ● ● ● ● *2½ km to A Santiago da Guarda with its medieval Tower and fortified Palace and nearby accommodation at* **Casa Vázea** ℭ *236 679 057].* To continue to Rabaçal proceed in the direction of A Santiago but turn right>

(100m) off the main road and right> again onto a short stretch of path by Casais da Granja. The route now alternates between asphalt and narrow lanes with dry stone walls and paths (overgrown in places – push through or seek alternatives). Just before entering Junqueira (small hamlet ahead) the route leaves the asphalt road to take a track up through scrub and woodland to:

3.7 km **Alvorge** *Albergue* Igreja *Par.[8÷1]* €5 ℗ 913 132 477 (Vitor at *café Largo do Cruceiro/ Centro).* Welcoming village proud of their pilgrim hostel in the lower floor of the new community building adjoining the church with splendid views over the surrounding countryside (plans to extend the accommodation) This attractive hilltop village has a grocery shop in the main square.

   The route continues steeply downhill on new asphalt access road to turn off left onto rough path **[0.4 km]** through scrubland down to the valley floor past lavadero to cross main road **[0.7 km]** onto lovely open path (see photo previous page) before turning down sharply onto secondary road **[1.7 km]** which we follow back down towards the main road, ignoring 1st path but taking the 2nd path off right> **[0.4 km]** the path maybe overgrown and can be wet underfoot, cross stream and turn right> on main road in a small hamlet **[1.5 km]**.

4.7 km **Ribeira de Alcalamouque** no facilities. Continue through the hamlet and turn off right> onto cobblestone lane that alternates between track and path past abandoned quinta (left) onto asphalt road, turn <left to cross river and up into Rabaçal turning right> at T-junction to *Café Bonito* menú:

3.9 km **Rabaçal** Casa de Turismo do Rabaçal €15+ ℗ 918 752 990 (Dª Alice) 917 620 982 (Hermínio) 239 569 371 (Serqueijo). 29 beds located on the main street adj. the cultural centre and *museo romano* ℗ 239 561 856 *[also arranges tours of the Roman Villa with its perfectly preserved mosaic floor – far end out of town). Café Ruínas* opp. the museum.

Residencial *(left)*   **Museo** *(right)*

(Detour ● ● ● ● 5 km to Penela, one of the oldest municipalities in Portugal founded by D. Afonso Henriques in 1142 as part of the defensive system in the re-conquest. Its beautifully preserved castle sits atop the hill pena *and is a listed monument. Penela has several pensões in the town including: P° Bigodes* ℗ 239 569 129. Penela Turismo ℗ 239 561 132).*

REFLECTIONS:

❏ **Live out of your imagination, not your history.** *Steven Covey*

08 *399 km (247.9 miles) – Santiago*

RABAÇAL – COIMBRA

‖‖‖‖‖‖‖‖‖	--- ---	10.3	--- ---	*35%*
	--- ---	15.6	--- ---	*53%*
▬▬▬	--- ---	3.6	--- ---	*12%*
Total km		**29.5 km** (18.3 ml)		

◣◢ 31.6 km (+^ 420 m = 2.1 km)
Alto(m)▲ Alto Santa Clara 215 m (705 ft)
< Ⓐ Ⓗ > *Condeixa a Nova* **12.8** *km (+1 km)*

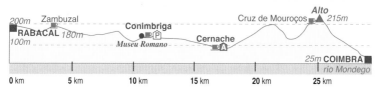

Practical Path: The terrain is gentler now as we leave the *serras* behind, our highest point of the day is Alto de Santa Clara at 190m overlooking Coimbra and the Mondego river valley. We follow part of the original Roman road that linked Olisipo (Lisboa) with Bracara Augusta (Braga) and pass the famous Roman ruins of Conimbriga. This first part of the day is through quiet countryside alongside the rio dos Mouros with a mixture of pine and eucalyptus woodland interspersed with vineyards and olive groves. However, the latter half of this stage ends less romantically as we navigate through the maze of roads and motorways that weave around the outskirts of Coimbra.

❏ **Mystical Path:** "Healing does not mean going back to the way things were before, but rather allowing what is now to move us closer to God" *Ram Dass.* Come back to the present – arrive into now – embrace the joy of this moment – inhabit your Self – laugh out loud – dance with the angels – come alive.

❏ **Personal Reflections:** I let my mind wander and my feet followed aimlessly, oblivious to the glorious Landscape Temple surrounding me; I might as well have been walking in my own back garden for all the benefit I was receiving or giving. As I retraced my steps I began to examine my choice – to stay dwelling on the past or focused on the glorious present – the switch is simple awareness.

0.0 km **Rabaçal** From the centre *residencial* proceed down the main street and turn right> (direction Panela) over **stream [1.1 km]** veering **right [1.0 km]** (not bridge 50m left) merging onto asphalt into **Zambujal [1.7 km]**.

3.8 km **Zambujal** central square with parish church and *community café.* Continue through the village and down over the river and over **road [0.9 km]** s/o into **Fonte Coberta [1.4 km]**.

2.3 km **Fonte Coberta** Chapel and image of Santiago (photo above). S/o out of this historic pilgrim hamlet onto path and <left onto a delightful track just *before*

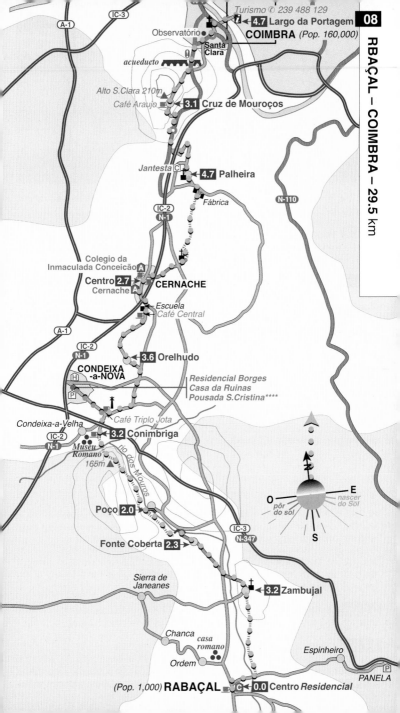

Turismo © 239 488 129

4.7 **Largo da Portagem** 08

COIMBRA *(Pop. 160,000)*

Observatório •

Santa Clara

acueducto

Alto S.Clara 210m

Café Araujo **3.1** **Cruz de Mouroços**

Jantesta **4.7** **Palheira**

IC-2 / N-1

Fábrica

N-110

Colegio da
Inmaculada Conceição

Centro 2.7 **CERNACHE**
Cernache

A-1

Escuela
Café Central

IC-2 / N-1

3.6 **Orelhudo**

**CONDEIXA
-a-NOVA**

*Residencial Borges
Casa da Ruinas
Pousada S.Cristina****

Condeixa-a-Velha

Café Triplo Jota

IC-2 / N-1

3.2 **Conimbriga**

*Museu
Romano*
165m

rio dos Mouros

Poço 2.0

Fonte Coberta 2.3

IC-3
N-347

*Sierra de
Janeanes*

3.2 **Zambujal**

Chanca

*casa
romano*

Espinheiro

Ordem

PANELA

(Pop. 1,000) **RABAÇAL** **0.0 Centro** *Residencial*

O — E
*pôr
do sol* — *nascer
do Sol*
S

the 17thc Ponte Filipina (see photo above). The track runs parallel to the rio dos Mouros into another tiny hamlet of Poço:

2.0 km Poço. We continue on a remote track alongside the river climbing gently up into woodland before dropping down more steeply to cross a tributary of the rio dos Mouros up to the historic Roman site at:

3.2 km Conimbriga *(Condeixa-A-Velha)* The largest and best preserved Roman settlement in Portugal and classified a National Monument. The Romans arrived here in 139 BCE under the command of general Decimus Junius Brutus who established a base on what was a Celtic settlement (*Briga* is Gaelic for 'fortified place'). Excavations have unearthed Iron Age remains going back to the 9thc BCE.

The extensive ruins occupy an attractive wooded site and include a museum with *Café* and good views down the valley. We exit the ancient site via a tunnel under the modern motorway IC-3 and make our way towards the antennae adjoining *Café-Bar Triplo Jota* where we have an option.

Detour ● ● ● ● *Condeixa-A-Nova 1 km off route. This regional centre for hand-painted tiles has a range of facilities and lodging. On the way into town we pass the up-market* Pousada de Santa Cristina €90+ ℗ 239 941 286. Residencial Borges €25 ℗ 239 942 350 Rua Dona Maria Elsa Franco Sotto Mayor Nº 65 + @ Nº 53 Casa de Hóspedes Ruínas ℗ 239 941 772 *with 11 rooms. This busy regional town supports a wide selection of bars and restaurants.*

Just before Bar Triplo Jota the waymarked route continues s/o right along a series of intersecting secondary roads. Stay focussed so as not to miss any of the frequent turnings into and through:

3.6 km Orelhudo. Continue up passing *café* **[1.5 km]** and turn <left after school over the IC-2 into Cernache past Correio to the town **centre [1.2 km]**.

2.7 km Cernache *Centro cafés* & *Albergue* ❶ Cernache *priv.[14÷3]* €9 ℗ 917 619 080 (Pedro) / 968 034 708 Rua Álvaro Anes, 37 in the centre of Cernache. at exit of town lodging available in Jesuit college ❷ Colégio da Imaculada Conceição €-donación ℗ 239 940 630. Turn right> roundabout and exit under the IC-2 and s/o at crossroads up to church and start of forest track [**1.6 km**] which continues for a tranquil [**2.5 km**] emerging by modern factories. Turn <left on main road and cross over into **Palheira** [**0.6 km**]:

4.7 km **Palheira** *Iglesia* the route now undulates sharply up to alto (190m). *[Here we have option for lodging at Jantesta Guest House Rua Da Jantesta, 35 (+0.5 km) €15-30].* We now drop down steeply again (previously via concrete pedestrian bridge over the IC-2) but now waymarked to cross under the motorway into Antanhol ascending once more turning right> at new roundabout and then sharp <left up to the high point of this stage Alto de Santa Clara (215m):

3.1 km **Cruz dos Mouroços** *Alto de Santa Clara Café.* From the church square *Plaza de la Iglesia* we get the first view over the Mondego river valley as we descend steeply down to the maze of roads and flyovers that bypass Coimbra 'old town'. Ongoing roadworks may obliterate some waymarks but the first obvious guide is the Roman **aqueduct** [**1.1** km] now sliced in half to allow one of the new roads to plough through the middle, as do we (but watch out for new or temporary waymarks that may offer a detour in this area). Continue down to the valley floor and turn up right> at **junction** [**1.8** km] into rua Central da Mesura and up into rua do Observatório passing the observatory (left) before cresting the rise into a modern suburb with *cafés & restaurantes* s/o over roundabout still with panoramic views over Coimbra.

We now begin the sharp descent to Santa Clara, satellite town of Coimbra with a population of 10,000. We pass a military barracks incongruously built adj. **Convento Santa Clara** [**1.8 km**]. The lower 'old' *Convento de Santa Clara-a-Velha* was the original resting place of its founder Santa Isabel, wife of King Dom Dinis and subsequently the patron saint of Coimbra. It also housed the murdered remains of the tragic Dona Inês de Castro (see below) but the waters of the Mondego River were constantly flooding the convent and so a new one *Convento de Santa Clara-a-Nova* was built during the 17th c further up the hill. The convent is an austere building; the two redeeming features include a fine cloister and Isabel's tomb (that of Inês was re-interred in Alcobaça).

The life and gruesome death of *Dona Inês de Castro* is the subject of many an epic story line and poetry and formed the subject (and title) of Victor Hugo's first play. Beautiful daughter of a Galician nobleman she caught the eye of Dom Pedro who vowed to marry her. Pedro's father King Afonso IV fearing Spanish influence on account of the Galician connection forbade the marriage. However they married in secret but Afonso hearing of the union had her murdered in the grounds of the mournful park close by (to the right of our route) known as 'The Garden of Tears' *Quinta das Lágrimas.* When Dom Pedro succeeded to the throne in 1357 he exhumed her body from the convent here and had her corpse crowned and seated on a throne in Santa Cruz (see Coimbra) where courtiers were forced to pay homage and obliged to kiss her decaying hand.

    The life of pilgrim Queen Elizabeth *Santa Isabel* 'The Peacemaker' is a somewhat less pitiful story. Daughter of King Pedro III of Aragon she was married off to the king *Dom Dinis* at the age of 12 and suffered greatly under his austere rule and bouts of jealousy. She used to infuriate her husband by giving constantly to the needy. One of the early miracles associated with her (that would lead eventually to her beatification) was when she hid gold coins to bring to the poor disguised in a basket and was stopped and searched by her husband but the gold had turned to roses thus escaping (or perhaps inflaming) his wrath. When Dom Dinis died in 1325 she distributed her remaining wealth to the poor and became a Poor Clare in the convent here.

We now make our way down and over the mighty river Mondego whose source is the Serra da Estrela and we cross the Ponte de Santa Clara into the welcoming square *Largo da Portagem* that marks the entrance to the city:

4.7 km Coimbra *Largo da Portagem* with cafés and helpful *Turismo* (right). Coimbra was capital of Portugal from 1145 until 1255 but is better known for its famous university founded in 1290 which crowns the hill and whose students bring a lively atmosphere to this ancient and historic city, formerly the Roman town of Aeminium. A population of 100,000 provides one of its main charms; its compact size which makes it easy to visit the main sites, some directly linked to the medieval camino de Santiago. Coimbra 'old town' was declared a World Heritage site in 2013. Spend a day in this enchanting city if you can for, like Tomar, there is much to do and see. The main historic and tourist sites are all grouped around the city centre and lie either directly on or within a few hundred metres of the waymarked camino. *Note: At Igreja Santiago* ❷ *the original route (yellow) turns left into R.Adelino Veiga. An alternative route s/o via R.Eduardo Coelho and R. Sofia is now waymarked.*

❏ *Turismo* Largo da Portagem ✆ 239 855 930. ❏**: Hoteles and Pensões:** on or imm. adjoining the waymarked camino (within 100 meters) includes: Largo da Portagem *P.* Larbelo ✆ 239 829 092. Adj. *left P.* Atlantico ✆ 239 826 496 *H°°°*Astória ✆ 239 853 020 *P.* Internacional ✆ 239 825 503. Adj. *right P.* Avenida ✆ 239 822 156. *P.* Parque ✆ 239 829 202. *P.* Jardim ✆ 239 825 204. Between Igreja Santiago and the rail station *P.* Moderna ✆ 239

825 413, rua Adelino Veiga 49. *P.* Dómus ✆ 239 828 584 rua Adelino Veiga 62. There are several other hotels and Pensões in the busy streets in the area of the railway station itself. *Note* there are 3 railway stations in Coimbra, the central station 'A' Estação Nova is the one referred to here. On the far side of the university in rua Henrique Seco is a modern youth hostel Juventud ✆ 239 822 955 Rua Dr. Henriques Seco, 14 a 20 minute walk or take bus Nº 46 from the central station 'A'. **Bombeiros Voluntários** Av. Fernão Magalhães.

Wide variety of restaurants catering to all tastes and pockets down virtually every street which includes the ever popular but tiny *Zé Manel* on rua Forno (behind the Astoria).

Sounding a different note but adjacent to the cathedral is fado restaurant *O Trovador* with its atmospheric interior of ceramic tiles and wood panelling. Coimbra fado shares the same sombre melodies heard in the fado houses of Lisboa and Porto but supposedly with more scholarly lyrics! Just above the cathedral is the renowned **Museu Machado de Castro** on Largo Dr. José Rodrigues and just above it we come to Largo da Sé Nova with the New Cathedral, which was

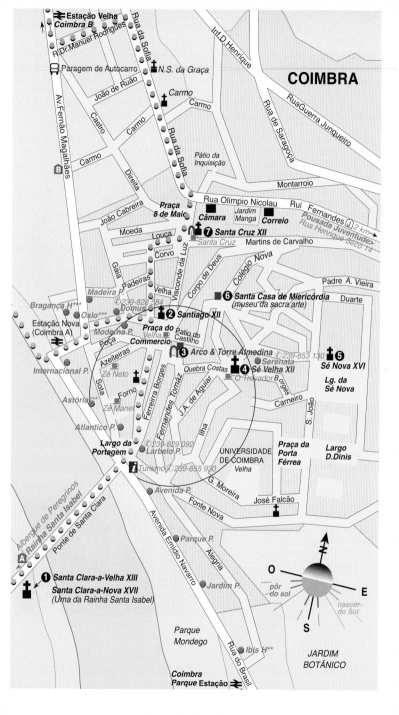

founded by the Jesuits. If you intend to visit the university buildings this is the time as you are now effectively at the crown of the hill where the various faculties are located. The end of the academic year is marked with rowdy celebrations *Queima das Fitas* the 'burning of the ribbons' held in April. From here you can find your way down (or get deliciously lost) amongst the maze of narrow winding streets. Providing you head north (sun to your left if its afternoon) you will arrive back in the main shopping street.

❏ **Historic Buildings and Monuments:** *(see city plan)* ❶ *Conventos Santa Clara* on the West side of the river (on the way in). From Largo da Portagem the waymarked route goes down rua dos Gatos into Adro de Cima and Adelino Veiga passing the 18ᵗʰc Igreja de São Bartolomeu and the ancient Hospital Real

into Praça do Comercio lined with bars and restaurants and open air market to ❷ **Igreja de Santiago** 12ᵗʰc evoking the medieval pilgrimage. The flight of steps (right) brings us (off route) up to the main pedestrian shopping street rua Visconde da Luz. Turn left to the heart of the city in *Praça 8 de Maio* and ❹ **Igreja de Santa Cruz** (photo far right). The monastery was founded in 1131 making it one of the oldest buildings still extant and housing the tombs of King Afonso Henriques and Sancho I.

Igreja de Santiago *(with waymark left)*

The Manueline 'Cloister of Silence' was added in 1517 and the triumphal arch in the 18ᵗʰc. Adjoining it (right) and built on the original monastery buildings is the popular neo-Manueline café Santa Cruz with its vaulted stone interior. Also on the square is the Câmara Municipal behind which is the Jardim da Manga.

This minimal 'tour' would not be complete without a visit to the historic cathedral. Return via the pedestrian shopping street, past Santiago church and turn left up steps under ❺ **Arco de Almedina** the original main gate in the medieval defensive wall that ran for 2 kilometres around the base of the hill. This is still the main entrance to the Old City or *High Quarter*. Continue up steeply into largo da Sé Velha where we find ❻ **Sé Velha** the old (original) cathedral before that function

was transferred to the soulless Sé Nova situated further on up. One of the most important Romanesque monuments in Portugal built in 1162 on a former ecclesiastical site dating from the 9ᵗʰc. Amongst the many ancient tombs is that of a former archbishop of Santiago de Compostela, D. Egas Fafes with a scallop shell emblem set in azulejos tiles. A side door provides access to a lovely Gothic cloister – the oldest extant cloisters in Portugal and well worth the minimal entry fee with proceeds going to community services.

Sé Velha – Cloisters

REFLECTIONS:

❏ **Bacchus hath drowned more men than Neptune.** *Thomas Fuller*

---

09 *369.5 km (229.6 miles) – Santiago*

COIMBRA – MEALHADA

⊪⊪⊪⊪⊪⊪⊪	--- ---	7.1	--- ---	32%	
▬▬▬▬	--- ---	12.2	--- ---	54%	
▬▬▬▬	--- ---	3.1	--- ---	14%	
Total km		**22.4 km** (13.9 ml)			

23.3 km (+^ 180 m = 0.9 km)
Alto(m)▲ Santa Luzia 145 m (475 ft)
< 🅰 🅷 > Fornos **7.8** km

Practical Path: The terrain is now markedly different from the previous stage being virtually flat as we pass along various river valleys crisscrossed with flood and irrigation channels *acequia* (reminiscent of the Ribatejo plains). Our high point is around Santa Luzia at 145m. While we have short stretches of the roman road *calzada romana* much of today is spent on asphalt and there are several stretches of main roads where extra vigilance is required. A forest track has now been waymarked from Santa Luzia. Do *not* follow old waymarks along the dangerous N-1 into Carqueijo.

❏ **Mystical Path:** Between inebriety and sobriety lies a state of equilibrium; embracing a super-sensible reality while honouring the god of harvest and grapes. Robbie Burns reflected thus: "I love drinking now and then. It defecates the standing pool of thought. A man perpetually in the paroxysm and fears of inebriety is like a half-drowned wretch condemned to labour unceasingly in water; but a now-and-then tribute to Bacchus is like the cold bath – bracing and invigorating."

❏ **Personal Reflections:** It was like a battlefield, the bodies of the vanquished strewn all over the square. Some students were still comatose, others lay moaning in the cold light of dawn trying to awaken from the festivities. I picked my way out of the city and recalled my own youthful period of excess. Perhaps I am now more interested in quality rather than quantity, waking rather than sleeping. Despite the chaotic scenes around me, the light of this new day filled me with a sense of hopefulness, we will arise from our stupor.

0.0 km Coimbra *Largo da Portagem* This stage is measured from *Largo de Portagem*. You can [1] proceed directly down Av. Emídio Navarro alongside the river to rejoin the waymarks at the central rail station [100 m] or [2] follow the waymarked route to the *Igreja de Santiago* and thence back to the central station *'A' Estação Nova* [0.5 km] and out along the rio Mondego past the bus station and under [!] the maze of high level roads giving access to **Ponte do Açude [1.0 km]** (N-1 and IC-2) under the railway to the **roundabout [0.9 km]:**

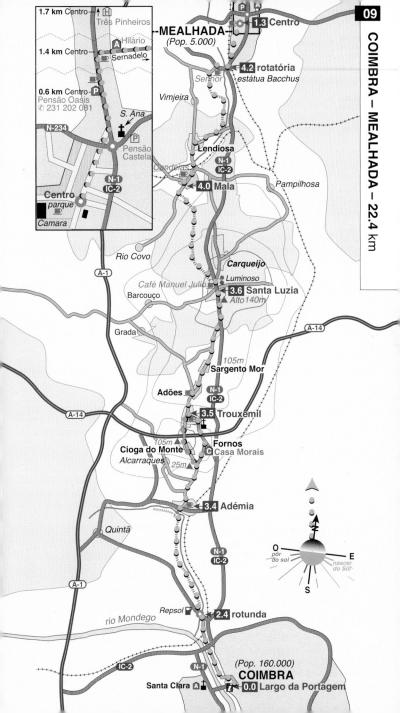

MEALHADA
(Pop. 5.000)

1.3 Centro

1.7 km Centro — Três Pinheiros

A Hilário

1.4 km Centro — Sernadelo

0.6 km Centro
Pensão Oasis
☎ 231 202 081

N-234

S. Ana

Pensão
Castela

N-1
IC-2

Centro
parque

Camara

4.2 rotatória
estátua Bacchus

Senhor

Vimjeira

Lendiosa

Candeiras

N-1
IC-2

Pampilhosa

4.0 Mala

Rio Covo

Café Manuel Julio

Barcouço

Carqueijo

Luminoso

3.6 Santa Luzia
Alto 140m

A-1

Grada

A-14

105m

Sargento Mor

Adões

N-1
IC-2

A-14

3.5 Trouxemil

Fornos

105m

Cioga do Monte

C Casa Morais

Alcarraques

25m

3.4 Adémia

Quinta

N-1
IC-2

A-1

rio Mondego

Repsol

2.4 rotunda

O
*pôr
do sol*

E
*nascer
do Sol*

S

IC-2

N-1

(Pop. 160.000)

COIMBRA

Santa Clara

7 **0.0** Largo da Portagem

2.4 km Rotunda continue s/o over roundabout and veer **right>** [0.3 km] (before Repsol petrol station) onto an old asphalt road with the environs of Coimbra now firmly behind. Continue alongside overgrown canal parallel to rail line and turn right> **over bridge** [2.9 km] up to main road **crossing** [0.2 km].

3.4 km Cruce *Adémia da Baixo café* s/o at **Trouxemil water works** [1.4 km].

[Option: for the original route turn left to Cioga do Monte (opp. Water dept.). continue up to Cioga [0.9 km] café and on up steeply to cross over A-1 motorway and down gently to Trouxemil [1.2 km]: Same distance as new route].

The new route is waymarked via **Fornos** [0.6 km] Casa Morais €50 Ⓒ 967 636 029 Rua Da Capela (formerly a medieval pilgrim inn). Up steeply by main road under the A-1 passing Manueline church (right) visited by Santa Isabel into **Trouxemil** [1.5 km] where the original route joins from the left.

3.5 km Trouxemil *Plaza café, bar e restaurant* turn up right> into **Adões** [0.7 km] *café e mercado* through **Sargento Mor** [1.1 km] *café e mercado* and up gently to join the busy N-1 *café* to traffic lights in **Santa Lúzia** [1.8 km]:

3.6 km Santa Lúzia *Luminoso cafés.* **Note**: a new route woodland track is now waymarked to the left of the N-1 *behind restaurante Manuel Julio.* Do *not* follow old waymarks along the N-1 but veer s/o left and join the **track** [0.4 km]. The rough woodland path emerges onto a secondary **road** [2.2 km] and we turn right> into **Mala** [1.4 km].

4.0 km Mala *Cafe/Pastelaria Candeias.* We continue over disused rail line into **Lendiosa** with chapel but no facilities. Veer right past *[F]* and onto path by river through woodland to rest area with *Café Senhor* turn right to main road at roundabout at the entrance to Mealhada.

4.2 km Rotunda with god Bacchus astride a wine barrel. Cross and turn <left over rail veering right> at Instituto da Vinho, past Correios to the town centre.

1.3 km Mealhada *Centro* town park with *cafés* and shops.

Mealhada is a busy town just off the A-1 and straddling the N-1 and rail line with a population of 5,000. The name derives appropriately from Meada 'meeting of the ways' and it was also a major crossroads town in Roman times being mile-post *miliário* XII on the Coimbra *Aeminium* – Porto *Cale* highway. A famous wine growing area where the municipal pamphlet takes a quote from Victor Hugo

"God created water but man made wine." and urges us to "… render homage on our knees our hands in prayer, this is Bairrada wine, the divine liquid awaiting us." Praise indeed! And so that the culinary highlights of the district are not left out it leaves us with another popular saying, "God created the suckling pig, the devil the hedgehog!" Mealhada is famous for its spit roasted month-old piglet dish *Leitões*. However, our focus is, perhaps, more on accommodation possibilities and the pilgrimage ahead.

❏ **Accommodation:** Pensão Castela ℂ 231 202 275 basic but centrally located adj. to the church. Further out but directly on our route (and the N-1) Residencial Oasis €25 ℂ 231 202 081 Estrada Nacional N.º1. *H°°°*dos Três Pinheiros €40 ℂ 231 202 391 Best Western Estrada Nacional N.º1. *Alb.* Hilário *Par.[18÷2]*+ €10-15 + priv. rooms ℂ 231 202 117 m: 916 191 721 E.N.1 Av. da Restauração, 30 (Sernadelo). *Note that the Bombeiros Voluntários are longer receiving pilgrims.*

REFLECTIONS:

❏ **"If we are not fully in the present moment, we miss everything."**
Peace Is Every Step: *The Path of Mindfulness in Everyday Life* Thich Nhat Hanh

10 *347.1 km (215.7 miles) – Santiago*

MEALHADA – ÁGUEDA

⦙⦙⦙⦙⦙⦙⦙⦙⦙⦙ --- ---	3.1	--- ---	12%
▬▬▬▬ --- ---	20.9	--- ---	82%
▬▬▬ --- ---	1.4	--- ---	6%
Total km	**25.4 km** (15.8 ml)

▰▰ 26.2 km (+^ 160 m = 0.8 km)
Alto(m)▲ Anadia 85 m (279 ft)
<🅰 🄷> Sernadelo **1.5** km / Anadia **7.7**

Practical Path: Another fairly level stage as the gently undulating terrain follows the path of the Cértima river valley (a tributary of the Vouga which we will pass tomorrow). It's also another relatively short stage but with much asphalt to contend with as we skirt several industrial areas. Vineyards and a stretch of woodland relieve the monotony of the road network and we have the town of Águeda, built around the banks of the river, to explore on our arrival.

❏ **Mystical Path:** Between alertness and stupor lies a liminal space of mindlessness. Day-dreaming can be a restful if the dreams are peaceful but it is not a place from which to navigate the paths of life with authority and power. To come fully alive we need to come fully present and act from mindfulness.

❏ **Personal Reflections:** I had feasted on the local speciality and fallen under the spell of Bacchus and was feeling somewhat the worse for wear. So much for my judgement and condemnation of the youthful citizenry of Coimbra. Here I am the following day lost because my mind is foggy from an excess of wine the previous night and I missed a key waymark. Mindfulness is the way of the pilgrim.

0.0 km Mealheada *Centro* from the town centre we make our way back to the N-1 passing *Residencial Oasis* and turn **right>** [**1.4 km**] by *restaurant Espelho d'Agua* in the *direction* of Sernadelo and **Albergue Hilário** veer off **right>** by house with modern concrete slatted windows [**0.2 km**] onto path through **woodland** [**0.6 km**] take left hand fork [**0.2 km**] s/o into **Alpalhão** [**1.0 km**].

3.4 km Alpalhão *Igreja* turn **right>** past church through **Aguim** [**1.5 km**] (no facilities) and turn **right>** onto another woodland **track** [**1.0 km**] and s/o main road and roundabout *towards* Anadia past modern sports grounds *zona desporto* and continue up to next roundabout at top of the hill above **Anadia** [**1.8 km**].

4.3 km Rotunda *Anadia* here we have an option to detour into the town for refreshments of to stay the night:

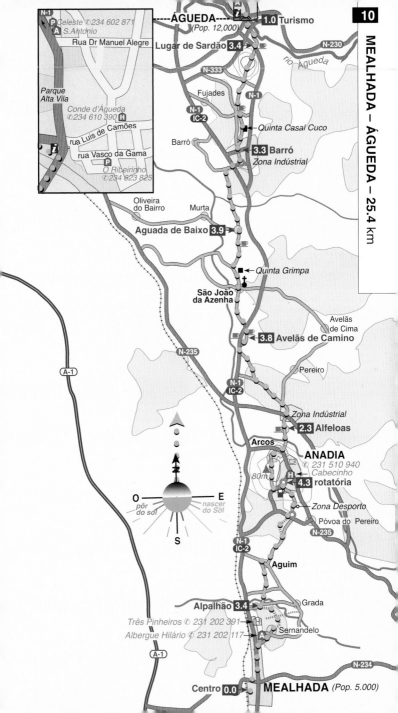

ÁGUEDA (Pop. 12,000)

1.0 Turismo

N-230

rio Águeda

Lugar de Sardão **3.4**

N-333

Fujades

N-1

IC-2

Quinta Casal Cuco

Barró

3.3 Barró
Zona Indústrial

Oliveira
do Bairro

Murta

Aguada de Baixo **3.9**

Quinta Grimpa

São João
da Azenha

Avelãs
de Cima

3.8 Avelãs de Camino

N-235

Pereiro

N-1
IC-2

Zona Indústrial

2.3 Alfeloas

Arcos

ANADIA
© 231 510 940
Cabecinho
80m **H**

4.3 rotatória

Zona Desporto

Póvoa do Pereiro

N-235

N-1
IC-2

A-1

Aguim

Alpalhão 3.4

Grada

Três Pinheiros © 231 202 391

Albergue Hilário © 231 202 117

Sernandelo

A-1

N-234

Centro 0.0

MEALHADA (Pop. 5.000)

O
pôr
do sol

E
nascer
do Sol

S

Inset (Águeda town map)

N-1

P Celeste © 234 602 871
A S.António

Rua Dr Manuel Alegre

Parque
Alta Vila

Conde d'Águeda
© 234 610 390 **H**

rua Luis de Camões

rua Vasco da Gama

P O Ribeirinho
© 234 623 825

i

88

Detour ● ● ● ● *Anadia* *1 km off route.*
The waymarked route bypasses this
lively market town with a good range of
facilities and accommodation including:
*H***Cabecinho* €40 Ⓒ 231 510 940
Av. Eng. Tavares da Silva (by the
roundabout). *Alb.* Centro Social de São
José de Cluny *Par.[48÷2]* € donativo
Rua São José de Cluny 231 504 167.

Turn <left at the roundabout past the petrol station *café* and shops and turn up
right> past the cemetery s/o up to our high point of this stage (75m) to drop
steeply down passing *[F]* into **Arcos *Igreja*** **[1.4** km] *café* turn <left and s/o over
river into **Adfeloas [0.9** km].

2.3 km Adfeloas *café* s/o over the busy N-235 past various factories back down
to the main road (traffic lights) into **Avelas de Caminho**.

3.8 km Avelãs de Caminho variety of *cafés-restaurantes* adjacent to the main
road including the popular *Queiróz*. The suffix *caminho* denotes associations
with the medieval camino. At the far end of the town we veer off <left by chapel
into **São João da Azenha** past Bodega
offices and **capela St. João [1.9** km]
continue along the quiet country lane
passing **Quinta da Grimpa [0.4** km]
connected with the Bodega in São João
and the famous Bairrada grape. The
quinta's fine Manueline features were
restored with stone from another site.
We now head into the Município passing
Café Rossio **[1.0** km] and up into the
village of **Aguada de Baixo [0.6** km].

3.9 km Aguada de Baixo *Centro* *café-pastelaría* s/o over river **bridge [0.6** km]
turn right under the IC-2 / N-1 **[2.2** km] into the industrial area of **Barró [0.5** km]:

3.3 km Barró *Zona Industrial* as we leave the industrial area veer right> off,
but parallel to the main road on the original Royal Way *Estrada Real* passing
Quinta Casa dos Cucos turning up <left by *café* and drop down steeply to cross
the busy [!] N-1 at:

3.4 km Lugar de Sardão *café* s/o through this ancient quarter with murals onto
open ground (flood area) and through a tunnel under the by-pass and up over the
old bridge *Ponte Velha* across the rio Águeda to:

1.0 km Águeda *Turismo* Largo Dr. Elísio Sucena with helpful tourist office
in this attractive tree-lined square at the bottom end of the town by the river.
Águeda, a lively town with a municipal population of 14,000. The main activity
is centred around the lower town and the river area and main shopping street rua
Luis de Camões with interconnecting mosaic-lined pedestrian streets off. *The*
camino continues left along the river in the direction of A Parades.

Turismo *©* 234 601 412 (by the bridge). In the ***lower town*** (summer only)***:***

❑ **Lodging:** *P*° **O Ribeirinho** *©* 234 623 825 rua Vasco da Gama, 88 welcomes pilgrims with 7 rooms above the restaurant (see photo right). *H******Conde d'Águeda** €45 *©* 236 610 390 Praça Conde de Águeda. **Bombeiros Voluntários** *©* 234 623 122 Av. 25 de Abril. *(an 'hotel' in the lower town masquerades as a brothel)* **Residencial Celeste** €22incl. *©* 234 602 871 Rua da Misericórdia, 713 (N-1 /) and its adj. *Alb.* **Sto. António** €12-15 incl. *©* 234 602 871 now welcomes pilgrims

[note the original hostel **Casa Azul** *on Rua Dr Manuel Alegre is closed].*

REFLECTIONS:

_____

_____

_____

_____

_____

_____

_____

_____

_____

_____

_____

_____

_____

_____

_____

❏ **We are all prostitutes… no matter how moral one takes oneself to be.**

R. D. Laing

11 *321.7 km (199.9 miles) – Santiago*

ÁGUEDA – ALBERGARIA *A-VELHA*

⠿⠿⠿⠿⠿⠿ --- ---	3.1	--- ---	*19%*
▬▬▬ --- ---	13.2	--- ---	*81%*
▬▬▬ --- ---	0.0	--- ---	*0.0%*
Total km	**16.3 km** (10.1 ml)		

◢◣ 17.9 km (+^ 320m = 1.6 km)
Alto(m)▲ Serém de Cima 125 m (410 ft)
< Ⓐ Ⓗ > None

Practical Path: Another easy day's walking and the shortest stage with reasonably flat terrain, the high point being Albergaria itself at 130m. Again the majority is on asphalt roads relieved by a magical path through pine and eucalyptus woods along the original Via Romana XVI over a beautiful stone bridge across the rio Marnel – the ancient ambience and tranquillity marred only by the main road. While there is not much to do in Albergaria A Velha it is a pleasant town that provides an opportunity to just hang out and soak up its peaceful atmosphere.

❏ **Mystical Path:** The rape and pillage we see all around us, of our earth, our children and each other is calling for urgent change. The masculine principle is out of balance and requires the restoration of the Sacred Feminine as a crucial phase in the evolution of human consciousness. It is time for healing as we begin to embody the qualities of Love, Wisdom and Compassion – the Divine Mother, Mary, Sophia… Known by different names but One and the same Source.

❏ **Personal Reflections:** The goddess of love appears to have joined Bacchus god of harvest along this ancient stretch of calzada romana; Venus tempting the modern traveller with her charms. The fishnet tights looked out of place on the Roman bridge but blended easily in the modern motel. I, too, sell myself every time I try and manipulate the universe around me to meet my own needs. The Coimbra students have taught me not to be too hasty in judging others.

0.0 km Águeda *Turismo* we continue out along the river via *rua 5 de Outubro* in the direction of *A Parades* and veer off right> **[0.5 km]** up steeply and cross over railway **[0.5 km]** down steeply and up right again *rua do Portinho* to industrial estate **[1.6 km]** and s/o over the N-1 [!] **[1.3 km].**

3.9 km Cruce welcoming *café-pastelería* on the far side. We now follow a secondary road (parallel with the N-1) directly into **Mourisca do Vouga [1.3 km]** with large mansions built in more prosperous times, many now semi-derelict. The town offers various *cafés, restaurantes e mini-mercados* we continue back over the N-1 **[0.8 km]** by traffic lights into **Pedacães [1.2 km].**

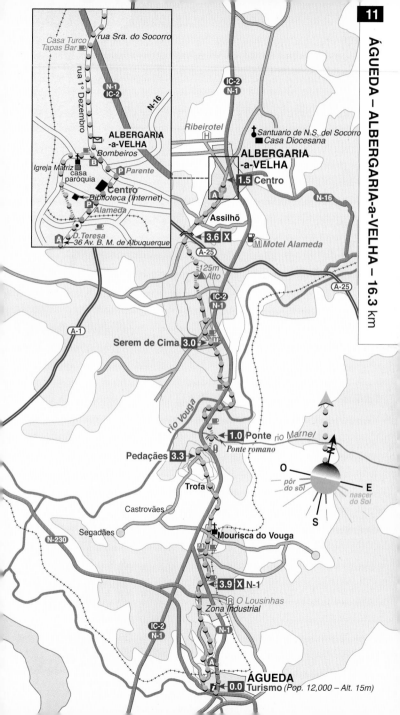

Casa Turco Tapas Bar

rua Sra. do Socorro

rua 1° Dezembro

N-1
IC-2

N-16

ALBERGARIA -a-VELHA

Bombeiros

B

Igreja Matriz

casa paróquia

P *Parente*

Centro

Biblioteca (Internet)

P

Alameda

A *D.Teresa*
36 Av. B. M. de Albuquerque

IC-2
N-1

Ribeirotel
H

† *Santuario de N.S. del Socorro*
■ *Casa Diocesana*

ALBERGARIA -a-VELHA

A   **1.5** Centro

N-16

Assilhõ

3.6 X

M *Motel Alameda*

A-25

125m Alto

A-1

IC-2
N-1

A-25

Serem de Cima 3.0

rio Vouga

1.0 Ponte   *rio Marnel*

Ponte romano

Pedaçães 3.3

Trofa

Castrovães

Mourisca do Vouga

Segadães

N-230

O

pôr do sól

E

nascer do Sol

S

3.9 X N-1

R *O Lousinhas*
Zona Industrial

IC-2
N-1

N-1

A

0.0 Turismo *(Pop. 12,000 – Alt. 15m)*

ÁGUEDA

3.3 km Pedacães veer right> into *rua de Espanha* and head down steeply, passing the Concelho Lamas do Vouga (school) to a dangerous bend on the **N-1 [0.7** km] cross over [!] onto a stretch of Roman road *rua da Ponte Romana* passing over the restored medieval bridge (with Roman foundations) **[0.3 km].**

1.0 km Ponte de Marnel dating from the 2nd century, part of the original Via XVI. On the far side is *Café Espírito Santo*. Cross back [!] over the **N-1 [0.4 km]** into Lamas do Vouga and under flyover and up to a bridge over the river Vouga at **Pontilhão [0.8** km] (Roman remains in the area; site of an archeological dig) and s/o to cross [!] the **N-1 [0.8** km] *café* and up steeply to **Serém de Cima [1.0** km]:

3.0 km Serém de Cima *Café S.António Mini-Mercado Casa Leonel* continue up past *Café-Pastelaría O Pelurinho* **[0.4** km] cross road and at T-Junction continue s/o ahead into eucalyptus forest **[0.9** km] the welcome respite from the asphalt road brings us to our high point of this stage (125m). The woodland track leads us to a bridge over the motorway **[2.3** km]:

3.6 km Ponte-A-25 and s/o at roundabout up into Largo da Misericórdia on the outskirts of Albergaria. S/o along wide tree-lined access past the primary school *escola primaria adj.* the pilgrim hostel *Alb.* **Rainha D. Teresa** *Asoc.[21÷3]* €8 (with bicicletas €12) *✆* 234 529 754 Bernardino Máximo de Albuquerque 14 (managed by Via Lusitana). (photo right) which still awaits formal opening. Continue to the roundabout with fountain.

1.5 km Albergaria-a-Velha *Fonte Note:* to access the main square continue 200m s/o into *Plaza principal.* The waymarked route bypasses the town centre by taking a path to the left of the roundabout over the rail line and up into town where we turn right by the parish church *Igreja Matrix* (possibility of accommodation on the floor in the adjacent parish hall).

❏ **Other Lodging:** *Residencial* **Casa da Alameda** €15-30 *✆* 234 524 242 (see photo below) adj. the atmospheric restaurant cum hardware store (same ownership also own motel). *P* **Parente** *✆* 234 197 226 rua Doutor Brito Guimarães. *H* **Ribeirotel** €30 *✆* 234 524 246 Areeiros, Zona industrial (½ off route). *Motel* **Alameda** *✆* 234 523 402 N-1 (+1.9 km adj. estação de gasolina Total). *Casa Turco* tapas bar (*menú peregrino*) rua 1° Dezembro. There is an appealing harmony to Albergaria-a-Velha, founded in the 12th century on the royal command of Dna. Teresa in 1120 to provide hospitality and refuge to pilgrims, a command that the townsfolk seem happy to fulfil 9 centuries later. Here is a place where old and new blend seamlessly – the façade of the historic Capelo Santo António sitting easily with the art-deco of the Cine Teatro. Whether writing your inner reflections in the shade of the alameda or availing of the free internet in the municipal library, enjoy the welcoming atmosphere.

Casa da Alameda

Igreja Matrix

Concelho

REFLECTIONS:

❏ **Life is like riding a bicycle. To keep your balance you must keep moving.**

12 *305.4 km (189.8 miles) – Santiago*

ALBERGARIA-*A*-*VELHA* – SÃO JOÃO *DE MADEIRA*

‖‖‖‖‖‖‖‖‖	--- ---	5.2	--- ---	18%
════════	--- ---	20.6	--- ---	70%
▬▬▬▬▬▬	--- ---	3.4	--- ---	12%
Total km		**29.2 km** (18.1 ml)		

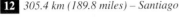

▲▬ 31.5 km (+^ 460 m = 2.3 km)
Alto(m)▲ São João da Madeira 240 m
< 🅰 🅷 > *N. Sra. do Socorro 3.4 (+0.5 km)* / Oliveira de Azeméis **19.8 km**

Practical Path: We start today with a stretch along a lovely forest road through eucalyptus and pine but the route becomes progressively more urbanized as we approach São João da Madeira and have to cross the main road and railway many times. The terrain is now more irregular as we pass through several river valleys separated by gentle hills. Facilities along this stretch are good with several opportunities to eat and sleep along the way.

❏ **Mystical Path:** When we are out of balance we begin to wobble and fall further from our centre. We become irritable, tired, confused with the apparently limitless choices around us and distracted from our true purpose. As we move forward with awareness we regain our balance and find a new sense of peace and poise amid the mayhem. We become free to choose the right direction.

❏ **Personal Reflections:** The bundle on her head was almost as big as her body yet she carried it with such poise. This theme of balance continues to flirt with me along the way. Between the sacred and the profane, between love and fear lies a place of acceptance and equilibrium. If I judge another as inferior or superior I make a distinction that drives the wedge of separation ever deeper into my human drama and psyche. I will keep moving forward and restore my equanimity.

0.0 km **Albergaria-a-Velha** We leave town via the fire-station *Bombeiros* and post office *Correio* (see town plan) and cross over the N-1 to forest **track [1.6 km]** turning <left at junction of **tracks [1.3 km]** to **crossroads [0.5 km]**

3.4 km **Cruce** *N. Sra. do Socorro* statue of Our Lady *[modern retreat house in woodland setting and viewpoint Casa Diocesana ℭ 234 522 422 ½ km off route up road to the right. Lodging may be available (generally pilgrims to Fátima].* The waymarked route continues s/o along a quiet asphalt road before turning off <left **[0.8 km]** onto woodland path emerging onto asphalt road to cross over railway onto **N-1 [2.0 km]** before veering off left to bypass town centre to re-emerge on the far side of Albergaria-A-Nova back on the **N-1 [0.9 km]**.

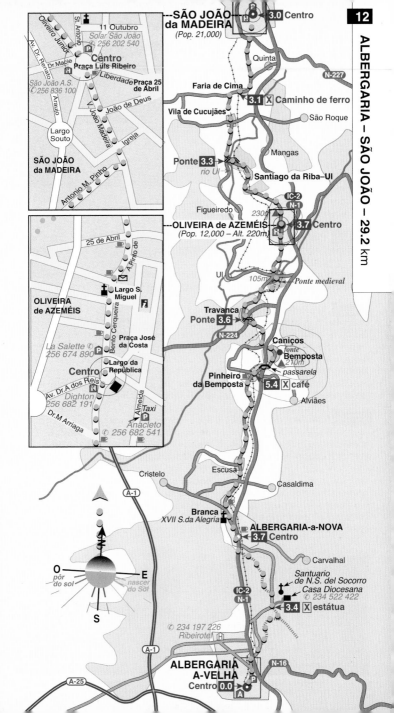

---SÃO JOÃO da MADEIRA (Pop. 21,000) — 3.0 Centro

Quinta

N-227

Faria de Cima

3.1 X Caminho de ferro

Vila de Cucujães

São Roque

Mangas

Ponte 3.3 → rio UI

Santiago da Riba–UI

Figueiredo

230m

IC-2
N-1

---OLIVEIRA de AZEMÉIS (Pop. 12,000 – Alt. 220m) — 3.7 Centro

UI

105m

Ponte medieval

**Travanca
Ponte 3.6** →

N-224

Caniços

fonte
Bemposta
210m

passarela

**Pinheiro
da Bemposta**

5.4 X café

Alviães

Cristelo

Escusa

Casaldima

A-1

O — pôr do sol
E — nascer do Sol
S

Branca
XVII S.da Alegria

ALBERGARIA-a-NOVA
← 3.7 Centro

Carvalhal

Santuario
de N.S. del Socorro
Casa Diocesana
© 234 522 422

IC-2
N-1

← 3.4 X estátua

© 234 197 226
Ribeirote H

A-1

**ALBERGARIA
A-VELHA**
Centro 0.0 →

N-16

A-25

Inset map: SÃO JOÃO da MADEIRA

Oliveiro Junior

St. Antonio

11 Outubro
Solar São João
© 256 202 540

Av. Dr. Renato

Dr. Macie

Centro
Praça Luís Ribeiro

São João A.S.
© 256 836 100

Liberdade

Praça 25
de Abril

V. João Madeira

João de Deus

Largo
Souto

Igreja

**SÃO JOÃO
da MADEIRA**

Antonio M. Pinho

Av. Dr. Araujo

Inset map: OLIVEIRA de AZEMÉIS

25 de Abril

A.Pinto de

**OLIVEIRA
de AZEMÉIS**

Largo S.
Miguel

Benito Cerqueira

La Salette ©
256 674 890

Praça José
da Costa

Centro

**Largo da
República**

Av. Dr.A dos Reis

Dighton
256 682 191

Dr.M Arriaga

Almeida

Taxi

Anacleto
© 256 682 541

`3.7 km` **Albergaria-A-Nova** with *café*
mini-mercado. *Note: from here to São
João da Madeira we crisscross the N-1,
the railway and a series of secondary
roads that makes it impossible (and
unnecessary) to detail all the twists
and turns. It is sufficient to know that
waymarking is adequate and with
attention to signs no undue problems
in navigating should arise).* Continue
along the N-1 and turn off <left [**0.5**
km] to join railway line over crossroads
bypassing **Branca** [**1.8** km] (no
facilities) with *Igreja Matrix* consecrated in 1695 (left). The terrain now becomes
more undulating as we crisscross our way up to **Pinheiro da Bemposta** [**3.1** km].

`5.4 km` **Pinheiro da Bemposta** *café-pastelaría Sorveto [F]*. Continue up and
over the N-1 via *pasarela* and up again steeply passing *Escola Primária da
Areosa* to high point (alto 217m) with view over the valley (left) and ancient
fonte (right). Continue down and over the N-1 (traffic lights) at **Caniços** [**1.9** km]
cafés through industrial estate and urbanised area over motorway [**1.7** km] into:

`3.6 km` **Travanca** continue down over stream and turn up sharp right to pass
under the **N-1** [**0.9** km] onto path alongside railway [!] *(it may look abandoned
but there are several daily services).* We now have a delightful one kilometre
stretch of original pilgrim pathway as we descend down into the river valley along
the *rua do Senhor da Ponte no Caminho de Santiago* over the rio Anceira via the
Roman bridge [**0.6** km] over railway back onto the asphalt road turning left into
rua Cruceiro up rua da Portela through the suburbs into the (part) pedestrianised
street *rua António Alegria* to the **central square** [**2.2** km].

`3.7 km` **Oliveira de Azeméis** *Centro* Largo da República with the historic
town hall *Câmara Municipal*. This town presents a confident air with a growing
population in excess of 12,000. It has all the facilities associated with a modern
town but also an historical centre. The waymarked route brings us past the parish
church of saint Michael *Igreja Matrix de São Miguel* mentioned in documents as
far back as 922 and an adjoining Roman milestone *Miliário* as evidence of the
towns earlier foundations as part of the Via Romana XVI. We also find links with
the camino de Santiago and the first 'official' camino bollard from the Xunta de
Galicia. The town also has an important Marian shrine *La Salette*. The feast day
of N. Sra. de La Salette takes place on 2nd Sunday in August and attracts huge

Igreja de São Miguel

Câmara Municipal

crowds when beds are virtually impossible to find. The fine houses built at the end of the 19th century are known as *casas de brasileiro* built by former emigrants returning with their new found wealth. The story of their lives is captured by Portuguese writer Ferreira de Castro whose own house has been turned into a museum *casa-museu* in the village of Ossela 5 km to the East.

❏ *Turismo* (Summer only) ℂ 256 674 463 Praca José da Costa (see map). ❏ **Lodging Oliveira de Azeméis:** *P*°Anacleto ℂ 256 682 541 rua António José Almeida (beside the taxi rank). *R* La Salette ℂ 256 674 890 rua Bento Carqueja. *H*°°°°Dighton €50 ℂ 256 682 191 rua Dr. Albino dos Reis (opposite the *Câmara*) pilgrim discount available. **B.V.** ℂ 256 682 122 Rua dos Bombeiros Voluntários. Wide choice of **restaurants**, several directly en route including the trendy *Art Club* opposite Residencial La Salette in the centre.

We continue our way up along rua Bento Cerqueira past the Correios crossing rua 25 de Abril and then heading steeply down over the river turning <left at roundabout [**1.0** km] and up through the northern suburbs and industrial area, crisscrossing the railway with several short stretches of cobblestone as we make our way out through the historic area **Santiago de Riba-Ul** passing *café Santiago* [**1.2** km] and down to the bridge over the river Ul [**1.1** km].

3.3 km **Ponte do Salgueiro** ancient stone bridge with miniature *alminhas* carved into the granite columns. We now make our way up past *café O Emigrante* [**0.4** km] through Vila da Cucujães (Galp) [**1.1** km] *café* with the former Benedictine monastery *Mosteiro de Cucujães* prominent on the hill. We now have a short section of path leading to bridge and railway [**1.6** km].

3.1 km **Ponte do Caniço** cross over rail for the last time and over the bypass and the major roundabout at the start of the modern suburbs of São João da Madeira. Here we continue s/o *(The Park of the Lady of the Miracles Parque da Senhora dos Milagres right)* as we head up Av. Dr. Renato Araújo signposted *Centro* veering right at the 2nd roundabout into rua Padre António Maria Pinho past the parish church of St. John the Baptist *Igreja Matriz (the original roman military thoroughfare Via XVI passed to the rear)*. We now turn left into rua Visconde de São João da Madeira up into the central square.

3.0 km **São João da Madeira** *Centro Praça Luis Ribeiro* with range of *cafés, bares, restaurantes* and *Hotels (see over)*.

São João da Madeira is an historic town of Roman origin but you wouldn't know that from the modernity that surrounds us. An industrial town built on the back of its worldwide reputation for the manufacture of hats and shoes with *Museo da Chapelaria* on the camino in rua Oliveira Júnior, 501. The area around the central square (a rotunda) is pedestrianised and has the 2 best hotel options and several café-bars including *café Concha Doce* with its prominent pilgrim shell, the only evidence that we are actually directly on 'the way'.

❏ **São João da Madeira:** *Turismo* ℂ
256 200 285 kiosko Praça Luís Ribeiro /
Av. Liberdade.

❏ **Accommodation:** On central rotunda
Praça Luís Ribeiro *Residencial* Solar
São João €35 ℂ 256 202 540 (popular
with pilgrims, photo right) and *H¨* A.S.
São João ℂ 256 836 100. *H¨¨¨*Ever São
João Business €55 Rua Adelino Amaro
da Costa *(Av. Liberdade)*. Bombeiros
Voluntários ℂ 256 682 745 rua Dr. José
Henriques / ℂ 256 837 120 Largo Conde
Dias Garcia / rua Oliveira Figueiredo.
Santa Casa da Misericórdia
€-Donativo ℂ 256 837 240 Rua Manuel
Luis Leite Júnior 777.

Amongst the more notable buildings
are: ● Chapel and Park of Our lady of
the Miracles *Capela e Parque de Na
Sra dos Milagros* built in the 1930's in the Neo-Romanesque style located near
the roundabout on the way into town close to the railway station. ● The Parish
church of St John the Baptist *Igreja Matriz de S. Joao Baptista* reconstructed in
1884 with an altarpiece dating from the previous century, Off rua Visconde de São
João da Madeira (also on the way in). ● Chapel of St. Anthony *Capela de Santo
António* built in 1937 in the Neo-Romanesque style and located immediately
behind the central square in Largo de S. Antonio. ● House of Culture *Casa da
Cultura* one of the best examples of a *Casa de Brasileiros* housing the town's Art
Centre, exhibition rooms and auditorium, located off Alão de Morais beyond the
Bombeiros.

REFLECTIONS:

❏ **Greater is He that is in you
Than he who is in the world.** *1 John 4:4*

13 *276.2km (171.6 miles) – Santiago*

SÃO JOÃO DA MADEIRA – PORTO

ⅢⅢⅢⅢⅢⅢⅢ	--- ---	2.8	--- ---	8%
▬▬▬▬	--- ---	20.6	--- ---	60%
▬▬▬	--- ---	10.9	--- ---	32%
Total km		**34.3 km** (21.3 ml)		

▰▰◣ 36.8 km (+^ 505 m = 2.5 km)
Alto(m)▲ Malaposta 315 m (1,033 ft)
< 🅰 🏠 > Malaposta **7.6** km – Grijó **19.0** km.

Practical Path: As we approach Porto the road network becomes ever more congested so prepare for the long slog into the centre along hard city pavements This is a *very* long stage, much of it on main roads with fast moving traffic across undulating terrain, so you will need to leave São João at first light. The noise and danger of the roads is relieved by a short but delightful stretch of medieval road through woodland beyond Grijó and the medieval monastery here offers respite around halfway with pilgrim hostel *(also pensãos 1½ km off route – see map)*. Consider taking a rest day in Porto to recover from your exertions and to explore this fascinating city crammed with historic monuments.

❏ **Mystical Path:** Physical sight shows us the superficial world of the ego fashioned by humanity with its incessant demands. Below the surface lies our true Identity. This higher Self is recognised by seeing it in others. The confusion between outer and inner between the ego and the divine forms the crux of our problem – one problem, one solution. It is time to awaken our spiritual vision.

❏ **Personal Reflections:** How many more crossroads will I meet today – each one requiring a choice of direction... but I need to remind myself that I journey on two different levels. If I heed only the signs to Santiago I head towards an empty casket. The signs to the Source are not so obvious… but I miss them at my peril. I need to stay alert amongst the labyrinth of highways and byways of the inner camino if I am to reach my true Destination.

0.0 km **São João da Madeira** *Centro* from the Praça Luís Ribeiro we head out along rua Oliveira Júnior (to the left side of the Banco Espiritu Santo) passing *Museo da Chapelaria* (left) [**0.5** km] veering <left opposite Repsol garage past disused industrial buildings s/o over crossroads by *supermercado* and over crossroads in **Arrifana** [**1.1** km] *Igreja Matriz* with fine façade of blue and white tiles *azulejos*. Continue up steps into rua S. António and turn <left as the road follows the undulating terrain to a bridge over the **N-227** [**2.3** km].

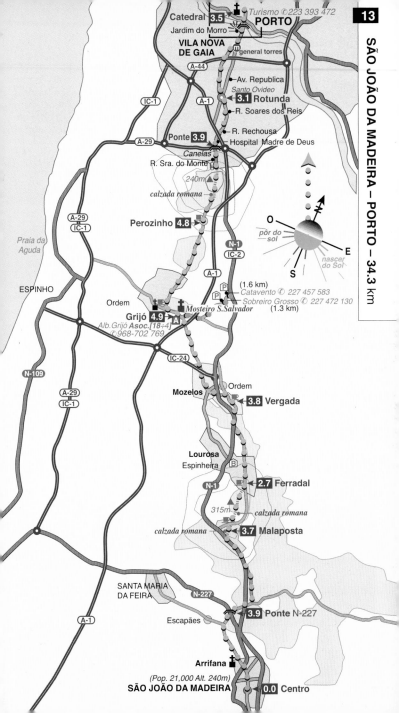

Catedral **3.5**
Turismo © 223 393 472
PORTO
Jardim do Morro
VILA NOVA DE GAIA
m general torres

A-44

IC-1   A-1

• Av. Republica
Santo Ovideo
3.1 Rotunda
• R. Soares dos Reis

• R. Rechousa
• Hospital Madre de Deus

A-29   Ponte **3.9**

Canelas
R. Sra. do Monte
240m
calzada romana

Perozinho 4.8

N-1
IC-2

A-1

Praia da Aguda

(1.6 km)
P ◄ Catavento © 227 457 583
◄ Sobreiro Grosso © 227 472 130
(1.3 km)

ESPINHO

Ordem
Grijó 4.9   Mosteiro S.Salvador
Alb.Grijó **Asoc.**[18÷4]
© 968-702 769

IC-24

Mozelos   Ordem
■ **3.8** Vergada

Lourosa
Espinheira   B
■ **2.7** Ferradal
N-1
315m   calzada romana
calzada romana ◄ **3.7** Malaposta

SANTA MARIA DA FEIRA
N-227
A-1
Escapães   **3.9** Ponte N-227

Arrifana
(Pop. 21,000 Alt. 240m)
SÃO JOÃO DA MADEIRA   **0.0** Centro

O   N
pôr do sol   E
S   nascer do Sol

A-29
IC-1

N-109

A-29
IC-1

3.9 km Ponte *N-227* We cross the bridge over the N-1 *restaurante Concorde* pass Galp petrol station *café* through Sanfins and turn off right> to the Roman road in Malaposta. This marks the high point of this stage at 315m.

3.7 km Malaposta *Calzada Romana* *Café Solar*. We enter a well preserved stretch of the original Via XVI which is rudely cut off 90m later by the main road. Modern Hotel Pedra Bela €35 ℗ 256 910 350 Rua Malaposta just off route on N-1. The cobblestones continue the far side in rather less pristine condition but with an additional 400m through shaded woodland. [The Calzada Romana becomes, variously *Rua da Estrada Romana* or the Royal Way *Estrada Real*]. We emerge in the straggling village of:

2.7 km Ferradal *café Ferradalense e mini-mercado*. The route winds itself through the urbanised neighbourhoods of Souto, Redondo, Carvalhosa, Monte Grande, **Lourosa** *café* and B.V. ℗ 227 443 189 on Av. Principal 4030 and into:

3.8 km Vergada *café / mini-mercados*. We now turn <left into rua Joaquim do Porto through **Mozelos** crossing the N-1 [!] down steeply *[good viewpoint of the complicated web of roads ahead and the distant sea. However, waymarking is good so keep focused on the friendly yellow arrows but with one eye on the fast moving traffic.]* Continue down through **Vila de Nogueira da Regedoura** and down under the IC-24 and down again under the A-1 into the lush and relatively tranquil Grijó valley turning <left at roundabout *Estadio Municipal* (See detour option) continue along the stone walls of Grijó monastery.

4.9 km Grijó *Albergue* S. Salvador de Grijó *Par.[14÷2]* € donativo António Pires ℗ 968 702 769 rua Cardoso Pinto, 274 – opposite the XIII[th]c **Mosterio S. Salvador de Grijó** where the medieval Italian pilgrim Confalonieri stayed during his pilgrimage from Rome to Santiago. The original buildings were consecrated in 1235 and were an important stop for both physical and spiritual nourishment to pilgrims. A sense of peace continues to pervade the parkland and offers the modern pilgrim respite from the traffic. Adjoining the monastery are the council offices *Freguesia de Vila Grijó* and public toilets. The waymarked route continues s/o down the Av. do Mosteiro into Grijó town.

Detour 1.6 km (uphill): ● ● ● ● Porto is still 4 hours away along busy main roads and, while not ideal, there is alternative accommodation in the area (a steep climb uphill). Turn right at the roundabout *Estadio Municipal* and continue s/o under a different section of the **A-1 [300m]** into Rua do Sr. do Padrao taking 3rd left uphill at **junction [600m]** into Rua da Quinta Fabrica and pass modern chemist to join the 'main' road **Rua de Americo Oliveira [300m]** at a staggered crossroads and continue s/o uphill (ignoring roads to left and then right) to next sharp fork **[400m]** and here 50m (left) **Pensão Sobreiro Grosso** ✆ 227 472 130 rua Américo de Oliveira, 807. Continue up past the restaurant for *another (500m)* to **Pensão Residencial Catavento** ✆ 227 457 583 Largo das Vendas, 88 / N-1.

Note: Despite the proximity to Porto there are still a few stretches of the original medieval pilgrim route ahead over the Serra dos Negrelos to relieve the noise and monotony of the roads. Waymarks now have to compete with other signs and you also need to stay alert to the fast moving traffic. Note the position of the sun and as you head due north keep it in the same general position which should be behind you over the left shoulder in the early afternoon to guide you into and through Vila Nova de Gaia which offers a range of intermediate accommodation. If you are not familiar with Porto it is probably best to go direct to the cathedral (along the *top* of the bridge – see alternative route later). This is the logical 'end point' of the Lisbon section where you can give thanks for your safe arrival, pick up a pilgrim passport *credencial* and / or stamp your existing one. Adjacent to the cathedral is a tourist office with map of the town and list of hotels. Just below the cathedral is a range of budget hotels and other accommodation (see under Porto).

From the Mosterio S. Salvador de Grijó head on down the Avenida do Mosteiro turning up right around the walls of the monastery in the general direction of Vila Nova de Gaia. At this junction is the Capela de S. António (directly ahead) and *cafés*. This marks the low point of this stretch (95m) and we now climb steadily along a maze of roads (well waymarked) passing various roadside cafes all the way up through Sermonde to:

4.8 km **Perozinho** welcoming *café-restaurante* and just beyond the crossroads the council office and parish church and suddenly we find ourselves amongst the pines and eucalyptus of the delightful Serra de Negrelos on the ancient Roman road *calzada romana*. This brings us to the high point (240m).

We now head into the residential suburbs at Senhora do Monte down rua da Serpa steeply to the N-1[!] Antalis HQ where we turn <left along a dangerous stretch of the rua da Senhora do Monte [!] with no pavement (photo right) into Rechousa and Vila de Pedroso and bridge over the motorway.

   Ponte A-29 *cafés (there are now roadside cafés all the way into Porto).* Continue s/o over the motorway still on the N-1 passing Hospital Madre de Deus and Galp filling station and head down *under* the A-1 motorway **[1.6** km] and up tree-lined rua da Palmeira into the commercial rua Soares dos Reis and to major roundabout **[1.5** km].

3.1 km **Rotunda de Santo Ovídio** [*Note: The N-1 now becomes the Avenida* *de República which we follow parallel to (and join later) all the way to* **Ponte de Dom Luis I** *– the main bridge over the rio Douro linking Vila Nova de Gaia with Porto and the cathedral.]* We head across this busy high level crossroads still on rua Soares dos Reis and wend our way over the city bypass A-44 *Cintura Interna* [**1.2** km] also referred to as Avenue of the Discoverers *Avenida dos Descobrimentos* into the Mafamude district past public gardens past *Casa de Juventude (right) this is* not *a hostal* continue s/o into rua S. Francisco Sá Carneiro and s/o at roundabout (following signs to *Centro Historico*) over a wide grass platform (over the railway) to the metro station Estação de General Torres [**1.1** km] back onto the Av. República to the delightful gardens overlooking the mighty rio Douro **Jardim O Moro [0.5** km] **OPTION** [?]:

Note [1]: Jardim O Moro is a good place to pause for breath – this has been a long stage and we are near the end point. [2] Take a moment to get your bearings – the viewpoint here gives a panoramic view of Vila Nova de Gaia spilling down *this* side with the Southern banks of the river with its Port wine lodges. On the *far* side is the city of Porto with the cathedral up to our right and the harbour area Ribeira down to the left and the main shopping area and hotels spread out behind it. [3] If you don't have reserved accommodation then decide now where to head for. [4] at this point the waymarked route goes sharply down via Calçada da Serra to cross over the lower tier of the iconic metal bridge and then proceeds either back up (steeply) to the cathedral or into and through the city centre. If you have no fixed plans it may be better not to loose the high ground but continue over the upper level of the bridge directly ahead [**0.1** km] and continue up to the next crossroads [**0.5** km] and turn <left straight down to the natural end point of this stage – the cathedral [**0.1** km].

3.5 km **Porto Catedral** *Sé* the waymarked route from Porto starts from this point. Adjoining the cathedral entrance (by the statue of Vimara Peres atop his steed) is a *Turismo* and the offices of *Porto Tours* in the tower just below. See city map and details of accommodation in the next section.

REFLECTIONS:

Serra de Negrelos *calzada romana.*

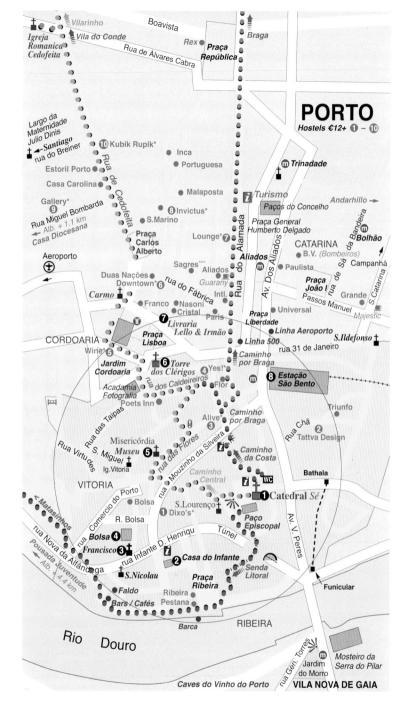

Boavista

Vilarinho

Vila do Conde

Rex

Braga

Praça República

Igreja Romanica Cedofeita

Rua de Álvares Cabra

PORTO

Hostels €12+ ① – ⑩

Largo da Maternidade Julio Dinis

† **Santiago**
rua do Breiner

⑩ Kubik Rupik*

Inca

Portuguesa

† **m Trinadade**

Estoril Porto

Casa Carolina

Malaposta

i **Turismo**

Paços do Concelho

Andarhillo →

Gallery*
⑨

Rua Miguel Bombarda
← Alb. + 1.1 km
Casa Diocesana

⑧ Invictus*

S.Marino

Praça Carlos Alberto

Lounge* ⑦

Alameda

Praça General Humberto Delgado

CATARINA

m Bolhão

Aeroporto ✈

Duas Nações *

Downtown*⑥

rua do Fábrica

Sagres****

Aliados

Guarany

Intl.

do Aliados

Rua

B.V. *(Bombeiros)*

Paulista

m Dos Aliados

Campanhã

Praça João I

Passos Manuel

Grande

S. Catarina

Majestic

Carmo

Franco

Nasoni

Cristal

Paris

Praça Liberdade

Universal

⑦ Livraria Lello & Irmão

Linha Aeroporto

CORDOARIA

Wine*⑤

Jardim Cordoaria

m **Praça Lisboa**

⑥ **Torre dos Clérigos**

Academia Fotografia

Poets Inn

⑤ **Linha 500**
rua 31 de Janeiro

S.Ildefonso †

Caminho por Braga

Yes!* ④

Flor

m ⑧ **Estação São Bento**

Triunfo

Misericórdia **Museu** ⑤

S. Miguel †

Ig. Vitoria

Alive* ③

Caminho por Braga

Rua Chã
② **Tattva Design**

VITORIA

Comercio do Porto

Caminho da Costa

i

Bolsa

R. Bolsa

Caminho Central

S.Lourenço †

① Dixo's*

i WC

① **Catedral** *Sé*

Bathala

← Matasinhos

rua da Alfândega
← Alb. + 4.4 km
Pousada Juventude

④ **Bolsa**

③ **Francisco** †

rua Infante D. Henriqu

i ② **Casa do Infante**

S.Nicolau †

Faldo

Bars / Cafés

Ribeira
Pestana

Túnel

Praça Ribeira

Paço Episcopal

Senda Litoral

Av. V. Peres

Funicular

Barca

RIBEIRA

Rio Douro

m

rua Gen. Torres

Jardim do Morro

Mosteiro da Serra do Pilar

Caves do Vinho do Porto

VILA NOVA DE GAIA

Arriving in Porto. If you are starting your pilgrimage in Porto and arrive by air there is a tourist information counter in the arrivals hall ✆ 229 432 400 (08:00 – 23:00) with a map of the city and hotel information. A regular bus operates to the city centre and takes around an hour for the 14 km trip. Or take the efficient metro from the station in the airport itself. If you arrive by train note there are 2 rail stations. The main station *Estação de São Bento* is in the centre. The modern *Estação de Campanhã* is a few kilometres east and the old *Estação de Trindade* has now been revamped as the ultra modern hub of the efficient metro.

■ *Turismo Central:* *(09:00–19:00 / (20:00 summer)* top of Av. dos Aliados at *rua Clube dos Fenianos 25* - adj. the *câmara.* ✆ **(Portugal +351)** 223 393 472. ■ *Ribeira*: 63 Rua do Infante D. Henrique *(down near the river)* ✆ 222 060 412. ■ *Cathedral* Terreiro da Se ✆ 223 325174 (10:00 – 18:00). ■ For information outside Porto: ✆ 927 411 817 Praca D. Joao I, 43.

■ *Albergues de Peregrinos:* €-*Donativo:* N.S. do Rosário de Vilar *Asoc.[12÷2]* ✆ 910 274 982 Casa Diocesana, rua Arcediago Vanzeller, 50 *(centro + 1.1 km).* ViaPortuscale *Asoc.[20÷2]* ✆ esencial 960 227 134 Rua Vasco Santana, 264, Senhora da Hora *(+ 9.2 km).* Bombeiros Voluntários *BV.[2÷1]* ✆ 222 055 845 rua Rodrigues Sampaio, 145. ■ Pousada de Juventude ✆ 925 664 983 rua Paulo da Gama, 551 *(+ 4.4 km).*

■ *Hostales (booking: www.hostelworld.com:* *(dormitorios €12+privados €18+):* ❶ **Dixo's** Rua Mouzinho da Silveira 72. ❷ **Tattva Design** Rua do Cativo 26-28 *(Near Sé/ São Bento).* ❸ **Alive** Rua das Flores 138. ❹ **Yes!** Rua Arquitecto Nicolau Nazoni 31. ❺ **Wine** Campo dos Martires da Patria 52. ❻ **Downtown** Praça Guilherme Gomes Fernandes 66. ❼ **Lounge** Rua do Almada 317. ❽ **Invictus** Rua das Oliveiras 73. ❾ **Kubik Rupik** Rua de Cedofeita 229. ❿ **Gallery** Rua Miguel Bombarda 222.

■ *Hostales Centro:* *(€35-55)* ● **Flor Bragança** ✆ 222 082 974 Rua Arquitecto Nicolau Nazoni 12. ● **Oporto Poets** ✆ 222 026 089 Travessa do Ferraz 13. ● **The Poets Inn** ✆ 223 324 209 Rua dos Caldeireiros, 261. ● **França** Praça de Gomes Teixeira,7 ✆ 222 002 791. **Nasoni** ✆ 222 083 807 rua Galeria Nº82 *(Near Lello books)* + **Cristal** ✆ 222 002 100 @ Nº48. ● **Duas Nações** ✆ 222 081 616 Praça de Guilherme Gomes Fernandes Nº59 + **VivaCity** ✆ 222 085 831 @ Nº35. ●**Casa Carolina** Rua de Cedofeita 159 ✆ 912 088 249 + **Estoril** ✆ 222 002 751 @Nº193. ● **Triunfo** rua do Cativo 9. ● **Andarilho** ✆ 222 010 252 Rua da Firmeza 364 (Metro Bolhão) *desconto a peregrinos.*

■ *Hoteles Central:* *(€35-75)* ● **Internacional** ✆ 222 005 032 rua do Almada 131. **Grande Hotel Paris** ✆ 222 073 140 Rua da Fábrica 27 *(with olde-world garden).* **Paulista** ✆ 222 054 692 Av. dos Aliados 214 + **Universal** ✆ 222 006 758 @ Nº38 + **Aliados** ✆ 222 004 853 / Elísio de Melo 27 *(above Cafe Guranay with entrance off side road).* For old-fashioned luxury *H***°°°Grande Hotel do Porto** ✆ 222 076 690 Rua de Santa Catarina 197 (near café Majestic). Downtown value at *H***°°°da Bolsa** ✆ 222 026 768 rua Ferreira Borges and by the river *H***°°°Riberia do Porto** ✆ 222 032 097 Praça da Ribeira Nº5 or double the price at adj. *H***°°°°Pestana** @ Nº1 ✆ 223 402 300 or top of the town and price bracket *H***°°°°°Infante De Sagres** €150 Praça D. Filipa De Lencastre 62.

❑ **Eating Out:** A tourist menu on the popular Ribeira will cost €20+ such as the *Taberna de Bebobos* with local specialities (pork). *Adega S. Nicolau* on rua S. Nicolau is popular and has a few outside tables with views of the river or try the basic *O Muro* for value on Muro dos Bacalhoeiros 88 pedestrian walkway above street level with views of the river. If you want to experience the haunting Portuguese music *fado* two popular fado houses are in this area *Casa da*

Cais da Ribeira with river barges *Barcos Rabelos* and **Catedral** *Sé (top left)*

Mariquinhas on rua São Sebastião and *Mal Cozinhado* on rua Outeirinho – both will try and sell you an expensive and mediocre dinner but it is possible to prop-up the bar instead and drink overpriced wine while you listen to the melancholy voices accompanied by the Portuguese guitar. For economy you can still find a basic menu in the old town away from the main tourist areas for around €10. Try the atmospheric *Taipas I Feijao* on rua das Taipas,17 while around the corner in rua de S. Miguel 19 is a rare vegetarian/vegan option at *O Oriente no Porto*. Back towards the centre on rua da Fábrica is the traditional grill *(parilla in Spanish) Churrasqueira Central Dos Clérigos*. At the other end of the scale (and other side of Av. dos Aliados) *A Brasileira* rua do Bonjardim 118 (opp. the old city theatre). Here you might start with an aperitif in the adjoining *Art Deco cafe*, dine in the restaurant and then make your way up to the *Majestic Café* on rua de Santa Catarina for liqueur and coffee. The majestic is one of the best known Belle Epoque cafés in Portugal with beautiful interior and possibility of live piano music in the background, but don't expect much change out of €50 for the evening's entertainment. However rua do Bonjardim also offers @Nº724 *Ginjal do Porto* a basic menú *prato do dia* for €5! and in between @Nº87 *Regaleira* seafood *par excellence*. ❏ *Self-service Lavandaria* Rua da Conceição, 23 (off Rua Cedofeita). ***Onward baggage transfer SEUR*** Rua Eng. Frederico Ulrich, 3620 Maia (by airport) ✆ 229 433 600 offices throughout Spain and Portugal.

Historical Sketch: Porto is beautifully situated on the 'River of Gold' *Rio Douro*. A city full of vitality and authenticity and justifiably proud of its long history. It was here in the 12th century that Portugal took its name as an independent nation. By the 14th century it had well-established trade links and we begin to see the emergence of a wealthy merchant class and the building of substantial civic structures. Henry the Navigator was born here in 1394 and we can still visit his house below the square bearing his name. By the 15th century the city was playing a leading role in the maritime discoveries of the New World. The historical centre was declared a World Heritage site in

Henry the Navigator & Cathedral Towers

1996 and in 2001 Porto was chosen as the European City of Culture. In 2004 it proudly hosted the European football championships – Porto and football are synonymous! Today the city has a population of around ½ million with 1½ million in the greater catchment area. All this grew out of a modest Celtic settlement atop what is now Cathedral Hillock *Colina da Sé*, a rocky promontory from which the old quarter tumbles down to the river at the *Cais da Ribeira*.

❑ **Historic Buildings and Monuments: City Excursion:** Allow time to visit the historic city centre and absorb some of its magnificent sights. From the west door of the Cathedral (the start of stage 14 to Santiago) in the old medieval quarter known as the *Bairro da Sé* to the beginning of the pedestrian street rua Cedofeita in the quarter known as *Cordoaria* is less than 2 km (see city map). You can walk this stage in under an hour. However, if you intend to visit the interior of any of the buildings along the way then you need to allow more time. Indeed to soak up the atmosphere of the Cathedral and its cloisters would require at least an hour in itself. Several further options are available from the Cathedral. You can take the tourist tram for a 90-minute tour of Vila Nova do Gaia. If you shudder at the notion, don't! For around €10 you can rattle instead over the cobblestones and over the famous bridge Ponte de D. Luís I. Your money buys you a visit to one of the oldest port wine lodges in Portugal, including a tasting session where you get to sample a ruby and perhaps a less familiar white port. The tour then returns to the Cathedral via the lower section of the bridge, past the old customs hall *Alfândega Nova* and up past the main rail station *Estação de São Bento*.

If a port wine lodge is not of interest, then just behind the cathedral at 32 rua Dom Hugo (around the back of the Archbishop's Palace) is the beautiful former house and museum (mostly Islamic art and artefacts) of the Portuguese poet *Guerra Junqueiro*. The office of the tour company *Porto Tours* is situated in the medieval tower 50m below the Cathedral. Here you can book for any of the extensive city and river Douro tours operated by the company. These include bus tours of the city and environs and a one-day cruise up the Douro, returning by train. There are also tours to the prehistoric rock art valley at Vila Nova de Foz Côa, off the river Douro. The following Porto 'excursion' follows the waymarked route from the cathedral to the start of the pedestrian street rua de Cedofeita (1.6 km) – and then loops back to the river – mopping up the remaining 'must see' sights on the way!

Praça da Liberdade & *Rua dos Aliados leading to* **Paços do Concelho** *(centre)*

❶ **Cathedral** *Sé* occupying a strategic site overlooking the city and river Douro. Like most medieval cathedrals it has been altered and embellished many times since its inauguration in the 12th century, most notably in the Baroque period. However it never lost its austere Romanesque form of fortress-church (see photo). Enter the west door below its fine rose window and just inside is the information desk where you can obtain a *credencial* (€2) or have your existing 'passport' stamped. €2 secures a ticket to visit the 14th century Gothic cloisters and provides access to the Chapter House *Casa do Cabido* and the cathedral treasury on the first floor. Many visitors never discover the wonderful notary chamber room on the second floor (imm. above). Richly adorned with hand painted tiles *azulejos* and a stunningly beautiful painted ceiling, with St. Michael making up the central panel overlighting proceedings below. But, most significantly, here you will find a delightful 16th century statue of Santiago Peregrino, pilgrim staff in hand – an opportunity, perhaps, to obtain a blessing on your own pilgrimage ahead.

Pick up the first waymark opposite the cathedral west door and proceed down the cobbled ramp past the offices of Porto Tours located in the medieval tower (right) and down the steep steps into the Largo Dr. Pedro Vitorino with the imposing 16-18th century Mannerist façade of *Igreja de S. Lourenço* (*St. Laurence* with museum of religioius art) built into the steep rock-face (left) and down again to cross the busy rua Mouzinho da Silveira and up into Largo São Domingos turning right into rua das Flores passing ❺ *Igreja da Misericórdia* 18th century Church of Mercy with museum and on to the imposing edifice of the former Companies office *Casa da Companhia* on the corner of rua das Flores 69 and rua do Ferraz. *Note*: [!] This is the point where the alternative route, *caminho interior* via Braga separates from the main way *caminho central* – don't confuse them.

The main central route turns up sharp <left into rua do Ferraz past the tiny chapel dedicated to Saint Catherine of the Flowers *Capela de Santa Catarina das Flores*. [*Formerly the pilgrim office* Associação Dos Amigos do Caminho de Santiago *whose Djalma de Sousa e Correia did so much to waymark the modern camino.*] At the top of rua do Ferraz turn right> into rua dos Caldeireiros and up to the large open area at the top *Campo Mártires da Pátria* that merges into the *Jardim de João Chagas* and here on the left is the imposing façade of the former remand prison *Cadeia da Relação* which is now a refurbished arts and photographic exhibition centre. On our right is one of Porto's most emblematic buildings ❻ *Torre dos Clérigos* Clergymen's Tower an impressive 18th century baroque tower and, at 75m high, the city's main landmark and worth the €2 entrance fee for the 225 steps and the grand 360 degree vista from the top. After you have stretched your quadriceps, the adjoining church *Igreja dos Clérigos*, built in a beautiful elliptical shape, is a delightful environment in which to flex your soul muscles. The architect, Nicolau Nasoni, is buried in the church in recognition of his dedication and skill in, 'creating such a beautiful and towering monument to God'. Pick up the waymarks again at the *Jardim de João Chagas* and cross diagonally over the park past the former Polytechnic Academy *Antiga Academia Politécnica* to the blue and white tiles *azulejos* of the 18th century *Igreja do Carmo*. It is separated from the neighbouring

Carmelite convent church *Igreja das Carmelitas* by one of the narrowest building in the world – barely a metre wide! It acted as a physical barrier between the monks and the nuns who, by convention, could not live in adjoining buildings. The waymarked camino now continues straight on (s/o) into rua de Cedofeita.

To continue this excursion of Porto's main sites head down towards the city centre, past the handsome statue of the Lions and into rua das Carmelitas where at number 144 is the intriguing bookshop *Livraria Lello (see photo)*. Described as, 'the most beautiful bookstore in the world', it really is an architectural delight but now has an entry charge (summer). Have a browse or a cup of coffee atop the sweeping

staircase. Continue down to join the rua Clérigos just below the church and s/o into Liberation Square *Praça da Liberdade* with its impressive statue of D. Pedro IV. At the top end is the imposing façade of the town hall *Paços Concelho Câmara*. No need to walk up the intervening Avenida dos Aliados unless you want to visit the main tourist office *Turismo* on the left side of the Câmara. It is now only a short hop *under* the Praça de Almeida Garrett to ❼ *Estação de São Bento* Main rail station named after the Benedictine monastery built here in the 16th century. Step inside its grand entrance hall with magnificent display of *azulejos* (over 20,000) depicting transport scenes and historical events including the battle of Valdevez in 1140 when the king of Portugal *Afonso I (Afonso Henriques)* defeated the Spanish under king Alfonso VII of Leon thus securing Portugal's independence from Spain. Other panels show the Conquest of Ceuta in 1415 and the arrival in Porto of D. João I and Philippa of Lancaster.

At this point we can return to the cathedral now visible up Av. Vimara Peres or head down the wide rua Mousinho da Silveira towards the river into Praça do Infante Henrique where we find an impressive statue to this most famous son of King D. João I – Henry the Navigator (1394 – 1460) who was a major force in the Portuguese discoveries of the New World. He looks down to the harbour and the house where he was born ❷ *Casa do Infante* (also referred to as House of the Navigator) and museum in the rua Infante Dom Henrique.

Perhaps it's time to cool off by the harbour and quench your thirst at any of the numerous bars, cafés, restaurants and fado houses that surround this historic and lively riverside area *Cais da Ribeira* or take a river trip on one of Porto's iconic river barges *Barcos Rabelos* now converted to transport tourists rather than Port wine. Around €10 will secure a memorable 1 hour boat ride under 6 of the city's bridges and down to the river mouth. If you have time or energy to spare head back up to Praça do Infante Henrique to visit the fabulous interior of

❸ *Igreja de São Francisco* now de-consecrated and turned into a museum but well worth the €2 entry fee to soak up some of its quiet and cool interior bedecked with gilded carvings (some of the most impressive in all of Portugal). A combined ticket provides access to a small museum opposite the church entrance (adjoining the ticket office) and the sombre catacombs below. A short walk back into Praça do Infante Henrique and we arrive at the city's splendid stock exchange building ❹ *Palácio da Bolsa*. You can see the vast inner courtyard at the entrance without having to take the €7 guided tour, although you will miss the magnificent Arab Hall (worth the visit) and a chance to dine in the adjacent restaurant.

Starting Out – Options for Stage 14 (the first stage for the majority of pilgrims). *Listen up!* Read this carefully as there are arrows pointing in every direction placed by different pilgrim associations, municipal authorities and hotel owners with little or no cooperation between them! Don't panic – you have 3 basic options (ignoring the little used caminho por Braga).

❶ **Camino Central:** ● ● ● ● ●
The main route chosen by around 60% of pilgrims. A delightful route well waymarked and served with excellent pilgrim hostels and facilities. However, the first stage through Porto is mostly on city pavements, main roads or the traditional cobblestone lanes with granite setts *adoquín pavés* which are hard underfoot and carry fast moving traffic. The route has been greatly improved

by eliminating hazardous sections and waymarking via the Monastery in Vairão which has been restored as a pilgrim hostel (and museum) and makes a welcome first stage stop-over. From Vairão / Vilarinho onwards the route is a delightful mix of quiet country lanes, agricultural tracks and forest paths that undulate over gentle hills separated by wide river valleys and coastal inlets *rias*.

❷ **Caminho da Costa:** ● ● ● ● ●
Has grown in popularity in recent years and now accounts for around 35% of pilgrims. However, the first stage out of Porto has been hobbled together by local authorities with scant knowledge of the needs of the modern pilgrim. It skirts the airport runway is uninspiring and *all* by road. While generally well waymarked there are stretches with no signposts at all. **Note** this refers *only* to the first stage

out of Porto; the rest of the Coastal way is a delightful mix of small country lanes and forest paths in the hills above the coast dropping down to stretches of sandy paths and boardwalks by the sea. It crosses over the Minho river estuary into Spain and reconnects with the Camino Central in Redondela. These two routes out of Porto involve a long slog through the suburbs and like any stage through a major city there will be challenges and these include the difficulty of seeing the waymarks with all the competing signs and street advertisements. The routes *are* well waymarked but you have to stay focussed and this attentiveness must also be directed towards the fast moving city traffic. The following alternatives are worth considering.

❸ **Senda Litoral (alt.):** ● ● ● ● ●
This makes a good alternative for the first stage out of Porto, depending on prevailing weather as strong winds make walking difficult with sea-spray and wind-blown sand. A tourist vibe replaces the camaraderie of the main route but the majority is on boardwalks *paseos de madera* which makes for pleasant walking alongside the beaches and through the sand dunes which are

protected on account of their fragile habitat. A new hostel in Labruge and several campsites offer lodging and the historic town of Vila do Conde makes a good stop-over for this stage from where it is possible to reconnect with the Camino Central either via Arcos or Rates (see next stage for details). However, waymarks have been removed in order to discourage this option as pilgrims can easily get lost and end up seeking help from hard pressed voluntary pilgrim organisations. If you are comfortable with 'finding your way' this remains a reasonable option...

...otherwise continue on the main Coastal route *Caminho da Costa* or the largely unwaymarked seashore path **Senda Litoral** ● ● ● ● ● which from this point on is shown with brown dots. It is generally *not* waymarked but follows the coastline. However, this is sometimes difficult in practise as pathways often peter out on some remote beach requiring a hard walk on soft sand or retracing steps. There are also countless pathways providing a bewildering array of options. In those situations where a coastal stretch connects easily with the main Caminho da Costa a tick ✔ suggests a good optional alternative; otherwise it makes sense to stick with the main waymarked route.

All routes start at the **Cathedal in Porto** Ⓐ Routes 1 and 2 effectively follow the same waymarks until Pedrão de Légua where they split. *Nota Bene* the maps in this guide cover an average of 26 km per stage but this has been designed for page layout purposes. We each have a different pace and level of fitness so decide where you wish to start and end each day. Note that the first day on the Senda Litoral covers a total distance of 33.9 km from the cathedral to Vila do Conde. Pilgrims choosing this option can stopover en route (accommodation is limited and often full during the busy summer tourist season). Alternatively start in **Matasinhos** Ⓑ by walking along the Douro estuary or take bus 500 from Praça Liberdade, tram #1 from Praça Ribeira or metro from Trinidade to Mercado.

Most pilgrims will have committed to walk the entire route from the cathedral but those who wish to skip the rigours of the road out of the city have a range of possibilities. The simplest is take the Metro from Trinidade in the *direction* of Póvoa de Varzim and alight at **Vilar do Pinheiro** Ⓒ to connect to the *Camino Central* by turning right (east) out of the metro station and s/o over the N-13 [0.6 km] and turning left at T-junction to join the waymarked route Mosteiró [0.5 km]. *Note: Vilar do Pinheiro - Rates 19.4 km.* Another option is to take the Metro to **Fórum Maia** and pick up the alternative (grey) waymarked route at *Igreja de Maia [+0.7 km].*

❏ **Look at every path closely and deliberately. Then ask yourself, and yourself alone, one question, 'Does this path have a heart?' If it does, the path is good; if it doesn't, it is of no use.** *The Teachings of Don Juan*

14 *241.9 km (150.3 miles) – Santiago*

PORTO – VILARINHO

VILA DO CONDE

IIIIIIIIIIIIIIIIIII --- ---	0.5	--- ---	2%
▬▬▬ --- ---	16.1	--- ---	60%
▬▬▬ --- ---	<u>10.3</u>	--- ---	38%
Total km	**26.9** km (16.7 ml)		

◣◢ 28.0 km (+^ 220 m = 1.1 km)
Alto*(m)*▲ Igreja Maia 125 m (410 ft)
< Ⓐ Ⓗ > Maia **12.4** (+0.7) km – Moreira Maia **14.0** km

The Practical Path: Despite the comprehensive waymarking, this first stage out of Porto is likely to prove taxing (see alternatives previous page). Commercial advertising and street signs compete for your attention and if you get distracted it is easy to get lost – stay focused. The various waymarked routes also require you to cross busy main roads [!] take special care. The city pavements and cobbled laneways are hard underfoot and today there is little respite from traffic. While the highest point of this stage is Maia at only 125m there is plenty of demanding undulations to test our reslove. All grist for the mill and remember – things can only get better... and they do!

The Mystical Path: Have you found the first waymark that points you in the direction of our true Destination? Does it look familiar or are you left in doubt as to the right course to take? One thing is certain, it will only be found by following the wisdom of the heart. Everything we see with the physical eye is likely to lead us away from the mystical. We have become intoxicated with the things of this world and fallen into a deep stupor. We search for relics housed in stone buildings that mask the true home of spirit. In our drunkenness we have forgotten the way Home... and yet feelings of alienation and loss stir us to awaken.

Personal Reflections: "...in the distraction of the city roads I forgot the waymarks to the inner path. I pause to clear my mind of the anger I directed towards a dangerous driver. Psychic rubbish is every bit as noxious as the physical rubbish that I now observe all around me... I start to pick up litter and, feeling momentarily self-righteous, remind myself of the many times that I have littered the landscape and suddenly become aware of a bright red rose just above my head – still part of the sense-perceptible world but reflecting, perhaps, a deeper reality; symbol of a higher truth. Yet in my initial anger I so nearly missed it..."

0.0 km **Catedral** we pick up the first waymark opp. the entrance and zigzag down (as described on page 110) and cross the busy **rua Mouzinho da Silveira** **[0.3 km]** up into Largo São Domingos veering right> into rua das Flores passing

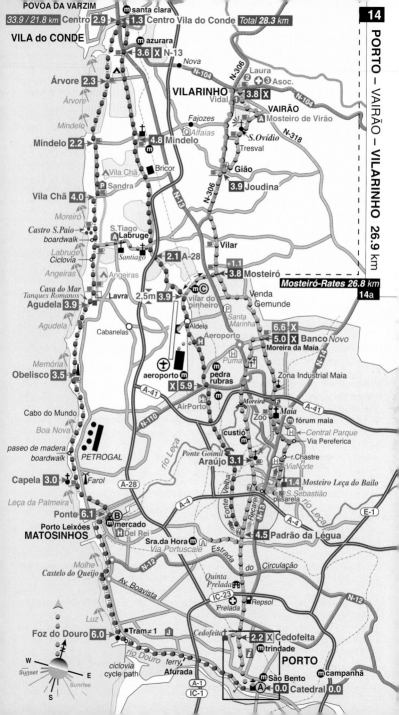

the Igreja da Misericórdia and then up sharp <left into the narrow **rua do Ferraz [0.3** km] [!] (*Note the route to Braga 'caminho interior' continues s/o along rua das Flores into rua do Almada. Be careful not to confuse these waymarks at this early stage*). Continue up steeply to the top and turn right> into rua da Vitória and then sharp <left into rua dos Caldeireiros and up to the expansive plaza at the top *Campo dos Martires da Patria* with Torre dos Clerigos (right) and the imposing former remand prison *Cadeia da Relação* (left) **[0.5** km]. Cross over to the park past (right) the neoclassical building (part of the university's science faculty *faculdade de ciências*) into Praça de Gomes Teixeira. On the corner (left) is the Carmelite church *Igreja do Carmo* evident from its distinctive blue and white tiles *azulejos*. From here we pass into the Praça de Carlos Alberto and the start of the pedestrian shopping street **rua de Cedofeita [0.5** km] which now runs in a straight line to the crossroads at rua de Álvares (Sacadura) Cabral **[0.6** km]:

`2.2 km` Cedofeita *Option*. Crossroads and optional short detour 200m *down left* into rua de Sacadura Cabral to Cedofeita church. (Note: Praça da Republica is *up right* rua de Alvares Cabral 500m for those accessing the route from there):

Detour ● ● ● ● ● **Igreja de Cedofeita:** 250m detour to the *site* of one of the oldest Christian buildings in Europe. The foundations of the Igreja de Cedofeita were laid in the middle of the 6th century, viz. 555 A.D. by the Suevian king Theodomir. What remains is, in most part, a 12thcentury Romanesque building constructed over the original foundations (see photo).

Continue s/o over the crossroads into rua do Barão de Forrester over the wide rua da Boavista passing under railway up to the chapel at largo da Ramada Alta veering <left into rua de Nove de Julho. Cross the busy rua de Egas Moniz *under* block of apartments over rua da Constituição under more apartments veering <left to pass pilgrim cross (left) and up to the crossroads at **Igreja de Carvalhido [1.6** km] recognisable by its exterior adorned with *azulejos*. Continue s/o into rua do Carvalhido merging into rua do Monte dos Burgos past the Hospital da Prelada (left) and Repsol station (right) under city bypass *Via de Cintura Interna* A-20 past entrance (left) of Quinta da Prelada (*formerly city camping now an equestrian centre*). S/o over [!] city ring road **Estrada Circunvalação [1.5** km] into rua Nova do Seixo to past Clínica Médica Padrão da Légua and taxi rank (right) to crossroads and option point **[1.7** km].

`4.8 km` Padrão da Légua ¡ *Opción!* Roadside cross *cruceiro*. Option point for: *[Albergue* **ViaPortuscale** *Asoc.[20÷2]* €-donativo Ⓒ *960 227 134 Abel (phone in advance)*. Directions: *continue over Rua Fonte Velha (100m) into Rua de São Gens into rua Vasco Santana 264 (Senhora da Hora) 1.5 km off route]*. Also...

➠ Caminho da Costa ● ● ● ● ● turns <left into Rua do Senhor and Rua Fonte Velha (one way) from *café Magnólia*. S/o through Santiago de Custóias at Jardim largo do Souto under the A-4 into Rua do Cal over the medieval Ponte Goimil (recently restored) into Rua das Carvalhas. The route continues over the A-41 into Rua da Estrada past pilgrim *Hs* AirPorto €13-35 Ⓒ 229 427 397 at Nº. 244 and up to the N-107 at the roundabout for the **Airport** `5.9 km` Several hotels incl. *H***Aeroporto €38+ Ⓒ 229 429 334 on rua Pedras Rubras. The route is now well waymarked all the way to Vila do Conde.

The main **Camino Central** continues s/o Rua do Recarei under **A-4 [1.6 km]**. ▼

Opción Detour to **Mosteiro Leça do Balio** and/or alternative road route to Moreira da Maia (Banco Novo): This newly waymarked route replaces the dangerous section over the Ponte de Barreiros and the leap of faith over the N-13! It adds 1.5 km to the main route via Igrexa Maia (8.0 km-v- 6.5 km). ***Directions:*** (*not* waymarked) just beyond the A-4 underpass turn right into Rua Dr. Silva Santos (Escuela Básica) and take the footbridge *pasarela* over the rail line and then over the N-14 and take the cobblestone lane through Largo S. Sebastiao *Café* down to the monastery and park *Café*. Return the same way, or continue on alt:

Detour 1.4 km: ● ● ● ● **Mosteiro Leça do Balio:** Romanesque monastery founded by the Order of St. Benedict and dedicated to San Salvador in 986 AD. In the 12th century the monastery was donated by queen D. Teresa to the Military Order of St. John and it became the burial place of various Hospitaller knights. In 1372 King Fernando I married Dona Leonor Teles in secret at the monastery. In a complex and gruesome plot Leonor's sister Maria was

also subsequently married secretly to Dom João, son of King Pedro and Inêz and thereby heir to the throne. The tumultuous love affair threatened the power of Leonor who falsely accused her sister of infidelity and arranged for her gruesome murder in the Palace at Coimbra (see Coimbra).

0.0 km To continue on the newly waymarked route to Moreira da Maia carry s/o past the Monastery and pick up the waymarks which run between the brewery (left) and shopping complex (right) along Rua da Lionesa and over the **rio Leça [1.0 km]** up to Rua do Chartre. *[Note: Back sharp left 300m off route on the N-14 H*** ViaNorte €35+ © 229 448 294].* Continue s/o to the new Maia bypass and turn left along the **Via Pereferica [1.0 km]** (Av. de João Paulo II) down across the valley and N-14. When the Pereferica ends turn up sharply **right> [1.1 km]** past *Café* and at the T-junction turn up <left. *[Note: the connecting route from Metro Fórum Maia joins from the right 700m off route. Also H**** Central Parque €50 © 229 475 563 Av. Visc. Barreiros].*

Continue up past the **Igreja da Maia** *Capela de Na. Sa. do Bom Despacho* with its façade of *azulejos* and the high point of this stage at 120 m. Just past the church is the shaded *Zoo do Maia* with *Café* (left). Turn right at the crossroads by Quinta de Santa Cruz past *cafe Saloã de Jogos* over the new eco-camino ciclovia to pass **Fonte do Godim [1.1 km]** fill up with its invigorating waters (often a queue of locals filling up on its high chemical quality!). Now it's up again under the motorway underpass in the direction of Gemunde. Veer <left by shaded park in Guarda with its tiny chapel dedicated to S. António. Follow sign for the industrial zone (Z.I. Maia 1) up to another high point 120m passing sports *Café Leões* the road (no margin!) continues through woodland and maize crops to the next major crossroads and option point **[2.4 km]**:

6.6 km **Moreira da Maia** *Cruce* crossroads with bank *Espirito Santo* and adjoining *café*. This is where pilgrims taking the main road route join from the left. See main route for accommodation options ½ km (left) at the main crossroads at *Cruz das Guardeiras* on the N-13.

▼ For the main waymarked route (from A-4 underpass) continue s/o Rua de Gondivai over railway to **Araújo [1.5 km]**.

3.1 km Araújo with small chapel *Capela* (right) adj. the Sacred Oak Cafe *Café Carvalho Santo* and shaded park with seating. The café is named after a miraculous event 200 years ago when a hurricane tore through Araújo and demolished everything in sight, save the ancient oak that stood here. Wood from the tree is used in the pulpit in the adjoining 19thc chapel of St. Peter *Igreja de São Pedro de Araújo*. A

tiny statue of St. Peter is embedded in the oak which still occupies the centre of the square. Note the ancient *curceiro* with scallop shells and other pilgrim motifs on the shaft. *[Note: The route down adj. D. Frei Manuel Vas Concellos and over ponte de Barreiros and the dangerous N-13 is now permanently closed]*. Continue s/o Rua de Custío, cross metro line down to the Río Leça and **Ponte de Moreira [2.0 km]**. Continue s/o over the IC-24 /A-41 and turn right> on Av. do Aeroporto (N-107) and s/o over new roundabout with the A-13 (Quinta do Mosteiro left) and veer right> by cemetery past *café Mosteiro* and turn right> at T-junction *(hotels left 300m see below)* into Rua Eng. Frederico Ulrich to rejoin alternative route at crossroads **[3.0 km]**.

5.0 km Moreira da Maia *Cruce* Banco Novo *Cafetaría*. If you need accommodation at this point there is a selection ½ km back down Rua Eng. Frederico Ulrich on the N-13. *Hs* **Puma** €37 ℂ 229 482 128 on Rua Cruz das Guardeiras 776. Other possibilities ½ km adj. airport: *Hs* **AirPorto** €13-35 ℂ 229 427 397 rua da Estrada 244. *H* **Aeroporto** rua das Pedras Rubras ℂ 229 429 334 (by metro). On the N-13 towards Vilar do Pinheiro *Hr* **Santa Marinha** €25 ℂ 229 271 520 (Anna Maria da Silva) also accessible from Gemunde).

We now leave behind the asphalt and city pavements and head onto quieter cobblestone laneways *calçada portuguesa* which are attractive but the granite setts are hard underfoot and make up much of Portugal's rural road network. Lack of maintenance compounds the problems as missing setts are a hazard to walkers and walking poles stick in the gaps.

The camino continues s/o between industrial buildings to **crossroads [2.5 km]**. Continue s/o (signposted Mosteiró) passing *café* (left) in Venda into the village square in **Mosteiró [1.3** km]:

3.8 km Mosteiró with pleasant shaded square *café*. *[pilgrims from the Metro option at Vilar do Pinheiro join here. See page 113 for details]*. S/o past the café up into **Vilar [1.1 km]** s/o over crossroads along the busy N-306 past *bar* (left) *café-snack bar* (right) **[2.2 km]** to crossroads in Joudina **[0.6 km]:**

3.9 km Giao/Joudina *Cruce/Option.* Turn right for recommended route via **Mosteiro de Vairão** *[this avoids continuing along the N-306 which has dangerous bends and continues s/o at this point directly to Vilarinho 3.6 km]*. Turn right at crossroads (signposted Tresval) along rua da Igreja veering left in **Gião [0.5 km]** passing *Café* (opp. Campo de Gião) and s/o to *Café Lemos* **Capela S. Ovidio [1.5 km]** with viewpoint over the distant coast (well worth the short 100m climb to the chapel in a sheltered grove of ancient oak trees left). S/o past *Café Jardim* **[0.3 km]** into rua do Convento to Largo do Mosteiro in **Vairão [0.9 km]**.

3.2 km **Vairão** Monastery founded in the XIth century and recently refurbished to provide pilgrim lodging, meditation room and museum. *Alb.* **Mosteiro de Vairão** *Asoc.[50÷12]* €-donativo ✆ 936 061 160. Kitchen & BBQ area *(if communal meal is not available restaurant Catiago* ✆ *252 663 304 will deliver dinner €6!).* Check-in with José Maria / Dna. Alice in the village square. The hostel and pilgrim museum is  the inspiration of Pedro Macedo and a dedicated team of volunteers who have created this peaceful oasis at the end of this first tiring stage out of Porto city.

Continue via rua das Oliveiras over N-104 and N-318 into rua Estrela to rejoin main waymarked route in **Vilarinho [1.4 km]**.

1.4 km **Vilarinho** small but busy town at junction of the N-306 and N-104 *(The latter links Vila do Conde on the coastal route (left/west) with Trofa (right /east on the Braga route.)* The town has a welcome shaded central park off which are several bars and cafés including the popular *Café Nova Aurora* and the adj.*Restaurant Castelo* at the far end (right) of the square. Vilarinho now has 3 centrally located albergues. ❶ **Casa Família Vidal** *Priv.[9÷3]* €10 ✆ 252 661 503 m: 914 413 500 rua Salterio 87 (adj. Gelataria Paulos). ❷ **Casa da Laura** *Priv.[6÷1]*+ €10 ✆ 917 767 307 rua Estreita 112 with peaceful garden adj. to *café CJ's* with pilgrim menú. The original hostel is located ½ km east ❸ **Escuela** *Polideportivo Muni.[4÷1]* ✆ 252 661 610 along Rua D. Ildefonso past the helpful chemist *Farmácia Rei* ✆ 252 661 610 (09:00 – 19:00) who hold a key.

Next albergue Rates (11.4 km – allow 4 hours at end of day pace) or detour to Vila do Conde (6 km – allow 2 hours or take a taxi (10 mins c. €10) or the infrequent bus. See alternative coastal route for lodging in this seaside town.

Reflections:snoitcelfeR
The dao that can be spoken is not the Dao...

Seashore Path *Senda Litoral* ● ● ●
● *(as distinct from the Coastal Way Caminho da Costa).* **Porto –Vila do Conde 33.9** km. *[An alternative is to start in Matosinhos crossing the lifting bridge* ponte móvel *makes a good symbolic start to the journey and reduces the distance to Vila do Conde by 12.3 km to a total 21.6 km].*

`0.0 km` **Cathedral** Turn left diagonally over Cathedral Square *terreiro da sé* down Escades das Verdades (orange arrows) into Rua do Barredo under niche to the Lord of Good Fortune *Senhor da Boa Fortuna* into the ancient Rua dos Canastreiros and out into **Praça da Ribeira [0.4** km]. From here we essentially follow the Río Douro and the coast by pavements, cycle tracks *ciclovia* and

boardwalks *paseos madera* all the way to Vila do Conde. Continue past the museu dos Transportes (left) and do Vinho (right) and out under the **suspension bridge [2.9** km] passing the mini ferry port where €1.50 buys you a ticket to cross the river to visit Afurada on the far side. We pass a bird observatory and park (detour to Pousada de Juventude right) and s/o along the estuary to the #1 **tram terminus [2.7** km]

`6.0 km` **Foz do Douro** we now leave the river estuary and traverse the shaded gardens out along the coast to pass Fort S. João and **Queijo Castle [3.2** km] on the Boavista roundabout. Head into Matosinhos *Posto de Turismo* ℃ 229 386 423 Av. Gen. Norton de Matos and head into the busy port area of Leixões to **Mercado [3.0** km].

`6.1 km` **Matosinhos** *Ponte Móvel* Variety of lodging in the area incl. on Rua de Brito Capelo @Nº 843 *Hr* **Del Rei** €30 ℃ 229 372 914. @Nº 599 *P* **Central** €30 ℃ 229 372 590. @Nº169 *H**** **Porto-Mar** €35+ ℃ 229 382 104. Cross the bridge over Río Leça which provides a symbolic start of this next stage as we leave Porto city behind. Waymarks direct us down Rua Hintze Ribeiro to the promenade at **Praia Leça da Palmeira** and we head North by Av. Liberdade towards the lighthouse *farol da Boa Nova* built to alleviate the shipwrecks along this notorious stretch of sea known as the Black Coast *Costa Negra*. The lighthouse gives us our bearing to the Capela Boa Nova built on a rocky promontory opposite:

`3.0 km` **Capela Boa Nova** *café* we now join the extensive network of wooden boardwalks *paseos de madera*. These provide welcome relief from the hard pavements and soft sand. They also provide useful signage and there are information panels all along the coast to Vila do conde. We leave behind the giant Petrogal plant (right) and pass through Adeia Nova & Cabo do Mundo to arrive at Remembrance Beach and Obelisk *Praia da Memória e Obelisco* [**1.7** km].

`3.3 km` **Obelisco da Memória** *café* we cross Ribeira da Agudela separating praias de Agudela *café Pedras do Corgo* W.C. and Marreco in the area of **Fontão** site of megalithic remains from the 3rd millenium BC and Roman artefacts of 3rd Century AD to traditional stone fisherman's houses *Casas do Mar de Angeiras*.

4.2 km Angeiras *Casas do Mar* and adj. *replica* Roman salt tanks *tanques romanos salga* used both for salt collection and salting fish. The Lavra area was also used to harvest seaweed *Sargaço* to fertilize the sterile sandy soil for agricultural purposes. *[Detour Camping* Angeiras *Orbitur* © *229 270 571 Rua de Angeiras ½ off route].*
Continue past Fishermens Beach *Praia dos Pescadores* and take the wooden bridge over the Río Onda which separates the town parishes of **Lavra** (Matasinhos) from **Labruge** (Vila do Conde). to Praia Labruge:

1.7 km **Praia Labruge** *Detour Café Novo Rumo [Detour up Av. Liberdade to Labruge town centre 0.8 km Albergue* Santiago Labruge *Mun.[8÷1] €-donativo. School house renovated in 2015 for pilgrim use with all modern facilities. The parish church is dedicated to Santiago]*. Continue on boardwalks that skirt the next sandy cove and wind our way around the S. Paio headland past **Capela S. Paio [1.0** km] *café S. Paio*. Archeological investigations continue and panels explain the rich history and geology of the ancient area. Continue past Praia de Moreiró and into the fishing village of **Vila Chã [1.3** km].

2.3 km **Vila Chã** *Largo dos Pescadores* W.C. *Hr* Sandra €20-30 © 919 254 629 behind *'Tony' Café* in the centre. Continue along Rua Facho to turn off right *Parque Campismo Sol* **Vila Chã** €5!+ © 229 283 163 Rua do Sol (+200m). S/o pick up boardwalks to **Praia Mindelo [2.2** km] *Cafés* W.C. This is a vast expanse of beach that continues all the way to the Ave estuary. New boardwalks skirt the dunes and the beaches of **Praia Árvore [2.3** km] *Cafés* and **Azurara** where we turn inland at the round tower (ruins) over small stream **[1.5** km] turning <left into Rua Francisco Goncales Mosteiró past the shipyards through the suburbs of Azurara up to the main road A-13 where we join pilgrims from the Caminho da Costa to cross the bridge over the estuary of the Río Ave **[1.3** km] into:

7.3 km **Vila do Conde** *Centro* Praça da República forms the heart of this delightful town with its medieval quarter built around the harbour and dominated by the prominent white dome of the *Capela do Socorro*. This tiny circular chapel was built in 1603 in the Moorish style with *azulejos* displaying the adoration of the Magi. Nearby is the maritime museum and replica of a Portuguese caravel *(Vila do Conde was a major centre of boat building activity in*
Portugal's great exploration period). The narrow cobbled alleyways wind around the ancient fishing quarter and central square with the XVIth parish church *Igreja Matriz*. If you want to swim in the sea head west past to the sandy beach around St. John the Baptist Fort (15 minutes from the town centre). Overlooking the town is the impressive *Convento de Santa Clara*. The walk up to the top is rewarded with fine views of the town and coastal area and the remains of a remarkable aqueduct built in the early 18th century that fed the entire complex with water from the nearby hills.

■ *Turismo* ✆ 252 248 473 the helpful tourist office occupies an ivy-clad building on rua 25 April in the town centre by taxi rank ✆ 252 631 933. ■ **Accommodation:** *Hs* Bellamar €10-35 ✆ 252 631 748 Praça da República. *P* Patarata ✆ 252 631 894 on the harbour front Cais das Lavandeiras with restaurant / bar and adj. *Hs* Erva Doce €14-35 ✆ 919 058 715. *R* A Princesa Do Ave €25 ✆ 252 642 065 Rua Dr António José Sousa Pereira 261. *Hs* Venceslau €20 ✆ 252 646 362 rua das Mós 13 (+500m). *H*********Estalagem do Brazão €38+ ✆ 252 642 016 Av. Dr. João Canavarro. *H**********Forte de São João Baptista €100 ✆ 252 240 600 Av. Brasil. **Azurara:** *H**********Spa Santana €60 ✆ 252 641 717 rua de Santana. *H**********Villa C Spa €70 ✆ 252 240 420 on the N-13. The town merges into its modern neigbour **Póvoa do Varzim** which offers additional lodging (see Coastal route p.198).

▲ To continue to **Esposende / Marinhas** on the **Caminho da Costa** go to p.198.

▼ To return to the **Caminho Central** you have 2 options (neither are waymarked).

❶ **Arcos** *via Junqueira* **[9.8 km]:** Follow the river Ave past Convento de Santa Clara and over **metro S.Clara [0.4 km]** and turn right> at **T-Junction [1.6 km]** under the A-28 into **Touguinha** *café* up and s/o over the **roundabout [1.3** km] and down to join the N-309 in **Touguinhó** passing *cafés* to bridge over the **Río Este [1.4** km] (tributary of the Ave). Cross the bridge (cascades upstream *cascatas de Touguinho*) into rua Rio Este past Quinta da Espinheira (right) to turn <left off the N-309 up into rua Central **[0.9** km] veering <left past Centro Médico *café* (right) s/o past *Igreja Matrix* **[1.2** km] and down past school (right) *café Panidoce* (left) to crossroads with *café* and central cruceiro at **Junqueira [0.5** km]: 7.3 km

Continue s/o to monastery church ahead *Igreja de São Simão da Junqueira* (statue of Santiago Peregrino in the right-hand niche). Narrow road [!] to cross the A-7 motorway **[1.5** km]. *Megalítico do Fulom (Mamoa do Fulão)* prehistoric Megalithic mound located in the pine forest (right). The burial chambers date back to 3,000 B.C.E. The west-facing opening is discernible in the second of the two mounds. It is little visited which adds to the mysterious atmosphere that pervades this peaceful glade despite is proximity of the new motorway. Continue along the road down to join the main waymarked route from Vilarinho at the bridge over the **Rio Este [0.7** km] and up into **Arcos [0.3** km]. 2.5 km
From here the route follows the main Caminho Central to Rates (see next stage).

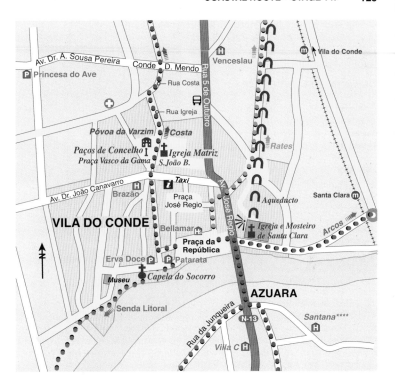

❷ **Rates** *via Beiriz* [12.7 km]: Waymarks have now been removed to discourage it's use. If you are experienced at route-finding and orientation then it is relatively easy to follow and the first 5.4 km is due north alongside the aqueduct.

From the central Praça da República head up the steps by Museu José Régio *Escaleras y Calçada S. Francisco* and follow *aqueduto* **aqueduct [0.4 km]** turn <left into Rua Tras de Arco to **metro Vila do Conde [1.0 km]** crossing Av. Atlántico at roundabout into Rua dos Arcos. At the far end take a short **detour left [1.8 km]** around private property and back to the aqueduct to take the tunnel under the **A-28 [0.9 km]** into Rua de Calves. Follow the wall (right) and turn left into Rua Comendador Brandão (sign Tapetes de Beiriz – once famous for its carpets) and straight up to the **crossroads [1.3 km]** with *café S. Goncalo.* `5.4 km`

The route now takes a turn right to the north/east along Rua Cruceiro past *café Cruceiro* in **Beiriz [1.0 km]** turn right at the church into Rua Ezequiel Campo and s/o at crossroads *Adega 4 Amigos* and veer right past Quinta da Luna and then left to **farmhouse** *granja* **[1.1 km]** and take the left hand track up to Rua Toureiro (Seixo) and turn right and then left into Rua Bouçó and s/o at **crossroads [1.0 km]** *café.* Rua Bouçó has many bends but continue up to T-junction at Rua Central and turn right and then imm. left opp. **school [1.1 km]**. Follow this track up to newely paved Calzada and turn up left to next T-junction at asphalt **road [1.1 km]** (Rua Caminho do Porto). The easiest option is to turn down right to join the **Caminho Central [0.6 km]** and follow the waymarks into **Rates Igreja [1.4 km]** `7.3 km`

❏ **The Path around our home is also the ground of awakening.**
Thich Nhat Hanh

15 *215 km (133.6 miles) – Santiago*

VILARINHO – BARCELOS

ⅢⅢⅢⅢⅢ	--- ---	7.2	--- ---	26%
▬▬▬▬	--- ---	15.1	--- ---	56%
▬▬▬	--- ---	5.0	--- ---	18%
Total km		**27.3 km** (17.0 ml)		

28.3 km (+^ 210 m = 1.0 km)
Alto(*m*)▲ Goios 150 m (492 ft)
<❘A❘ ❘H❘> Arcos **7.5** km / Rates **11.4** km / Pedra Furada **18.5** km

295m ▲ Monte Franqueira
200m
VILARINHO — Arcos Rates — Pedra Furada ▲150m Goios — BARCELOS
Barcelinos
rio Ave — rio Este — rio Cávado
0 km — 5 km — 10 km — 15 km — 20 km — 25 km

The Practical Path: A varied day where we encounter our first delightful woodland paths around Arcos. 50% of this stage is along quiet country lanes, mostly screened by eucalyptus and pine woods, offering shelter from wind and shade from the sun. While this requires walking on asphalt this is somewhat kinder underfoot than the traditional granite cobblestones. There are also some stretches along the N-306 with poor sight lines that require extra vigilance. Improvements are ongoing including a new woodland path around Monte Franqueira.

❏ **The Mystical Path:** We have mastered how to travel to the moon but we don't know how to find inner peace. *Charity begins at home* is an old adage containing much wisdom. The breakdown of relationships is endemic in our affluent western world – we don't need to switch on the television to witness war. We are at war with ourselves, with our families, our own society... If we want to create peace in our world we don't need to step outside our own home – we just need to develop an open door, an open mind and an open-heart right here and now.

❏ **Personal Reflections:** "…I was covered in dirt and sweat and suffering from heat exhaustion and dehydration and nearly missed the café entrance. The cool interior and the smile on the patron's face embraced me in welcome. Before I had spoken a word he guided me to a table and poured a fresh orange juice – it was unasked for and tasted like nectar. But the greatest gift was the spontaneous display of generosity. Before I left this haven of hospitality António had pressed the key of his apartment into my hand, *'treat my home as if it were your own,'* he said simply… I write these notes in his apartment overlooking the broad sweep of the river Cávado. He is at work in his restaurant till late but I look forward to having breakfast with him. I want to understand what makes one man open his home to a total stranger while another bars it to his own family…"

0.0 km **Vilarinho** From the central crossroads continue s/o in the direction of Fontaínhas. Stay on the N-306 and turn **right> [1.2 km]** down to the beautiful medieval bridge over the río Ave **Ponte D. Zameiro [0.5 km]** with old mill

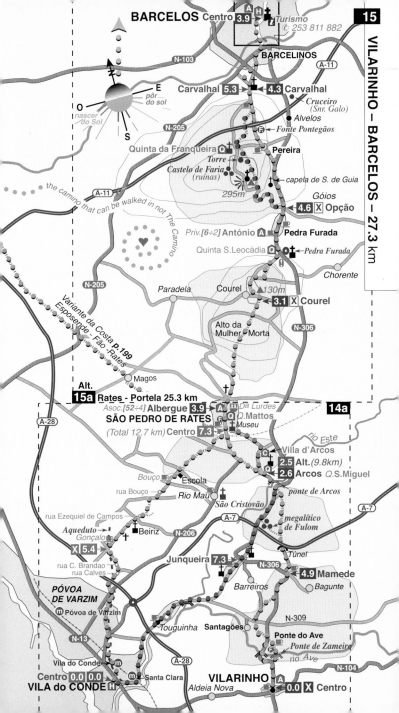

BARCELOS Centro **3.9**
Turismo
© 253 811 882

N-103
BARCELINOS
A-11

E
pór
do sol

O

nascer
do Sol
S

N-205

Carvalhal **5.3** **4.3** Carvalhal
Cruceiro
(Snr. Galo)
Alvelos
Fonte Pontegãos

Quinta da Franqueira
Torre
Pereira

Castelo de Faria
(ruínas)
295m
capela de S. de Guia

A-11

Góios
4.6 X Opção

the camino that can be walked in not The Camino

Priv.[6÷2] **António** A
Pedra Furada

Quinta S.Leocádia
Pedra Furada

N-205
Paradela
Courel
▲130m
Chorente

Variante da Costa P. 199
Esposende - Fão -Rates

3.1 X Courel

Alto da
Mulher ●Morta
N-306

A-28
●Magos

Alt.
15a Rates - Portela 25.3 km
Asoc.[52÷4] **Albergue** **3.9** A m *Dª Lurdes*
SÃO PEDRO DE RATES Q.Mattos
(Total 12.7 km) Centro **7.3** Museu

14a

rio Este

Vila d'Arcos
C
2.5 Alt.(9.8km)
2.6 Arcos Q.S.Miguel

Bouço
Escola
rua Bouço
Rio Mau
São Cristóvão
ponte de Arcos

A-7

rua Ezequiel de Campos
Aqueduto
Gonçalo
X 5.4 Beiriz
N-206

megalítico
de Fulom

Túnel

rua C. Brandao
rua Calves

PÓVOA
DE VARZIM

m Póvoa de Varzim

Junqueira **7.3**
Barreiros

4.9 Mamede
●Bagunte

N-309

N-13
Touguinha
Santagões

Ponte do Ave
Ponte de Zameira
F
rio Ave
N-104

Centro **0.0** **0.0**
VILA do CONDE H
m Santa Clara
A-28
Aldeia Nova

VILARINHO A
0.0 X Centro

buildings down river. The bridge has been damaged on several occasions in recent years. *(Note: If the bridge is impassable – don't panic! Continue along the river bank and veer up to rejoin the main road and proceed over the modern bridge ½ km down river (see photo right) and continue until you join the waymarks again).* Proceed over the river Ave to pass *[F.]* (left) and continue up to the hamlet **Ponte de Ave [0.3 km]** straddling the crossroads with *bar* and chapel *Capela de N.S. da Ajuda.* Continue up into woodland and back onto **main road [0.6 km]** *(alterative bridge route joins here).* Turn right> and then imm <left at new camino signboard. (Do *not* take old route s/o along the busy N-306) but continue left along quiet tracks and laneways in the direction of **Santagões** which we skirt around via ruas da Venda and José Cañdido back onto the N-306 at **Mamede crossroads [2.3 km]**.

4.9 km **Mamede** *Cruce* roadside shrine Outeiro Maior (right) Junqueira (left) s/o passing the **Casa do Alto** (high point of the day at 125 m) before veering right> onto the cobbled rua de São Mamede through **Boa Vista** passing the ruins of the old pilgrim and coaching inn *Estalagem das Pulgas* and under the new A-7 motorway where Arcos opens to view straight ahead. *[Optional detour (adds ½ kilometre to the waymarked route): a forest track to the left runs alongside the motorway to the megalithic burial mound **Megalítico do Fulom** described under alternative route from Vila do Conde].*

We now make our way s/o down the rough path to the **rio Este** A sandy riverbank makes a good place for a picnic, or a swim? Proceed s/o over the Ponte de Arcos and up the cobbled lane of this pretty hamlet with the walls of the Quinta São Miguel (right).

2.6 km **Arcos** Quinta São Miguel €30-70 incl. ℂ 919 372 202 (adj. the church). Delightfully restored 18th century manor house recently extended to 11 rooms with 2 swimming pools! The owner António Rodrigues speaks English and is very supportive of pilgrims. *Option:* At this point there are 2 waymarked routes to Rates. Main route (left) or s/o for road route as follows:

S/o past the church and *Café Barbosa* **[0.2 km]** s/o past Villa d'Arcos **[0.2 km]** €20-40 ℂ 916 344 308 Rua da Alegria, 38. S/o over N-206 at **crossroads** [!] **[1.5 km]** *Transporte Matos* and over disused **rail line [1.0 km]** [!] Be careful not to confuse waymarks (left) leading to the coastal route at Esposende that cross our path at this point *(pilgrims have found themselves, unintentionally, beside the sea!).* Continue s/o past pilgrim statue and up to the albergue in Rates **[0.6 km]**.

3.5 km **Rates** The original route is 400m longer at 3.9 km as follows:

Take waymarks <left at *cruceiro* adj. quinta and around the edge of the village onto earth **track [0.4 km]** into eucalyptus woods and over busy main road **N-206** [!] **[1.1 km]** by timber yard *(an alternative route from Vila do Conde, via Rio Mau joins from the left).* Continue onto cobble **lane [1.2 km]** over abandoned **railway [0.4 km]** to the parish **church** in **São Pedro de Rates [0.3 km]**.

The town is a delightful blend of old and new with the parish church dedicated to St. Peter, a local saint much revered in the area and reputedly ordained by St. James himself on his evangelization of the peninsula. It was

originally built as a monastery church by the Order of Cluny (a powerful influence on the camino) in the 11th century over the remains of earlier pagan temples of Roman and pre Roman origins. The church belfry is a separate structure to the rear. An adjoining ultra modern museum (with public toilets) displays some artefacts found during excavation, most dating from 12th century but with some exhibits from the Roman period.

Just beyond the church an extensive square opens up *Praça dos Forais* with the diminutive Chapel to Our Lady of the Square the *Capela do Sra. da Praça* with the historic Town Cross *Pelourinho* adjoining. At the far end of the square, opposite the clock tower, is the internet *Café-restaurante Macedo.*

Pick up the arrows behind the **Igreja de S. Pedro** and continue on past the drinking font *Fontenário de S. Pedro* into rua Direita past **Casa de Mattos** €40 © 919 822 398 rua Direita **[0.3 km]** directly on the camino (right) but not well signposted. Turn <left and on the left is the Rates albergue **[0.2 km].**

3.9 km São Pedro de Rates *Albergue Asoc.[50÷4]* €-donativo Rua S. António, 189. The first dedicated pilgrim hostel to open on the Portuguese side of the camino and was inaugurated on St. James Day 2004. The hostel was further renovated and extended in 2009 and now offers 50 beds in various small dormitories with ample shower and toilet facilities. A cosy living room, laundry room and kitchen make up the

amenities on the first floor. There is an extensive courtyard for clothes drying and relaxing and also provides access to a small museum displaying objects typical of rural life in the area. If the hostel is closed you can obtain the key from the well-stocked and welcoming shop located 100m further on opp. the *Capela de S. António* where Dª Lurdes and her family are usually open until 21:00.

Continue up past the albergue and shop and s/o over crossroads onto short stretch of asphalt road which becomes a delightful earth track **[0.7 km]** and veers right> down to a stream bed (wet) up through overhanging vines into eucalyptus woodland continuing along forest tracks up to a high point at Dead Woman's Peak *Alto da Mulher Morta* at which point we enter the administrative area of Barcelos. The natural path now undulates gently to cross over a road close to the village of Courel (left) **[2.4 km]**:

3.1 km **Cruce Courel** continue up through woodland ahead along a walled lane up to asphalt road and turn <left and then right> around high walls of quinta

[**1.7** km] and continue s/o right> off this road at next junction (*café Real* off route 100m left) then down <left onto track back to busy main road [!] [**1.4** km] turn <left along the N-306. Stay alert walking this stretch of road as it is narrow with little margin for the fast moving traffic with several blind bends. We pass the Igreja Pedra Furada [**0.2** km]. Adjoining the church is the perforated stone *pedra furada* that gives this area its name. Opp. the church is the austere Quinta de Sta. Leocádia 🕾 252 951 103

AT *Ag.Turismo* seldom open. S/o main road to **Pedra Furada [0.9** km] popular *café-bar restaurant Pedra Furada* on rua Santa Leocadia. António Martins Ferreira and his family have been welcoming wayfarers for many years and now have aa small *Albergue* **Pedra Furada** *Priv.[4÷1]+* €10 + adj. private room twin beds €25 🕾 António 252 951 144. Continue up past various *cafés* to crossroads at **Góios** [**0.6** km] and **option:**

4.6 km Cruce *Pedra Furada / Góios / Opção.* **Option** [1] Continue s/o along the main 'lower' route via **Pereira** or [2] Turn left uphill to **Monte Franqueira.**

This alternative has been waymarked through woodland around the slopes of Monte Franqueira (*Alto 290m*) with opportunity to visit [a] **Capela de Sta. da Franqueira** and viewpoint. [b] remains of Roman castrum and [c] the Manueline Convento da Franqueira adj. Quinta da Franqueira (luxury accommodation). *Note*: This is a strenuous uphill climb (+140m) and adds 1.0 km but it makes a delightful path through woodland. An annual pilgrimage to Monte Franqueria is held 2nd Sunday in August. Turn up <left at the crossroads and imm. right> by side of timber yard on asphalt road and turn off right [**2.1** km] onto forest path ❖.

[to access the chapel and viewpoint continue s/o along road for a further 800m to the top [a] Capela de Sta. da Franqueira XVIII. Cafe (summer only) adj. the chapel and panoramic viewing balcony with unsurpassed views west over the Atlantic and, allegedly, east into Spain! If you take this option then continue down the far side by steps to rejoin road 300m where there is an option to visit [b] Castelo de Faria a short detour 100 metres (left) along a sandy track to this ancient fortress built over a Roman Castrum and before that over a prehistoric settlement Citania. A brief climb up through the ancient woodland to the ruins built around a rocky outcrop evokes a sense of both history and mystery – this peaceful site is little visited. Continue back down the road to rejoin the waymarked route by the medieval tower 300m].

❖ For the waymarked route veer right onto the forest path that maintains this contour line *below* Monte Franqueira to cross the road down ancient granite steps past the healing waters of the Fountain of Life *Fonte da Vida* back to road and exterior [c] **Convento da Franqueira** [**1.4** km] built in the 16th century in the Manueline style (left) adjoining Quinta da Franqueira €60-90 🕾 253 831 606. The convent is under the guardianship of the Gallie family who own the Quinta which also acts as a starting base for pilgrims riding by horseback to Santiago.

To continue take the waymarked path back into the woodland over **A-11** [**0.6** km] steeply down through Monte de Cima to rejoin the main route in **Fulões** [**0.7** km] and then to **Carvalhal** [**0.4** km].

5.3 km Carvalhal Church, cafe and restaurant.

To continue on the *lower* route continue s/o at crossroads along the **N-306** passing *Capela de Senhora da Guia* [0.4 km] set back (left) from the road with *[F.].* Turn <left signposted Aldeia /Souto /Pedrêgo **[0.8 km]** off the main road and proceed down the cobblestones into **Pereira [0.7 km]**: *Café S. Salvador* small hamlet with churrasquería, shop and small chapel at the crossroads. We continue along a maze of small roads but the route is well waymarked as we pass the ancient *[F.]* **Fonte de Pontegãos [1.0** km] s/o under the motorway and veer right> at T-Junction **[0.8** km] *café-mercado* (left) *(here the alternative route from Monte da Franqueira joins from the left).* Follow sign for Barcelos to the parish church in **Carvalhal [0.6 km].**

4.3 km Carvalhal *Igreja.* Turn <left at church and 50m right> through Portocarreiro and over stream and up to Holy Cross chapel *Capela da Santa Cruz* [1.3 km] into the industrial area of Barcelinhos s/o **roundabout [0.6 km]** around car showrooms and through underpass (N-103) to rejoin the main road on the outskirts of Barcelinhos *cafés (Here the ancient way went directly to the river to the medieval ferry point before the bridge was built).* Turn right> along main road to crossroads and turn down <left opp. ancient drinking font past *Alb.* ❶ **Amigos da Montanha** *Asoc.[16÷2]* €5 ✆ 253 830 430 Rua Custódio José Gomes Vilas Boas 57 modern purpose-built hostel.

Continue down to the medieval bridge *Ponte Barcelos* in **Barcelinhos [1.2 km].** Chapel of Our Lady of the Bridge built in 1328 to provide shelter for pilgrims (the stone benches and basins for washing feet can still be seen). 100m (left) along the riverside past the **Bombeiros** *Alb.* ❷ **Residência do Senhor do Galo** *Folclórico Asoc.[20÷2]* €5 ✆ 253 833 304 Largo Guilherme Gomes Fernandes. Residence for folk-dance groups where lodging is also available for pilgrims.

❶ *Capela de Nª Sª da Ponte [*❶ *Numbers refer to historical monuments on the town plan, those with an asterisk* are national monuments* ● *from the bridge to the central square is 800m.]* Cross over the medieval bridge ❷ *Ponte Medieval* built by *D. Pedro* Earl of Barcelos in 1328. This acted as a great spur to the development and prestige of the town and facilitated early pilgrims to Santiago.

    Note: by taking your time along the following route you will pass most of the historic sites along the way. You can take time to visit them as you pass or return, perhaps, when you have found a place to stay for the night. Turn <left then first right> up past the 15th century ❸ *Solar dos Pinheiros** manor house of the Pinheiro family (left) with its gargoyles of the bearded one *Barbadão*. Next we come to the remains of the 15th century Palace of the Counts ❹ *Paço dos Condes* now an open air archaeological museum **Museu Arqueológico** with the Pillory **Pelourinho*** (see photo) portraying the legend of the Cock *lenda do Gallo* (see later) with the 14th century parish church ❺ *Igreja Matriz** fronting onto the municipal square *Largo do Municipio.* This Romanesque church, with later Baroque additions, was built in the 12th century and has a fine display of glazed tiles *Azulejos.* On the opposite side of the square is the sumptuously restored town hall and council office ❻ *Câmara e Paços do Concelho** formerly a hostel for pilgrims to Santiago de Compostela. Continue into ❼ *Largo do*

Apoio the original town square around which the nobility built their houses with central fountain (1621). *[At this point you can take a shortcut direct to the new pilgrim hostel in rua Miguel Bombarda by continuing s/o via rua da Barreta].* Turn right> into rua S. Francisco and the main pedestrian shopping street, rua D. António Barroso (rua Direita) to **[0.8** km]:

3.9 km Barcelos *Largo da Porta Nova.* The attractive main square is the hub of this lively town with the helpful tourist office located clsoe by the 15th century granite tower ❽ *Torre da Porta Nova** which is the only remaining medieval entrance into the town (formerly the tourist office and handicraft centre). At the other end of the square is a fine stone fountain with the interesting 18th century Baroque church dedicated to Good Jesus of the Cross ❾ *Templo do S. Bom Jesus da*

Cruz* *(Igreja de Senhor das Cruces)* built in 1704 in an octagonal shape over an earlier chapel. This is the venue of the 500-year-old Feast of the Crosses that takes place annually on 3rd May and is named after the miraculous appearance of a cross in the soil of the adjoining market square in 1504. By the church is the central Residencial Arantes on Av. da Liberdade and just beyond it Café Santiago with temporary Camino information adjoining.

BARCELOS: Opening out from the Largo da Porto Nova is the extensive market square *Campo da Feira* otherwise known as Campo da República. The whole area becomes one of Portugal's best-known and liveliest markets *Feira de Barcelos* every Thursday. At the top end of the square is the ❿ *Igreja do Terço* built in 1707; its plain façade belies its rich interior and ceiling depicting the life of Saint Benedict *São Bento*. Adjacent to it is the new shopping centre and hotel in the Centro do Terço built around the original Convent of that name. Barcelos makes an excellent stopover and there are several parks and squares in which to rest and enjoy the local scene and a municipal swimming pool if you want to cool off. If you have walked from the new albergue in Rates you will have plenty of time to explore. However the next stage to Ponte de Lima is a long day so you need to be refreshed and ready for an early start although intermediate lodging is now available. The tourist office has a list of accommodation, which includes the following (see town map for locations).

❏ *Turismo:* ✆ 253 811 882 Largo Dr. José Novais where Nuno Rodrigues and other helpful staff are on hand (also handicraft centre + internet). Summer: Weekdays 9.30-18.00 Winter 9.30-17.30. Weekends 10.00-13.00 /14.00-17.00.
❏ *Accommodation:* Alb.❸ Cidade de Barcelos *Priv.[20÷3]* €-donativo rua Miguel Bombarda, 36 adj. café Araujo where Emília has a key and menú peregrino. *R* Arantes €30+ ✆ 253 811 326 rua da Liberdade, 35 centrally located above the restaurant and pastelaría. *H****Bagoeira €45+ ✆ 253 809 500 Av. Dr. Sidónio Pais, 495 overlooking the main square with popular restaurant attached. Albergaria do Terço €40+ ✆ 253 808 380 rua de São Bento with pedestrian entrance through shopping mall off rua Manuel Pais – stylish modern hotel on upper floors of the shopping centre. *R* Dom Nuno €35 ✆ 253 812 810 Av. Nuno Alvares Pereira, 76 modern hotel off road to rail station. *R* Solar da Estação €25 ✆ 253 811 741 Largo Marechal Gomes da Costa opp. the rail station.

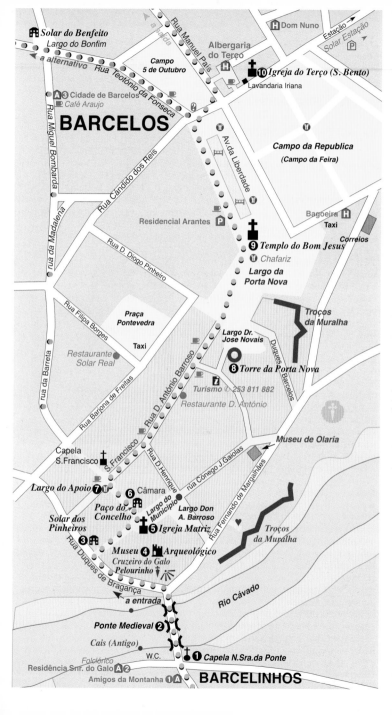

Solar do Benfeito
Largo do Bonfim

a alternativo   Rua Teotónio da Fonseca

A 3 Cidade de Barcelos
Café Araujo

BARCELOS

Campo 5 de Outubro

H Dom Nuno   Estação   Solar Estação

Albergaria do Terço

10 Igreja do Terço (S. Bento)
Lavandaria Iriana

Av. da Liberdade

Campo da Republica
(Campo da Feira)

Residencial Arantes

Bagoeira **H**
Taxi

Correios

9 Templo do Bom Jesus
Chafariz
Largo da Porta Nova

Troços da Muralha

Rua Cândido dos Reis

Rua D. Diogo Pinheiro

Rua Filipa Borges

Praça Pontevedra
Taxi

Restaurante Solar Real

Rua Berjona de Freitas

Largo Dr. Jose Novais

8 Torre da Porta Nova

Rua D. António Barroso

Turismo ☏ 253 811 882
Restaurante D. António

Duques Barcelos

Museu de Olaria

Capela S.Francisco

Rua S. Francisco

Rua D. Henrique

rúa Cónego J. Gaiolas

Rua Fernando de Margalhães

Troços da Muralha

Largo do Apoio 7

6 Câmara
Paço do Concelho
Largo do Município

Largo Don A. Barroso

Solar dos Pinheiros

3

Museu 4 Arqueológico
Cruzeiro do Galo
Pelourinho

5 Igreja Matriz

Rua Duques de Bragança

a entrada

Rio Cávado

Ponte Medieval 2

Cais (Antigo)
W.C.

1 Capela N.Sra.da Ponte

Folclórico
Residência Snr. do Galo **A 2**

Amigos da Montanha **1 A**

BARCELINHOS

rua da Madalena
Rua Miguel Bombarda
rua da Barreta
Rua Manuel Pais

❏ **Restaurants:** Wide range of cafes and snack bars around the main squares. For good value and atmosphere try *Solar Real* Praça de Pontevedra on the first floor with interesting interior and fading murals. ❏ **Transport:** Rail station ✆ 253 811 243 with rail services along the Porto – Santiago line. Bus Av. Dr. Sidónio Pais (Campo da Feira) ✆ 253 808 300. Also Linhares ✆ 253 811 517 rua Dr. Julio Vieira Ramos. Both have regular services to Braga.

Barcelos is a delightful town occupying an elevated site above the river Cávado and was the first Portuguese County established by D. Dinis in 1298 but its origins go back to the Roman period. The town retains much of its medieval atmosphere, the oldest remaining structure being the original town walls and Torre da Porta Nova, which date back to the 15th century and to the first Duke of Bragança. There are several museums including the Ceramic Museum *Museu de Olaria* housed in the 19th century *Casa dos Carvalhos Mendanhas* which contains a large collection of ceramics from around the world, especially from this region and particularly of the famous brightly coloured cockerel which has become a national symbol of Portugal and logo for Portuguese tourism.

The Barcelos cockerel is based on the same story that we may have heard in Santo Domingo de Calzada on the Camino Francés. The cross in the Paço dos Condes portrays the miraculous story of the roasted cock that rose from the table of the judge who had wrongly condemned a pilgrim to Santiago to hang from the nearby gallows (located south of the river). The pilgrim had proclaimed his innocence and stated that if he were wrongly condemned to hang then a dead cock would rise from the judge's table in proof of his righteousness. The innocent lad was hanged and sure enough a roasted cock stood up on the judge's plate as he sat for dinner that night. The bewildered judge hurried from his table to find the pilgrim alive on the gallows – saved by the miraculous intervention of St. James and the Barcelos cockerel!

Detour – Braga: Buses run throughout the day and the journey takes around one hour. If you are planning to visit Braga and the nearby Bom Jesus (the most popular tourist site in Portugal) you will need to allow an extra day. An easy way to do this is book an extra night in Barcelos and then you can travel to Braga without having to waste time looking for accommodation there and carrying your rucksack to boot (note the bus stop in Braga is 10 minutes walk west of the city centre). Braga is a city with a host of outstanding monuments. Sometimes referred to as the 'Rome of Portugal' it is the country's ecclesiastical capital with a somewhat pompous and grandiose atmosphere to match. Its name derives from the original Bracari Celts but Romans, Visigoths and Moors have all occupied it. Amongst the many historic buildings conveniently grouped around the city centre is the 11thc Romanesque cathedral *Sé* whose foundations go back to 1070 when they replaced an earlier mosque built by the occupying Moors and later underwent Gothic and Baroque embellishments. Access to the museum of sacred art is off a small cloister just inside the main entrance. Braga has more than 30 churches and several national monuments. The *Turismo* is housed in a prominent Art Deco building on Av. da Liberdade, 1 / corner of *Praça da República* ✆ 253

262 550 (09:00-19:00 weekdays summer / 09:00-17:30 & closed lunch during winter) and provides a useful map of the town and list of accommodation together with details of how to get to the famous ***Bom Jesus do Monte*** overlooking the city from its hilltop perch surrounded by ancient woodland and terraced gardens – a pilgrimage in itself if you want to climb the steps to the chapel at the top.

REFLECTIONS:

I only went out for a walk... and finally concluded to stay out till sundown, for going out, I found, was really going in. *John Muir*

16 *187.7 km (116.6 miles) – Santiago*

BARCELOS – PONTE DE LIMA

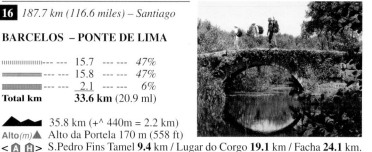

⊪⊪⊪⊪⊪⊪⊪⊪--- ---	15.7	--- ---	47%	
▬▬▬▬▬--- ---	15.8	--- ---	47%	
▬▬▬▬--- ---	2.1	--- ---	6%	
Total km	**33.6 km** (20.9 ml)			

▰▰▰ 35.8 km (+^ 440m = 2.2 km)

Alto*(m)*▲ Alto da Portela 170 m (558 ft)

< 🅰 🅷 > S.Pedro Fins Tamel **9.4** km / Lugar do Corgo **19.1** km / Facha **24.1** km.

```
200m - - - Alto da Portela-170m - - - - - - - - - - - - - - - - - - - - - - - - - - - -
    Tamel S. Pedro Fins 🅰            Portela ▲160m  🏨Facha
100m                                            Vitorino         PONTE DE LIMA
BARCELOS             Balugães    Corgo   dos Piães                     ■🅰
 ■               rio Neiva         🅰                      rio Lima ▼
0 km      5 km      10 km      15 km      20 km      25 km      30 km
```

The Practical Path: This is the longest but arguably the most beautiful stage. It includes two hill passes *portelas* separating the river valleys of Neiva and Lima and we have the natural landscape to lift our spirits and nearly half the route (47%) is on pathways through vineyards and woodland through the peaceful Neiva valley. From Portela (Vitorino) all the way is downhill into the beautiful Lima valley. The opening of several new albergues and casa rurales provide additional options if tiredness or nightfall overtakes.

The Mystical Path: The word hospitality comes from medieval Latin *hospitare; to receive a guest.* From this root we also find host, hospice, hospital and Hospitaller. The Knights Hospitaller provided welcome to the increasing numbers of pilgrims struggling across the remote landscape and now, centuries later, it is no different. The garb of the knight may have changed but the hospitality can still be found, "...ask and it will be given to you; seek and you will find; knock and the door will be opened unto you." *Matthew 7.*

Personal Reflections: "I heard there was the possibility of a place to stay in the area but had no idea where to start looking, it was getting late and I was exhausted. As if on cue 3 delightful children appeared 'out of nowhere.' Language was no barrier to their enthusiasm and insistence that I follow them... I sit under the starry sky and scribble these notes by the light of the fire lit from resinous pine needles. The fragrance now overtaken by the smell from the pork chops sizzling on the griddle. Framed in the light of the kitchen doorway is Mariana while her mother and father prepare the table in the background. The generosity of spirit that flows from this family leaves me humbled and filled with deep gratitude for the spontaneous hospitality offered to a total stranger."

0.0 km Barcelos *Centro* Igreja Bom Jesus continue up Av. da Liberdade by fountain to busy roundabout with *Centro Commercial Terço (right).* **Option**▼ An alternative (historic) route veers off left via **Abade de Neiva** (Romanesque church *Santa Maria XII)* to loop back and rejoin the main route in **Vila Boa**.

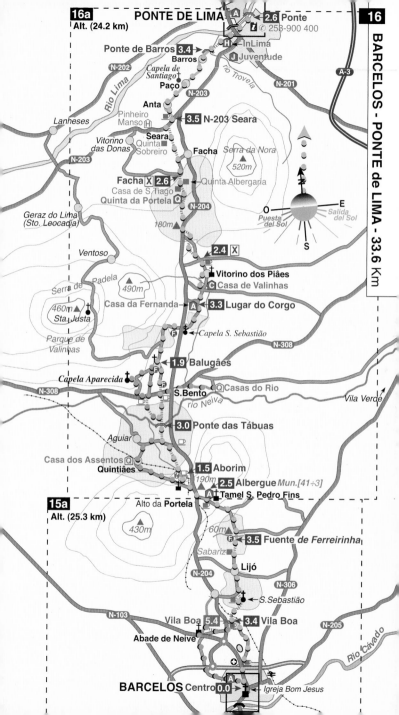

PONTE DE LIMA

16a Alt. (24.2 km)

2.6 Ponte
© 258-900 400

Ponte de Barros **3.4**
H InLima
J Juventude
Barros
N-202
Capela de Santiago †
Paço
N-203
Anta
3.5 N-203 Seara
Rio Trovela
N-201
A-3

Lanheses
Pinheiro Manso
Seara
Quinta Sobreiro
Vitorino das Donas
Facha
Serra da Nora 520m

Facha X **2.6**
Casa de S.Tiago
Quinta da Portela Q
N-204
Quinta Albergaria

Geraz do Lima (Sto. Leocádia)
180m

O — Puesta del Sol
E — Salida del Sol
S

N-203

Ventoso

2.4 X

Vitorino dos Piães †
C Casa de Valinhas

Serra de Padela
490m

Casa da Fernanda A **3.3** Lugar do Corgo

460m Sta. Justa †
Parque de Valinhas

F ‡ *Capela S. Sebastião*
N-308

1.9 Balugães
F

Capela Aparecida †
N-308
S.Bento
F
Q Casas do Rio
rio Neiva

Vila Verde

3.0 Ponte das Tábuas

Aguiar

Casa dos Assentos Q
Quintiães

1.5 Aborim
190m
2.5 Albergue *Mun.[41÷3]*
A † Tamel S. Pedro Fins

15a Alt. (25.3 km)
Alto da **Portela**
430m

60m
F **3.5** Fuente *de Ferreirinha*
Sabariz

Lijó
N-204
N-306

† *S.Sebastião*

N-103
Vila Boa **5.4**
3.4 Vila Boa
N-205

Abade de Neive

Rio Cávado

BARCELOS Centro 0.0
A †
Igreja Bom Jesus

Detour: ● ● ● ● *via Abade de Neiva* (well waymarked / 2 km longer + climb): At the top of Av. da Liberdade in Barcelos fork left by restaurante Galliano into rua Dr. Teo' da Fonseca into rua do Bem Feito (Solar do Benfeito right Albergue Cidade de Barcelos rua Miguel Bombarda left) and over the **dual carriageway [0.4 km]** Av. Sao José (use pedestrian crossing) onto local road CM 1069 which merges onto path up and over city bypass **[1.0 km]** veering right> into rua do Areal past **Capela S.Amaro [0.9 km]** over crossroads and turn <left on **N-103 [1.4 km]**. *[½ further up the N-103 is: CR Casa do Monte €70 Ⓒ 967 057 779 Rua de Santa Maria, 640 Lugar do Barreiro].* Turn up imm. right> to the romanesque church of *Santa Maria de Abade do Neiva* [National Monument] founded by D. Mafalda, wife of D. Afonso Henriques in the 12th century with niche in the form of a scallop shell connecting it to the camino de Santiago. Take the road imm. above the church that descends gently and then sharply down woodland path to cross the N-204 (pedestrian crossing) *Cafe* (left by service station) and down to rejoin the main route in **Vila Boa [0.5 km]**.

5.4 km Vila Boa *Lugar do Espirito Santo.*

▼ For the main route take R.Dr.Manuel Pais cross over city **bypass [0.9 km]** s/o past Casa de Saude to **roundabout [0.5 km]** veer right> by *Café* into rua de S. Mamede and veer right> again **[0.9 km]** (city football stadium ahead) and turn up <left past **school [0.2 km]** and <left at **Igreja de Vila Boa [0.4 km]** with open porch, past concelho and turn right> **[0.3 km]** into rua do Espírito Santo s/o into **Vila Boa [0.2 km]** *Lugar do Espirito Santo* where alt. route joins from main road 100m up left with *café.*

3.4 km Vila Boa village green *Lugar Espirito Santo [F.]* adj. *Quinta São João* manor house with annex for wedding functions. Continue down over **railway [0.3 km]** onto a lengthy stretch of sand road through eucalyptus woods on the original caminho de Santiago over bridge **Ponte de Pedrin [0.9 km]** through Lugar de Ribeira with *Cafe Arantes* **[0.4 km]** and chapel of St. Sebastian *Capela de S. Sebastião*. We then pass another chapel

dedicated to the miracle of the Holy Cross **Capela de Santa Cruz [0.2 km]** in the area of Lijó s/o over road onto a short stretch of cobblestone onto track and then cross over **road [1.3 km]** into mixed woodland of pine and eucalyptus continue to end of the asphalt **road [0.3 km] Casa do Sabariz** Ⓒ Fernanda Cunha 964 751 844 quinta-style country house with 2 double apartments with all facilities generally available for weekly let but may be available for overnight stay. Proceed down gravel track to wayside **fonte [0.1 km]:**

3.5 km Fonte da Ferreirinha *[F.]* ancient spring offering cool refreshing water. Track meanders through vineyards over stream past the gates of *Quinta de Revorido* (dogs) to join asphalt road **[0.7 km]** in the parish of *Tamel S. Pedro Fins* and we start a steep climb past •*Fonte Rua da Cruz (quality no longer monitored)* and continue the climb to junction with the main road and wayside cross **cruceiro [1.2 km]**. We have another steeper climb up past the parish council offices *Freguesia de Tamel São Pedro Fins* and *Capela Sra. da Portela* with ancient wayside cross with interesting pilgrim motifs of staff and gourd on the shaft and, adjoining is the new pilgrim hostel **[0.6 km]:**

2.5 km Tamel *São Pedro Fins Portela* *Alb. Asoc.[41÷3]* **Casa da Recoleta** €5. ℭ 967 096 576 restored parish house *Casa da Recoleta* adjoining the church (see photo) with excellent modern facilities. Opp. *Bar-Restaurant 2000.*

Continue up to a high point of today at the Portela (195m) junction with the main Barcelos to Ponte de Lima road [!] **N-204** and turn right> along the crest of the pass (caution on the dangerous bend in the road [!]) as we now start heading downhill into the Rio Neiva valley past Fonte da Portela (dry) and first <left (signposted *Quintiâes*) and then right> onto track over river and past the modern parish church down steps and turn right over the rail line in:

1.5 km Aborim / Option: ▲ The main waymarked route now turns right> and imm. <left onto sand road. **Note:** take care around Aborim as there are several other waymarked paths in the area. One is an alternative route in case the main camino is flooded (it is low lying). The Camino del Norte via Lanheses is also close by and you don't want to inadvertently stray onto it. The safest way to avoid confusion is to make sure you enter Aborim by the modern parish church and leave over the railway line. [100m (s/o) along the rail line opp. the station *Estação Aborim Tamel Café Oliveira.*

Detour: Quintiâes [+1.5 km] ● ● ● ● all by asphalt road (signposted s/o left before crossing the railway). The House of Agreements **Casa dos Assentos** €70 ℭ 253 881 160 (Machado family) historic 16th century manor house. On the way you pass by the old parish church of Aborim *Igreja Velha de Aborim* (right). *[The dense woods (right) just before crossing the railway at Quintiâes hide*

the ruins of a medieval castle and chapel. A visit is only recommended for the seriously adventurous as the area is very overgrown and close to the steep rail cutting]. Waymarks (to the Northern route) will lead you behind the cemetery (right) but the Quinta is located behind the parish Church located at the end of the road to the left. *Bar-cafe* and *mini-mercado* adjacent.

To rejoin the main route make your way down past the bar to the T-junction and shop in *Gândara [0.8 km]* and veer right> signposted Barcelos (Note: this is the opposite direction to the arrows which are for the Camino do Norte via Aguiar, Vilar Nova and the Ponte de Nova). Continue to the bridge over the small stream *[0.6 km]* and veer <left immediately over the *Ribeiro do Pico* to rejoin the waymarked route from Aborim by drainage pipe factory.

▲ From Aborim the path continues along alternating stretches of sand-tracks and cobblestone laneways (often wet as this is a low lying area) turning right> on asphalt road **[1.0 km]** (winter route in wet weather) to T-Junction **[0.5 km]** where we turn <left onto the Caminho de Santiago in the Quintiâes district *[100m right off the waymarked route is Café Gandera on the main road].* The route now meanders through an ancient hamlet to turn right> by factory **[0.5 km]** *(Alternative route from Quintiâes joins from left)* onto a cobble lane leading to the marvellous medieval bridge over the river Neiva **[1.0 km]**.

3.0 km **Ponte das Tábuas** 'Bridge of Boards' a reference to an earlier wooden bridge over the rio Neiva dating to the 12th century. The present medieval stone structure is very emblematic of the pilgrim way. Up ahead, just visible in the distance, is Capela da Aparecida (see detour). On the far side of the bridge is a small sandy beach by the weir, an idyllic spot for a picnic or perhaps a swim? **Option**: Several optional routes through Balugães commence at this points:

❶ ● ● ● ● For the main route veers right to take a 'middle' course (drinking fonts only). Veer right> on newly surfaced track along this low-lying area through vineyards veer up <left at fork up to main road [!] **N-308 [1.2** km] *(At this point café Aldeia on route 2 is 400m up left while the main crossroads at São Bento is 200m down right with shops and café).* Continue s/o onto track which leads into Balugães and *[F.]* **[0.5** km] and up to road junction *[F.]* and **signboard [0.2** km].

1.9 km **Balugães Cruce** ▲ *caminho tabuleta* all routes converge at this point.

❷ ● ● ● ● Follow the main route above and just before the N-308 turn down right to crossroads at **São Bento** (300m) café, mini-mercado, farmacia. A further 1.1 km off route in Lugar de Navió, Cossourado is the superb *CR Casas do Rio* €50+ ℓ 969 312 585 (José Lúis Amaro). A former pilgrim hostel beautifully restored with peaceful gardens fronting the original camino

real. **Directions**: from the crossroads head east along the N-308 and veer right> 300m and continue a further 800m.

❸ ● ● ● ● Just beyond Ponte de Tábuas turn up <left sign GR 11/ E9 onto path that winds its way up through woodland to cross over [!] **N-308** [900m] at timber yard and *Café Aldeia.* Continue s/o to rejoin the main route at caminho signboard ▲

❹ ● ● ● ● **Capela da Aparecida** 18th century sanctuary of the Apparition of the Virgin *Santuário da Senhora da Aparecida,* site of a miracle where a devout deaf and dumb penitent regained his hearing and speech after the appearance of the Virgin. The sanctuary is the venue for a pilgrimage held annually on 15th

August and the detour will add an extra 1 kilometre to the waymarked route – but allow yourself an extra hour to refresh yourself by the shaded drinking font, to visit the peaceful chapel and to climb underneath it to wash your sins away forever; according to the local tradition! Not a bad exchange for one hour of your time? However, if you started in Barcelos and intend making it to Ponte de Lima tonight you may need to leave remission for some future date.

Directions: turn up <left on the main road past the timber yard and then right> [400m] and wind up past drinking font and up the steep steps to the Sanctuary [300m]. Access to the tunnel under the chapel is at the side by iron railings. Climb underneath and out the other side – if you can't make it around the boulder you will have to back-out and reflect some more on the errors in your life! Return downhill by the asphalt road ahead (no need to return to the main road) ignoring any side roads and rejoin the main route at camino signboard [600]. ▲

▲ *caminho tabuleta* Continue downhill along the Stations of the Cross (that lead back up to the sanctuary) to a modern fountain cascade **fonte [0.2 km]**.

detour: Igreja Velha de Balugães (½ km) ● ● ● ● Romanesque church with covered portico and medieval cruceiro. *Directions:* At the fountain veer up <left to follow a quiet country lane to the church. To rejoin the main route continue along the road which curves back down to the camino.

The direct route continues right at the fonte past the return loop from the Romanesque church (left) onto path through pine woods **[0.6 km]** veering right> back onto minor road down to crossroads **N-204 [0.6 km]** *[F.]* (right) by bus shelter. Cross over by wayside chapel *capela de S. Sebastião* also dedicated to Fátima. The route now follows peaceful laneways along a small river valley *ribeira de Nevoinho (that flows into the Neiva just above the Ponte das Tábuas)*. We finally enter a small hamlet with **crossroads [1.9 km]** in:

3.3 km Lugar do Corgo in the parish of *Vitorino dos Piães* (2.4 km before the village of that name). Here on the left is the ever popular ♥ Casa da Fernanda *Priv.[14÷2]+* €-donativo © 914 589 521. the modern bungalow of Fernanda and Jacinto Gomes Rodrigues who have welcomed pilgrims to their home over many years providing hospitality with B&B, dinner or BBQ. This facility has been extended to accommodate 14 pilgrims in a new timber chalet

adjoining. This is a long day's stage and if you started in Barcelos you have already walked 19.3 kilometres (before adjusting for height climbed and possible detours) and have another 14.4 kilometres before we reach Ponte de Lima. A night at Casa Fernanda will refresh body and soul.

Continue s/o in Lugar do Corgo turn off <left onto **track [0.1** km] as we now crisscross over several roads to beautifully renovated 'stables' **Estábulo de Valinhas [1.0** km] Casa de Valinhas €20-30 Ⓒ 961 050 955. Continue and turn right along avenue up to the parish church **[1.2** km] *Centro Paroquial* in *Vitorino dos Piães* with interesting carvings and collection of sarcophagi in the forecourt. Continue up to the **crossroads [0.1** km].

2.4 km Cruce / **Vitorino dos Piães** *Café-Restaurante Viana / mini-mercado* (50m down right). Continue s/o *up* the hill turning <left **[0.3** km] past *[F.]* **[0.3** km] turning down <left and then up steeply right> onto **path [0.2** km] through woods turning <left to main road at Portela **N-204 [0.4** km]. We now turn right> by cement works along main road [!] and turn off <left onto **track [0.2** km]. The Rio Lima valley now opens to view as we proceed down through eucalyptus woods to quiet country lanes **[1.2** km] and:

2.6 km Facha Quinta da Portela *Priv.[6÷3]*+ €15-70 Han Ⓒ 964 257 171 manor house with private rooms and pilgrim beds in adj. annex. Dinner + breakfast €15 (vegetarians catered for). Just beyond is Casa de SanTiago (S.Tiago niche and fonte) where a bed may be available from Ceu Ⓒ 919 216 557 €35 incl. dinner + breakfast (phone in advance). Opposite we find *Quinta de Albergaria* (not open for 1 night stay). We now head s/o *up* asphalt road turning <left at sign for **Leiras [0.6** km] over the road onto lane past wayside cross with tile image of Santiago (see photo) and wayside chapel *capela de S. Sebastian* **[0.8** km] continue s/o past *Quinta do Sobreiro* (2 night min.) **[1.6** km] continue through vineyards and apple orchards to the main road N-203 [!] in **Seara [0.2** km].

3.5 km N-203 *Seara [400m left R* Pinheiro Manso €30-40 Ⓒ 258 943 775 *modern residencial on main road]*. Cross busy N-203 [!] by *Café Lotus* and turn <left **[0.2** km] to follow quiet country lanes through the sleepy hamlets of Anta, Bouça, Paço, Periera, Barros which all merge one in to the next. Pass *[F.]* **[1.2** km] s/o over several small crossroads and veer <left **[0.8** km] at Wayside shrine to S. Antonio. At the top of the gentle rise ahead in **Lugar do Paço [0.3** km] we come to the Capela de Santiago which lies in ruins behind the private house on our left. Here in the townland of Correlhã is the only chapel dedicated to San Tiago on the route in Portugal. It is incongruously situated just inside the privately owned yard (50m left off the road). The dilapidated Capela de Santiago has an interesting connection with the camino as the lands here at Correlhã were bequeathed to the city of Santiago de Compostela in the year 915, this bequest being ratified by D. Henrique and D. Teresa on their pilgrimage to Santiago in 1097. It may be possible to visit the chapel and to see the 18th century statue of *Santiago de Peregrino*, which is now kept in the house adjoining the chapel (on the road), which is in the private ownership of Fátima and her brother José Begerra Silva e Sousa.

Proceed s/o along the quiet country lane through Pedrosa with the ancient *Cruceiro da Pedrosa* (left) and *Bar* **[0.5** km] adj. the tiny Capela de S. Francisco and sign Ponte de Lima 1.0 *(note it is 2.8 km to the albergue)*. S/o into Barros to **Ponte de Barros [0.4** km]:

3.4 km **Ponte de Barros** medieval bridge over the rio Trovela. We now turn <left by bandstand and chapel to Our Lady of the Snows *capela da Sra. das Neves* continue s/o and pick up the pathway parallel to the river Lima *Ecovia* to junction with viewpoint and boulders **[1.2** km] *(Note: If you plan to stay in the Youth Hostel Pousada da Juventude* or *Hotel InLima take the short-cut up the narrow lane (right) to the main road. The YHA is on the opp. side of the main road – 250m)*. Continue under road bridge **[0.2** km] past the *Capela de N. Sra. da Guia* and along the tree-lined Av. D. Luis Filipe past the former *Hotel Império do Minho* **[0.4** km] (awaiting a new owner) past the medieval tower now the **Tourist office** along the river front to the central square Largo de Camões to the medieval bridge Ponte de Lima **[0.4** km]. For the new pilgrim hostel cross the bridge past the church to the hostel entrance **[0.4** km].

2.6 km **Ponte de Lima** Albergue *Casa do Arnado* pilgrim hostel in a central location by the bridge. Ponte de Lima is a delightful market town that retains a sleepy medieval atmosphere. Take time to amble around its narrow cobbled streets and historic buildings. This is an ideal place to take a rest day – if your schedule allows. The town has several museums and there are lovely walks along the Rio Lima itself. It prides itself on being the 'oldest' town in Portugal and there is certainly little doubt that it occupies one of the most beautiful riverside settings to be found anywhere. The Lima valley is outstanding in its natural surroundings and even the A-3 motorway is far enough away not to disturb its tranquillity. However, a fortnightly market, reputedly the oldest extant market in Portugal (Barcelos claims to be the most popular!) spreads itself along the sandy beach and creates a great deal of activity and several annual fiestas add to the action such as the *Vaca das Cordas* where a roped cow is led around the parish church before being maddened by darts and led down to the beach for slaughter to become part of this annual feast. It all harks back to ancient pagan fertility rights (whatever one thinks about animal rights) and takes place in June, the day before Corpus Christi *Corpo do Deus* when the town streets are covered with incredible floral displays. August generally sees a 'medieval' market arrive with juggling, jousting and joviality. The *Feiras Novas* takes place during the second weekend in September when a sea of humanity floods the town in the biggest party of the year that goes on 24 hours a day for 3 days.

❑ **Historic Buildings and Monuments:** The main sites of historic interest are clustered around the town centre area and are therefore easy to visit and include (from the start on the way in) ❶ **Igreja de S. Francisco e S. António dos Capuchos** *XVI* e **Museu dos Terceiros** with impressive baroque façade and museum of religious art and artefacts. ❷ **Torre da Cadeia** *XIV* the original prison now *Turismo* and to the rear library with internet entrance from the intimate square situated *behind* with evocative granite statue of a local woman carrying a water jar *Estatueta uma Cantareira*. ❸ **Igreja Matriz** *XV* parish church on the main street opp. **Igreja da Misericórdia** *XVI* ❹ **Paço do Marquês** municipal offices with viewing gallery from the roof. ❺ **Torre de S. Paulo** part of the original defensive walls of the town and adjacent to the **Chafariz** the beautiful fountain fashioned in 1603 and occupying pride of place in the centre of the main square *Largo de Camões* with popular *cafés and bars* overlooking the river. ❻ **Medieval stone bridge** rebuilt in 1368 on Roman foundations. This handsome bridge is 300 metres in length and 4 metres wide. It forms the pedestrian link between the busy southern town and the quieter northern quarter. ❼ **Capela do Anjo da Guarda / S. Miguel** an intriguing stone shrine dedicated variously to the Guardian Angel or Saint Michael. It is an open vaulted structure with interesting motifs located on the riverbank adjoining the **Capela de Sto. António da Torre Velha** *XIX*.

Just beyond the church is the new pilgrim hostel behind which are the beautiful ● **Thematic Gardens** *Jardims Temáticos* with their peaceful and well maintained sections each having a separate theme. Further downstream (adj. the road bridge) ● ***Clube Náutico*** with canoe hire and restaurant. Ponte de Lima is the headquarters of the *Solares de Portugal* part of the TURIHAB organisation that offers over 1,000 luxurious beds in historic Quintas and Manor houses in Northern Portugal where the Friends of the Portuguese Way to Santiago *Associação dos Amigos do Caminho Português de Santiago* is also housed.

❑ *Loja de Turismo: Torre da Cadeia Velha* ✆ 258 942 335 / 258 240 208 *(Tues-Sat: 9:30-13:00 & 14:00-17:30).***Turismo:** *Paço do Marquês* Praça de República ✆ 258 900 400. ❑ **Accommodation:** *Albergue* **Casa do Arnado** *Muni.[60÷2]* €5 ✆ m: 925 403 164 + peregrino S.O.S. m: 925 403 162 Largo Dr Alexandre Herculano / Alegria (see photo). Here also is: **Arc'otel** €45 ✆ 258 900 150. **Pousada de Juventude** *[50÷12]* €12 Rua Papa João Paulo II ✆

258 943 797. Nearby is the ultra modern *H***** **InLima** €50+ ✆ 258–900 050 r/ Agostinho José Taveira. Old fashioned luxury at **Casa do Pinheiro** €65 ✆ 258 943 971 Rua General Norton de Matos, 40. *H* **Mercearia da Vila** €60 ✆ 925 996 366 rua Cardeal Saraiva, 34 town centre adj. the church. **Casa das Pereiras** ✆ 258 942 939 Largo Capitão José de Magalhães adj. the 18th century capela das Pereiras with access off rua Fonte da Vila. *Pª* **São João** €30 ✆ 258 941 288 above the restaurant on Largo de S. João with entrance on rua do Rosário. *P* **Beira Rio** €25 ✆ 258 944 044 Passeio 25 de Abril. *P* **Morais** €20-30 basic rooms on rua Matriz (opp. church entrance).

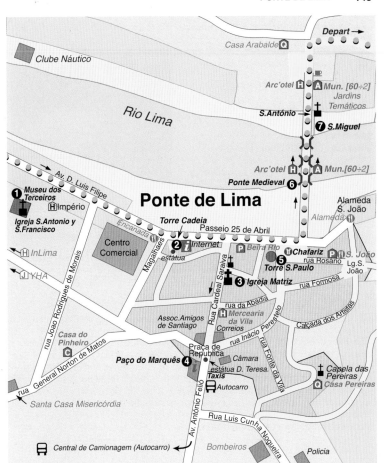

❏ **Restaurants** a wide variety to suit all pockets. Overlooking the river on Passeio 25 de Abril *Encanada* with terrace above the road or just behind (half the price) *Katekero* with menú from €6 (open all day). *Manuel Padeiro* on rua Bonfim set back from the busy *passeio* but with outside tables that get the evening sun. Along the *passeio* are: *Parisiense* with ground and first floor tables, pizzeria *Beira Rio* and just beyond it is the basic *Catrina*. Various snack bars spill out onto the central square *Largo de Camões* with its lovely central fountain *Chafariz* and behind the square in *Largo Feira S. João* and at the far end is the popular *Alameda* whose small dining room overlooks the river. On the far side of the river in the vicinity of the pilgrim hostel and theme gardens are a number of cafés.

❏ **I dwell in the high and holy place, with they who have a contrite and humble spirit.** *Isaiah 57:15*

17 *154.1 km (95.8 miles) – Santiago*

PONTE DE LIMA – RUBIÃES

‖‖‖‖‖‖‖‖	--- ---	10.3	--- ---	57%
▬▬▬▬	--- ---	7.8	--- ---	43%
▬▬▬▬	--- ---	0.0	--- ---	0%
Total km		**18.1 km** (11.2 ml)		

🔺 20.4 km (+^ 460 m = 2.3 km)
Alto*(m)*▲ Portela Grande 405m (1,329 ft)
< 🅰 🅷 **>** None

The Practical Path: We now have our first glorious day where natural paths account for over half the route and there are no main roads at all. This stage also marks our steepest accumulative climb almost entirely encountered in the one ascent up the Labruja valley to the high pass through the mountain ridge and into the Coura valley via the Alto de Portela Grande. Facilities along the way are limited but there is reasonable shelter amongst the pine woods on either side of the pass and a number of drinking fonts along the way – you will need to use them. **Intermediate Accommodation:** None.

❏ **The Mystical Path:** With all the great discoveries made within the sense-perceptible world of science we have never been able to see the super-sensible. Not even the most powerful telescope on earth has been able to glimpse even the tiniest fragment of God. Knowledge of Higher Worlds does not come from exploring the physical universe within the laboratory of the mind but in diving into the mysteries. Paradox is at the heart of the spiritual quest and so the top of the mountain becomes a symbol of the wisdom often found at the lowest point of the journey and within the humblest of hearts.

❏ **Personal Reflections:** "The steep climb is rewarded by stunning views back over the incomparable beauty of the Lima valley while the unexplored country to the north invites discovery. I drink deeply from the clear cool waters that flow from the mountain spring while all around me are the harmonious sights and sounds of nature. There is no sign of human activity apart from a vacant mountain hut… I like the idea that high places reflect Higher Mind – that place where clutter and illusion seem to evaporate in the rarefied air of the mountains. While fog hangs in the valleys, clarity abounds amongst the peaks. The wounded ego is nowhere to be seen and the mundane commitments fashioned in the lowlands all pale into insignificance from these lofty heights."

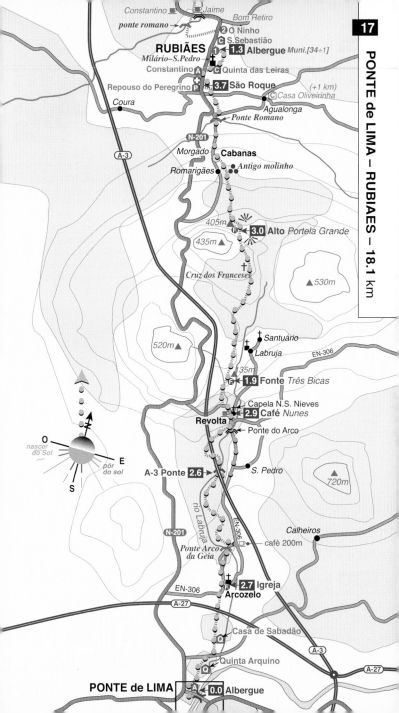

Constantino ■ *Jaime* *Bom Retiro*
ponte romano →
② O Ninho
Ⓒ S.Sebastião
RUBIÃES
1.3 **Albergue** *Muni.[34÷1]*
Milário–S.Pedro ■
Constantino Ⓐ ② Quinta das Leiras
Repouso do Peregrino P ✚ **3.7** **São Roque** *(+1 km)*
Ⓒ *Casa Oliveirinha*
Coura ●
Agualonga
→ *Ponte Romano*
N-201
Morgado **Cabanas**
A-3
Romarigães ● *Antigo molinho*
405m F ← **3.0** **Alto** *Portela Grande*
435m ▲
▲ 530m
✝ *Cruz dos Franceses*
520m ▲
✝ ✝ *Santuário*
■ *Labruja* EN-306
135m
F ← **1.9** **Fonte** *Três Bicas*
Capela N.S. Nieves
2.9 **Café** *Nunes*
Revolta
→ *Ponte do Arco*
O
nascer do Sol
E
pôr do sol
S
S. Pedro
← **2.6** **A-3 Ponte** →
720m ▲
N-201
EN-306
Calheiros ●
▭ – *café 200m*
Ponte Arco da Geia
✝ **2.7** **Igreja**
EN-306
Arcozelo
A-27
A-3
Q *Casa de Sabadão*
Q *Quinta Arquino*
A-27
PONTE de LIMA Ⓐ ← **0.0** **Albergue**

0.0 km Ponte de Lima from the albergue on the north side of the river Lima turn right> past café (signposted Quinta do Arquinho). We now make our way around the back of the theme gardens *Jardims Tematicos* veering <left and <left again onto **track [0.4 km]** beside the entrance to Quinta do Arquinho ℭ 258 742 306. and follow the low-lying path to cross over the **N-202 [0.8 km]** onto a cobbled lane past the fading opulence of Casa de Sabadão Lugar de Sabadão, Arcozelo ℭ 258 941 963. *(In winter this whole area can become marooned from the overflowing rivers Lima and Labruja).* We now head out under the A-27 **motorway [0.7 km]** along quiet country lanes to pass the Centro Social **[0.8 km]** in:

2.7 km Arcozelo with church *[F.]* onto track over the Rio Labruja by **Ponte da Geira [0.9 km]** continue up and turn <left onto path **[0.2 km]** *[Detour café 200m s/o on main road]* we now meander along lanes and earth tracks through the natural environment of the Labruja valley (disturbed only by the A-3 motorway that snakes above us). We pass (left) a newly renovated mill *Casa do Caminho da Beira Rio* to climb along a pathway that summits just above the A-3 *[F.]* (right) and then descend to option underneath the motorway **[1.5 km].**

2.6 km Option / A3 Underpass. Up to the right is the road route while the direct route lies over a partially collapsed metal bridge over the river Labruja and up a steep pathway that climbs up around the motorway to the Ponte do Arco where the other route joins from the right. Consider using the longer alternative route if the river is in torrent.

For the alternative route ● ● ● ● take the track to the right that climbs above the A-4. From here a wide farm track takes you to the main road [0.5 km] turn <left and continue along main road turning off <left [1.3 km] (signposted Labruja/ Sanctuario do Socorro) and cross the rio Lubruja over the Ponte do Arco [0.3 km] where the main path joins from the left.

For the direct route continue s/o over the rio Labruja which flows rapidly through a narrow gorge at this stage. Scramble up the far side underneath the A-4 flyover onto a narrow path that climbs up through scrubland at the edge of pine woods away from the A-3 as it flattens out and follows the contours around the side of the *Vale do Inferno*. We now rejoin the asphalt **road [2.3 km]** at Ponte do Arco at the point where the road route joins from the right. Continue past the capela de São Sebastião *[F.]* (left) in the area of Devesa / Revolta, veering <left (signposted Valinhos Valada) to cafe **[0.6 km]** in:

2.9 km Revolta *Café Cunha Nunes* cafe and shop run by Marcia and Manuel adjoining the chapel to Our Lady of the Snows *Capela de N. S. Das Neves* with wayside cross. This is the last chance to acquire food or drink (apart from water at drinking fonts) on this stage. We now start climbing alternating between paths and lanes with the village of Labruja and its distinctive parish church visible

over the valley to our right (with the Santuário do Senhor do Socorro in the far distance, behind it) and the A-3 motorway over to our left to:

1.9 km Fonte des Três Bicas *[F.]* where clear water gushes from 3 channels *três bicas* carved into the stone. Fill up your bottles with the cool and refreshing waters for the long climb ahead. Continue over bridge and turn up sharply <left past Casa da Bandeira and over road onto track through the pine woods ahead, much of which has recently been felled *(the tiny Capela Santa Ana is visible below in the valley*  *floor).* The path becomes a forest track and then turns up <left onto another path passing wayside cross *cruz dos Franceses* [2.2 km] where pilgrims to Santiago have placed stones to mark their passage and prayers. It is otherwise referred to as *cruz dos Mortos* a reference to the ambush that took place here on Napoleon's troops during the peninsular war (1808 – 1814). Cross over track back onto path by drinking tap (dry) and beehives and as we summit we have a magnificent view back over the Lima valley to the south. We make our way around the paddock ahead to finally reach our **high point [0.8 km]** at:

3.0 km Alto da Portela Grande (405m) *[F.]* 50m *off* route at entrance to the forester's lodge. A view north over the wooded rio Coura valley now opens up as we start our descent over a rough stony path [!] through pine woods, the terrain flattening-out as we cross a small stream with a series of ancient mill wheels running above and below the path **Moinhos de Cabanas [1.0 km]** This line of unusual wheels were used to mill grain, particularly maize (for the local bread found in these parts). A little further on we pass Quinta de Matos. The path now drops down into the hamlet of **Cabanas [0.5 km]** onto asphalt road s/o past **wayside cross [0.5 km]** s/o past *[F.]* (left) down to the medieval bridge **Ponte**  **Águalonga [0.9 km].** The track crosses minor road and continues over the N-301 to emerge at the main Ponte de Lima / Valença road N-201 in São Roque **[0.8 km]** with hostel opposite:

3.7 km São Roque *Hr* **Repouso do Peregrino** €20-40 incl. *℄* 251 943 692 (Silvia) adj. farmacia and: *Alb.* **Constantino** *Priv.[6÷1]+* €-10 +25 *℄* 968 432 059 (André) who also owns *Rest. Constantino* by Ponte Nova. *(Note: shuttle service to local restaurant(s) is offered by all hostals).* Note also Águalonga is 1.0 km *off* route up (steeply) with *CR* **Oliveirinha** *℄* 917 600 160 on Rua Trulha de Cima 218 (see map). Continue down hill

148

passing **Quinta S. Roque** (long term let only) and veer right> onto **path [0.3 km]** passing Quinta das Leiras €23–46 incl. © 967 813 689 (Ana Paulo) comfortable

modern home with laundry, games room and small swimpool. Continue through woodland to derelict *cruceiro* **[0.7 km]** and **option**: down (left) 100m to visit the enchanting 12th century Romanesque church dedicated to St. Peter *Igreja de São Pedro de Rubiães* and *miliário* the historic Roman mile marker on the Via XIX has been hollowed out to form a sarcophagus (see photo). Continue down the main road to **albergue [0.3 km].**

1.3 km Rubiães *Alb.*❶ Escola *Muni.* *[34÷2]* €-donativo © 917 164 476 m: 251 943 472 spacious conversion of former schoolhouse with kitchen and dining area and extensive lounge and outside patio. One large dormitory sleeps 34 in bunk beds with ample ladies and gent's toilets and showers with additional room on the top floor.

Just below (still Estrada de S. Pedro de Rubiães or the N-201) is *CR.* S Sebastião © 251 941 258 and below that: *Alb.*❷ ♥ O Ninho *(The Nest) Priv.[17÷2]* €10–25 © 251 941 002 (Marlene / Sra. Maria) 695. This new albergue is well named and provides welcoming lodging in a traditional stone family house with outside garden area. Laundry and breakfast available and well located 300m below the municipal hostel and 200m from the bar and restaurant *Bom Retiro* © 251 941 245 a popular pilgrim haunt with menú from €6.

On the far side of the road bridge (directly on the camino via the Roman bridge *2nd Century* - see next stage) is the newly extended shop and *Café Jaime* on Ponte Nova and just beyond that is *Rest. Constantino.*

REFLECTIONS:

❏ **Do not seek to follow in the footsteps of the men of old;**
Seek what they sought. *Matsuo Basho, 16ᵗʰ century Japanese pilgrim poet.*

18 *136 km (84.5 miles) – Santiago*

RUBIÃES – VALENÇA / TUI

ⅲⅲⅲⅲⅲⅲⅲ --- ---	9.1	--- ---	54%
▬▬▬▬ --- ---	8.8	--- ---	7%
▦▦▦ --- ---	1.4	--- ---	39%
Total km	**19.3 km** (12.0 ml)		

20.3 km (+^ 200 m = 1.0 km)
Alto(m)▲ S. Bento 270 m (886 ft)
< 🅰 🏠 > Cossourado **4.0** km – Passos **10. 4** km – Valença **16.3** km.

300m
■RUBIÃES S.Bento 270m Alto S. Bento
200m
100m río Coura   Fontoura   Paços Ponte VALENÇA   TUI
   🅰 Romano   N-13 🅰 🅰
   río Pedreira▽   río Minho▽
0 km   5 km   10 km   15 km

The Practical Path: Apart from the short stretch of main road into Tui the rest
of this stage is split between natural pathways and quiet country roads through
woodland affording shelter and shade. With the exception of a modest climb
out of the Coura river valley into the Minho basin the majority of this stage is
downhill from São Roque. The Minho now becomes the Miño and our clocks will
also need adjusting one hour as we make our way over the border from Portugal
into Spain. Most pilgrims head straight for Tui. However you have an option to
visit the historic old walled town of Valença and / or stay in the atmospheric old
town or the modern hostel just outside it.

❏ **The Mystical Path:** '*All roads lead to Rome*' was a truism in the time of
the Caesars but now we begin to understand that '*All roads lead Home*' and are
assured that all we need to do to realise the truth of this simple statement is to:
'Render unto Caesar the things which are Caesar's; and unto to God the things
that are God's.' *Matthew 22:21*. To whom do you pay tribute? Whose footsteps do
you follow? What is it you seek?

❏ **Personal Reflections:** "The dark grey clouds had been gathering all afternoon
but nothing could have prepared me for the downpour the moment I set foot in
Galicia. The ensuing deluge was so powerful that within minutes I was wet from
head to foot and the road turned to a river... The hot shower restored some heat
to my body. There is only one other pilgrim in this spacious hostel – a young
Japanese girl who walked to Santiago from France and just kept going! She
follows the blue arrows now towards Fátima but she has no destination in mind.
What are the hidden forces that drive us on, through the blistering heat, the bitter
cold, the torrential rain?

0.0 km **Albergue** From the municipal hostel turn right> downhill and sharp
<left **[0.3 km]** (directly opp. albergue O Ninho) onto muddy path that follows

Turismo ☏ 677 418 405
(Pop. 15,000) **TUI**
🚻 🅰 **3.1** Albergue
rio Minho

A-55
N-552

VALENÇA (Pop. 14,000)
Fortaleza 🚻
Mun.[85÷4] 🅰 Ⓨ **2.9** Ⓧ ❓ Fortaleza

ⓗ ← Valença do Minho
Casa Diego 🅀
P O R T U G A L

🍴 🅰 **2.3** Tuido Ⓧ N-13

N-13

S.Pedro da Torre ● ■ ← *Quinta da Bouça*
Pedreira
Ponte da Pedreira 3.2 → *ponte medieval*
< Caminha
Quinta Estrada Romana 🅰 rio Pedreira
N-13 **Paços**
N-201
A-3

✝ 🅕 **3.3** Fontoura Fuente

S.Julião ● N-201

▲ *365m*

✝ **4.5** São Bento da Porta Aberta

Casa da Capela 🅀 **Cossourado** *Pecene*

▲ *380m*
N-303
rio Coura

A-3
Constantino **Ponte Nova**
ponte romano → ■ *Bom Retiro*
RUBIÃES 🅰 **0.0** Albergue

E S P A Ñ A
< Monte Tecla

O
Puesta del Sol
E
Salida del Sol
S

the bed of a stream to a well preserved Roman bridge *Pons Romana 2nd century* (see photo) over the rio Coura whence we follow the surface (clearly visible) of the original Roman road to cross the N-201 at **Ponte Nova [1.0** km] *café* and shop s/o along track by the river Coura with old millrace and weir. The camino now alternates between quiet country lanes and earthen tracks up through a wooded valley to **Pecene Cossourado [2.7** km] Casa da Capela €60 ℃ 251 782 005 / 919 117 640 quinta adj. chapel s/o up to crossroads, high point of this stage 270m **[0.5** km].

4.5 km **São Bento da Porta Aberta** major crossroads *café* with adj. shop. The camino now crosses *behind* Santuario São Bento *XVII* onto path with distant views over the Minho valley as we begin our descent towards Valença along delightful woodland paths through pine, eucalyptus, holm oak and the occasional cork tree (Portugal is one of the world's largest producers of cork). The path alternates between these woodland paths, cobblestone laneways and short stretches of asphalt road (all well waymarked) into:

3.3 km **Fontoura** *Café Central* s/o up past chapel and pilgrim memorial plaque *Peregrino Caminhante* adj. *[F.]* (left) and access road to the parish church *Igreja de São Miguel*. The route alternates between road and track through woodland into **Paços** (Passos) **[2.1** km] *café-mini-mercado* to *Albergue* ♥ **Quinta Estrada Romana** *Priv.[18÷2]+* ℃ 251 837 333 m: 913 401 395 (Lesley & Geof) 2 trusty pilgrims + wellington Boot returning to 'give something back' to the camino. Wonderful restoration of traditional farmhouse offering dinner, bed and breakfast in bunk room suggested €20-25. Similar arrangement in private room €30-50. Proceed to rio Pedreira and the medieval bridge **[0.6** km].

3.2 km **Ponte da Pedreira** s/o up past Quinta da Bouça **[0.6** km] and s/o through woodland along quiet country lanes up to the N-13 **[1.7** km].

2.3 km **Tuido** cross N-13 [!] *cafés* the camino continues via cobblestone road (signposted Arão) parallel to the busy N-13 *[H°° **Valença do Minho** €30+ ℃ 251 824 211 Av. Miguel Dantas]*.past *Café A Toca* turn <left at **Capela do Senhor de Bonfim [0.7** km] past *CR* **Diogo** ℃ 251 823 926 Eido de Cima 2 in **Arão [0.5** km] turn down right> by lavadero cruceiro and *[F.]* (left) into rua da Cruz continuing along asphalt road past *Café* under **rail [0.6** km] to veer right across the modern outskirts of Valença, passing the main **bus station** and turning up <left into Valença by rail bridge up to main **roundabout [1.1** km] *Largo da Trapicheira*:

2.9 km **Valença** *Option* The bridge into Tui and Spain lies straight ahead and the first Spanish hostel only 3.1 km *or* turn up left along Av. Bombeiros Voluntários to the last pilgrim hostel in Portugal (see photo). *Albergue* **São Teotónio** *Muni.[85÷4]* €5 ℃ 966 473 409 Av. José Maria Gonçalves / dos Bombeiros Voluntários. *(not to be confused with the luxury Pousada São Teotónio in the old fort)* The Portuguese

hostel adjoins the fire station *Bombeiros* on the roundabout directly opposite the main entrance to the Fortaleza. The decision is whether to leave Portugal without first seeing the old quarter of Valença and the magnificent Fortaleza. Allow 2 hours to visit and soak up some of the atmosphere with a stroll through the colourful streets and a brief visit to the main historic buildings. The tourist buses tend to leave around 5 p.m. when the old fort reverts to a more relaxed mode and is a pleasant place for a drink or supper in the evening sunshine.

❑ **VALENÇA** *DO MINHO*: *Posto de Turismo* Avenida de Espanha Ⓒ 251 823 374. Praça Forte de Valença Ⓒ 251 823 329. *Táxis* Ⓒ 252 822 121. *Estação Caminhos do Ferro* Ⓒ 252 821 124. Bus *Autocarro* Ⓒ 251 809 588. ❑ **Accommodation:** Several modern hotels in the new town close to the main entrance to the Fortaleza in rua de São Sebastião. *H**Lara Ⓒ 251 824 348 €55. *H**Val Flores Ⓒ 251 824 106 €30. Within the old fort *Fortaleza: R* **Portas do Sol** €30-60 Ⓒ 251 837 134 Rua Conselheiro Lopes da Silva,51. *H*****Pousada de S. Teotonio* Ⓒ 251 824 392 €90 disappointing in its stark modernity. Try the adjacent **Casa do Poço** €90 Ⓒ 251 825 235 Travesa da Gaviarra where a similar price will buy luxury in more authentic surroundings. At the other end of the scale are a variety of rooms to let above the bars and shops in the old quarter.

Valença Detour: The main attraction is the huge fortress *Fortaleza* standing guard over the Rio Minho. The narrow cobbled streets are lined with souvenir shops, bars, restaurants, hotels and pensions. It is very busy during the day with bus tours but worth a walk through if you have the energy. Alternatively, stay the night and take a whole day to explore both Valença and Tui. There is much of interest in both towns and pleasant walks along the Minho. A ferry operated between these border towns until the rail and road bridge was opened in 1886.

Occupying an elevated position on the border of Portugal and Spain it has been a major military defensive establishment from the earliest times and more recently modelled on the design of the 17th century military architect Vauban. In 1262 The town received a royal charter from D. Afonso III and was renamed Valença (formerly Contrasta). In 1502 D. Manuel I stayed in the town on his royal pilgrimage to Santiago.

Among the sites worth visiting (see town map over): ❶ **Portas da Coroada** the main entrance to the fortress town opposite the pilgrim hostel. This leads directly to the tiny ❷ Capela de São Sebastião on the wide Largo Dr. Alfredo Guimarães. Next we come to ❸ **Capela do Bom Jesus** with its harmonious proportions in front of which is the statue to the illustrious son of Valença, S. Teotónio and in the square is the popular restaurant Bom Jesus which serves good value food throughout the day and has an outside terrace that gets the last of the evening sun. Down to the right is the alternative way to access (or leave) the fort through ❹ **Porto do Sol** also known as Porto de Santiago. Straight ahead over the dry central moat we come to the inner gate ❺ **Portas do Meio** which leads into the main square ringed with more shops and cafés in the busy *Praça do Republica*. Continue due North to ❻ **Igreja de Santo Estevão** 12th century and the adjoining ❼ **Roman Miliário** dating back to Emperor Claudius c.47 A.D. (National Monument). In the next square is the venerable ❽ **Iglesia Santa Maria dos Anjos** a fine 12th century Romanesque church and adjacent ❾ **Capela da Misericórdia** 18th century with sculpture by master Teixeira Lopes '*O Senhor Morto.*' Beyond this church (left) we find Pousada de S. Teotonio and beyond it the viewpoint over the Minho ❿ **Baluarte do Socorro.** Return to the Capela da Misericórdia and go behind it to the delightfully restored Casa do Poço below which is a little used side exit that brings you directly down to the international bridge via stone steps. To access these (to save you having to walk all the way back to the Porto do Sol) take the second *lower* gate out of the fort and make your way down the stone steps which lead to the bridge.

To proceed into **Spain** *España* from the main roundabout *Largo da Trapicheira* continue down hill passing the tourist kiosk (left) and over the International Bridge into Spain.

Portugal – GMT + 0 / ✆ internacional **+351** (telefone fixo: 2 ou 3 / móvel: 9)

Note: *Spain is 1 hour ahead of Portugal. Int. dialling code for Spain +34. You will also need to switch from asking directions in Portuguese to Spanish not forgetting that many signposts will now appear in a mixture of Galician* Galego *and* Castellano. *Some similarities remain: esquerda – izquierda, direita – derecha.*

Turn right> *gira a la izquierda* along the main road and right> again at crossroads passing Tui **Parador** down to the Rio Miño where we pick up the first of the official markers in Spain – PK 115.454 (the camino is changing constantly so these signs, supposedly accurate to 1/100m can no longer be relied on for accurate distances but are useful as waymarks). It was here at *Praia de Fábrica* that the ferry carrying pilgrims and merchants from Valença would land and this is the Camino starting stage in Spain. You also have an option here:

Option. Instead of the waymarked route up to the main road you can take the path (right) along the river for a delightful 1 km until you reach the steps opposite the marina. Ascend to the Praza da Estrela and on up the rua Bispo Castañon to its intersection with rua S. Telmo and turn <left under the arch to the Church of S.Telmo and then up right> to the entrance to the albergue (situated just below the cathedral). The distance is the same as the waymarked route but you enter along the river instead of the main road.

Spain – GMT + 1 / ℄ internacional **+34** (teléfono fijo: 9 / número de móvil: 6)

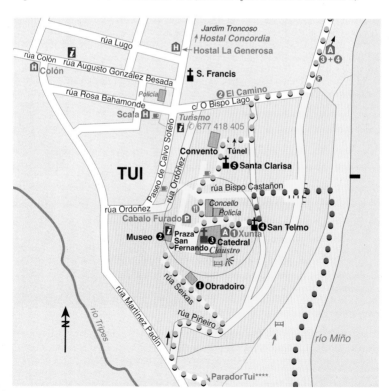

The waymarked route (left) winds its way up to the cathedral passing a handsome *Fonte* built into the side of the cliff. There is now a steep climb up into Tui onto the main road and turning off right> into the medieval heart of this border town passing the 16ᵗʰ century prison (now the Obradoiro school of Restoration) up to the west door of Tui Cathedral. Pass around the side of the cathedral into Praza do Concello and head down right> past the police station to:

3.1 km **Tui** *Albergue* ❶ *Xunta [36÷2]* €6 ℗ 638 276 855. Preference to pilgrims walking from Portugal (with no back up help). Well located stone building just below the cathedral. 2 dormitories with separate ladies and gents toilets and showers. Large lounge and kitchen On the ground floor and to the rear is a pleasant open patio with space to wash and dry clothes. Well located in the heart of the historic centre although a nearby nightclub can be noisy at weekends.

TUI: Historical border town with a population of 15,000. It has a more interesting modern profile than Valença but at its heart is still the well-preserved medieval town. ❶ **Obradoiro** *XVI* the original prison where the date of construction 1584 can still be seen over the door. ❷ **Museo Diocesano** *XVIII* originally a pilgrims hospice now the Diocesan office and museum with an interesting display of Celtic, medieval and religious artefacts and well worth the small fee just to savour an original pilgrim hostel with its central courtyard. Here also is the sarcophagus in which lay San Telmo's body after he died at the Bridge of Fevers in 1251 (which we pass on the next stage). On the opposite side of the square *Plaza San Fernando* is Tui's centrepiece the impressive Romanesque cathedral ❸ **Catedral**

de Santa María *XII* dating from 1120 but with later Gothic additions, most notably the fine portico. The cathedral has a handsome cloister, reputedly the only remaining example of a medieval cathedral cloister in Galicia. Off the cloister are steps down to a delightful garden overlooking the Miño (see photo below) and overlooking the gardens is the medieval tower with access off the far corner of the cloisters (light switch on wall to illuminate the spiral staircase). The interior of the cathedral itself is no less outstanding with a chapel dedicated to St. James 'the Moor Slayer' *Santiago Matamoros* and an interesting statue to the first black saint from Africa *Sta. Ypiîgenîa*.

Below the Cathedral is the chapel of Mercy *Capela de Misericordia* and ❹ **Igrexa de San Telmo** XVᵗʰc built over the crypt that housed the relics of S. Telmo. The waymarked route leaves town via the handsome town hall *Concello*, opposite the popular •*Jamonería Jaqueyi* past the •*Café Central* to the evocative Nuns Way *Rua das Monxas* with ❺ **Igrexa Santa Clarisa** XVIIᵗʰc (the work of master mason Santiago Domingo de Andrade with fine Baroque altarpiece) and opposite is the **Convento de Clarisas** *XVI s*urrounded by the walls of the convent of the enclosed order of nuns of St. Clare *Convento das Clarisas Encerradas.* The waymarked route continues through an arched passage below the convent known as the nuns tunnel ***Túnel das Monxas*** to leave the medieval city through the *Porta Bergana,* today nothing more than a memory.

If you are staying the night in Tui take a stroll along the Paseo de Calvo Sotelo with its lively pavement cafés and bars. At the far end is the statue of 'wild horses' overlooking the Troncoso gardens built around the old medieval city walls. Midway along the Paseo is the 18th century Church of St. Francis. There are several restaurants (expensive) in the old town near the cathedral *O Novo Cabalo Furado* on Praza do Concello is one of the best, but like most restaurants in Spain it doesn't open till 20.00 or later. The adjacent wine bistro *Jamonería Jaqueyi* has terraced seating in this elegant square. For less expensive fare and earlier options try around Paseo de Calvo Sotelo or *Cafe Scala* on c/Rua Rosa Bahamonde which serves food all day. If you need your backpack carried contact TuiTrans *transporte de mochilas* ✆ 986 627 979 / 646 983 906.

❏ *Turismo* ✆ 677 418 405 Praza de San Fernando or central kiosk on Paseo de Calvo Sotelo (summer). ❏ *Albergues:* ❷ El Camino *Priv.[24÷5]* €10-12 ✆ 646 982 906 c/ Obispo Lago,5 central location & popular cafe. ❸ Caracol Veloz *Priv. [6÷1]* €12 ✆ 986 604 324 c/Antero Rubín,55 on the way out of town opp. Convento Sto. Domingo *(provides beds at busy times).* nearby: ❹ Villa San Clemente *Priv. [26÷3]* €10 ✆ 678 747 700 c/ Canónigo Valiño,23 with garden patio. ❏ *Hotels:* O Novo Cabalo Furado €35 ✆ 986 604 445 c/ Seijas, 3 (by the cathedral). Hostal La Generosa €20 ✆ 986 600 055 basic old-fashioned on the central Paseo de Calvo Sotelo. *H* San Telmo €30 ✆ 986 603 011 Av. de la Concordia (past the Jardim Troncoso). Cafe Scala ✆ 986 601 890 c/Rua Rosa Bahamonde, 5 (above the cafe Scala). *H***Colón €70 ✆ 986 600 223 modern business hotel on Rua Colón. At the lower end of town on the way in (top price bracket) *H***Parador de Tui €90 ✆ 986 600 300. A walk around the old quarter will reveal a number of discreet signs for beds *camas* from €15.

❏ **Death – the last sleep? No, it is the final awakening.** *Walter Scott*

19 *116.7 km (72.5 miles) – Santiago*

VALENÇA / TUI – REDONDELA

ⅢⅢⅢⅢⅢⅢⅢ --- ---	8.6 --- ---	27%
━━━ --- ---	20.6 --- ---	63%
▓▓▓ --- ---	3.2 --- ---	10%
Total km	**32.4 km** (20.1 ml)	

◣◣ 33.9 km (+^ 300 m = 1.5 km)
Alto(m)▲ Alto Cornedo 235 m (771 ft)
<❒ ❒> Porriño 17.3 km / Mos 22.8 km

The Practical Path: Most of this stage is along quiet country roads (63%) and woodland paths that follow the rio Louro valley. There is good shade and several drinking fonts along the way. The challenge today is the stretch of main road entering and leaving the industrial town of Porriño. However, a lovely new route along the rio Louro avoids the slog through the notorious industrial estate. Porriño provides a useful half-way stopover with modern albergue. The busy N-550 runs parallel to our path and we crisscross it and the railway line several times on our way to Redondela. There is also a steep climb from Mos up the Road of the Knights *Rua dos Cabaleiros* around Monte Cornedo. However, this is rewarded by our first views of the sea since leaving Porto, the beautiful Ría de Vigo. The final part of the day is then all the way downhill into Redondela, an attractive town with good facilities and a superbly restored pilgrim hostel.

❏ **The Mystical Path:** 'when you live your life as though you're already dead, life takes on new meaning. Each moment becomes a whole lifetime, a universe unto itself… Our priorities change; our hearts open, our minds begin to clear of the fog of old holdings and pretendings. We watch all life in transit and what matters becomes instantly apparent: the transmission of love, the letting go of obstacles to understanding, the relinquishment of our grasping, of our hiding from ourselves.' Who Dies? *Stephen and Ondrea Levine*

❏ **Personal Reflections:** "… around me everything is silent but for the babbling of the brook whose waters make their way inexorably back to the ocean. The isolated cross marks the spot of a saint's death and the inner silence is broken with thoughts of death and dying. Like the busy waters of the brook, I too, will return to the Source. My body, like the Earth's, is already half way through its physical life-span. Body and Earth, both will dissolve back into the dust from which they were made. Only what is perfect and formless is eternal and created by the Love of God. All else is impermanent and ephemeral. How could I ever have believed that God created what was transitory? Even the sun will die…"

0.0 km **Tui Albergue** Leave the Xunta hostel via the Praza do Concello veering

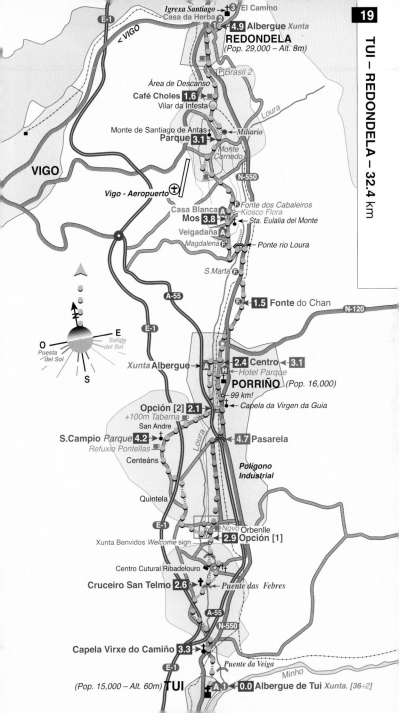

Igrexa Santiago → **†3** *El Camino*
Casa da Herba **2**
1 **†** → **4.9** *Albergue Xunta*
REDONDELA
(Pop. 29,000 – Alt. 8m)

P *Brasil 2*

Loura

Área de Descanso
Café Choles **1.6**
Vilar da Infesta

← *Miliario*

Monte de Santiago de Antas
Parque **3.1** **†**

Monte Cornedo

N-550

Vigo - Aeropuerto ⊕

VIGO

F *Fonte dos Cabaleiros*
Casa Blanca **A** *Kiosco Flora*
Mos **3.8** ← *Sta. Eulalia del Monte*
Veigadaña **A**
Magdalena **F** ← *Ponte rio Loura*

S.Marta **F**

O — *E*
Salida
Puesta *del Sol*
del Sol
S

A-55

E-1

F ← **1.5** **Fonte** do Chan **N-120**

Xunta **Albergue** → **A** **2.4** **Centro** ← **3.1**
H *Hotel Parque*
PORRIÑO *(Pop. 16,000)*
↙ *99 km!*
← *Capela da Virgen da Guia*

Opción [2] **2.1**
+100m Taberna
San Andre
S.Campio *Parque* **4.2** →**†**
Refuxio Pontellas
Centeáns

Loura

4.7 **Pasarela**

Polígono
Industrial

Quintela

E-1

Novo *Orbenlle*
2.9 **Opción [1]**
Xunta Benvidos Welcome sign

Centro Cutural Ribadelouro **†**
Cruceiro San Telmo **2.6** **†** ← *Puente das Febres*

A-55
N-550

Capela Virxe do Camiño **3.3** **†**

Puente da Veiga

E-1
Minho
(Pop. 15,000 – Alt. 60m) **TUI** **†** **A 1** ← **0.0** **Albergue** de Tui *Xunta.* [36÷2]

right> by *Café Central* into rua das Monxas past the convent of the St. Clares *Convento das Clarisas* and through the nun's tunnel *Túnel das Monxas (photo right)* down rua Antero Rubín to the ancient *[F.]* (below the overpass) to the XIV[th]c **Convento Sto. Domingo [0.7** km] *(the Dominicans have been associated with this site since 1330).* Past the adj. *Museo Municipal* under the archway (simulating an earlier medieval gateway) past Albergue Villa San Clemente and turn right> (sign Praia da Areeira) into Praza San Bartolomé one of the oldest suburbs of Tui with the XI[th]c Romanesque monastic church of St. Bartholomew **San Bartolomé de Rebordáns [0.6** km]. *(Recent excavations in the area have unearthed Roman and Visigothic ruins. The finely carved cruceiro dates from 1770).*

We now leave the town behind and turn down onto path to the medieval bridge over the rio Louro **Ponte da Veiga [0.6** km] which we do *not* cross but turn <left onto a wide earth track along the ancient Via Romana XIX. The camino is somewhat obscure here and has been realigned (to avoid having to cross rail tracks) and now does a wide loop *under* the railway and over the main road [!] **N-550 [1.1** km] (sign to Rebordáns) to the Virgin of the Way **Chapel [0.3** km].

3.3 km Capela da Virxe do Camiño. The camino crosses the new motorway A-55 where a red asphalt 'pilgrim' track replaces the earth path but at least it has an attractive timber covered safety barrier. We follow this all the way *under* the AP-9 **[1.8** km] and 200m later we turn right> **[0.2** km] [!] back *over* the motorway to enter a densely wooded section that is low-lying and can be wet and muddy after rain to emerge at an isolated glade by the river and wayside **cross [0.6** km].

2.6 km Cruceiro San Telmo – also known as the bridge of Fevers *Ponte das Febres*. Here San Telmo fell sick and died of a fever in 1251 on his way back from a pilgrimage to Santiago de Compostela. A cross marks this mournful spot *Aqui enfermo de Muerte San Telmo Abril 1251*. Turn <left over the bridge along a woodland path parallel to the river (there are several local walking routes around the river valley but stick to the yellow arrows to avoid confusion). We wind our way up onto the asphalt road past the **Centro Cultural de Ribadelouro [1.6** km] (left) through the straggling hamlet of A Magdalena recognisable by the roadside crosses marking the Calvario de la Magdalena. *[100m right off route café – often closed]* turning <left by cruceiros and then immediately right> down onto a path to cross over the river again via a medieval stone bridge. Shortly afterwards the scars of the open cast mines of Porriño appear on the horizon warning us of the intense industrial activity ahead. Continue up to the road where the Xunta has placed a Welcome *Benvidos* sign **[0.8** km]. Turn left here up to another signboard for local walk **[0.2** km] and option.

2.9 km Opción [2]. A new route was waymarked in 2013 along the course of the rio Louro. It is 1 km longer than the original but avoids the soulless slog through the Industrial area. [!] Watch carefully as waymarks at the start have been partially obliterated (cafés along the original route still want your custom). However, once you enter the woodland waymarks are obvious and appear at every turn on the maze of paths and country lanes ahead. *[Blacking out of yellow arrows also occurs at the next option point [2] and would deprive you of a tranquil riverside path into the centre of Porriño].* To take this new (recommended) route turn <left onto a woodland path over rio Louro and up to a series of quiet country roads that wind their way over the AP-9 **[2.2 km]** to pilgrim 'refreshment' area *Refuxio Pontellas* (often closed) adj. Ermida San Campio and park **[2.0 km]**:

4.2 km **San Campio.** The route now heads back over the AP-9 to the *Velodromo Municipal* **[1.2 km]**. *Here up left 200m off route is the welcoming Bar Taberna.* Continue over roundabout and under A-55 to option point [2] **[1.0 km]**.

2.1 km **Opción [2].** As we emerge under the A-55 is a sign s/o to cross the river and over the rail to join the route along the N-550. The sign to the join the recommended river path (left) may have been obliterated. However, the signs reappear shortly after but it is impossible to get lost as we simply follow the delightful river path all the way to the albergue and town centre **[2.2 km]**. *Albergue* **Peregrinos** *Xunta.[50÷2]* €6 Ⓒ 986 335 428 Av. de Buenos Aires; purpose built hostel with all modern facilities overlooking the river (to the rear is the noisy A-55 motorway). Continue into town over bridge and rail line past *Pº* **Louro** and up to the central roundabout *Banco Santander* and taxi rank **[0.2 km]** where the road route joins from the right.

2.4 km **Centro.** The attractive pedestrian town centre lies to the right.

For the road route: Continue s/o at option point [1] and follow the waymarks up to a recreation zone and back down to **Orbenlle [0.6 km]** *Bar O Novo Cazador* a 'last chance saloon' before the trek through the *polígono industrial de Porriño*. Continue to footbridge *pasarela* **[4.1 km]** over the rail and under A-55 flyover.

4.7 km **Pasarela** onto the N-550 past the chapel to the Virgin of the Way *Capela A Virxe da Guía* **[1.6 km]** turning <left at next traffic lights *Semáforo* **[0.5 km]** (waymark 99.408!) over rio Couro into Porriño town centre passing the XVI[th]c Capela San Sebastian with *F.]* (right) and Capela San Benito and *F.]* (left) past the Igreja Santa María into the main street *la calle principal Ramón González* and past the impressive stone façade of the Casa Consistorial (photo right) to the central fountain *Fonte y Parque do Cristo* and the steps leading up to the Igreja Bom Cristo (right) and s/o past the minerals museum *Museo Municipal de Minerals* to the central roundabout *Praza Central*. Plaza **[1.0 km]**:

3.1 km **Centro** where the recommended route joins from the left.

❏ **Other accommodation:** Around the centre: *H⁺⁺*Azul Ⓒ 986 330 032 c/ Ramiranes,38. *P⁺⁺* **Louro** Ⓒ 986 330 048 Av. Buenos Aires. *H⁺⁺⁺***Parque** Ⓒ 986 331 604 / 986 336 378 Parque del Cristo and on the outskirts (+0.5km) *H⁺⁺***Internacional** Ⓒ 986 330 262. c/ Antonio Palacios, 99.

The central area has a variety of bars and restaurants. Porriño is a sprawling industrial town of 15,000 sandwiched between the río Louro and the steep cliffs to the east where granite quarries provide much of the raw material for the intense industrial activity (see road route for museum). It is crossed by the main line rail, the N-550 and 2 motorways, the Autovía del Atlántico A-55 and the Autovía de las Rias Baixas A-52. To continue (from the central roundabout in Porriño) keep s/o along rua Ramiranes passing rail station (left) and cross over [!] the main roundabout by the Capela das Angustias *[F.]* under **motorway [0.8 km]** and up to a small hamlet with *[F.]* **[0.7 km]**.

1.5 km **Fonte do Chan** *(rest area with granite boulder that forms a dedication to local mountaineers and the first Galician to summit Mount Everest).* Continue back down again to cross the busy **N-550 [0.4 km]** which we to join for several short stretches. *(Note: A short detour along the Via XIX crosses the rail line here [!] and rejoins the official route beyond the timber yard where the Via XIX veers off up left again to rejoin the main route at Mos).* Continue along the left verge of the N-550 under rail bridge past petrol station and shop (opposite side of road) to turn off <left for brief respite and refreshment at *[F.] Fonte de Santa Marta* **[1.2 km]** to emerge once more onto the N-550 before finally turning off <left to cross **Ponte Rio Loura [0.5 km]** which we cross for the last time (local river walk right). Continue s/o up along a quiet asphalt road passing a picnic area and *[F.] Fonte Magdalena* **[0.7 km]** and shortly afterwards we pass new school building *Concello de Mos* and *Alb* **Veigadaña** *Asoc.[16÷1]* €7 Ⓒ 986 094 277 / 673 289 491 Asociación de Vecinos Santa Ana de Veigadaña Petelos-Mos. Now we begin the steep climb up the road of the Knights *rua dos Cabaleiros* over crossroad into the part pedestrianised village of Mos past Iglesia de Santa Eulalia del Monte and the newly renovated Pazo de Mos to arrive at the pilgrim hostel **[1.0 km]**.

3.8 km **Mos** *Alb.* **Casa Blanca** *Asoc.* *[16÷1]* €6 Ⓒ 986 334 269 rúa de Santa Eulalia, 19 *asociación vecinal.* key with Flora in *Cáfe Flora* and shop opp. Nearby is new albergue (2015) Continue up passing *Fonte dos Cabaleiros* to *Cáfe-Bar Victoria* **[0.8 km]** alternating between road and path through woodland climbing all the time to reach our high point of this stage (235m) at Monte de Santiago de Antas and extensive park **[2.3 km]**.

3.1 km **Parque** park with chapel dedicated to *Santiago Caballero* his mounted image carved above the door *Capela de Santiaguiño de Antas* 50m off route (right) and 50m further on *cáfe* on the main road. We now start our long descent towards the Ria Vigo which lies hidden by the woodland around Monte Cornedo but we can hear the aeroplanes landing at Vigo airport only 2 km to the West. We pass a Roman milestone *Marco Miliário* marking the military route Via XIX evidence that we are directly on the original pilgrim way to Santiago. Shortly afterwards we pass O Loureiro and Vilar *Pastelería O Parque* **[0.8 km]** and **Casa Figueroa [0.5 km]** turn <left **[0.3 km]** to:

1.6 km Restaurante *Churrasquería Choles* we now alternate between path and road through woodland with distant views of the Ria de Vigo as we descend to a small rest area *Área de Descanso* and follow a maze of small country lanes very steeply [!] down to level out where the new AVE rapid rail from Vigo to A Coruña crosses and up to our right *Pension* Brasil 2 ℂ 986 402 251 with 13 rooms from €27. Continue to the busy main road N-550 [3.6 km] *cáfes* to junction [0.6 km] and veer right> signposted Redondela town centre and continue to major junction with pilgrim hostel straight ahead [0.7 km].

4.9 km Redondela *Albergue* ❶ Casa da Torre *Xunta [44÷2]* €6 ℂ 986 404 196 Plaza Ribadavia. Originally a 16th century manor tower house *Casa da Torre* now renovated as a pilgrim hostel with good modern facilities. As if to compensate for its tiny kitchen, it has an enormous lounge! There is a council library upstairs and some museum pieces including a splendidly preserved Roman Miliário. The albergue is located just off the main paseo and alongside a culvert of the río Pexeiro and provides an atmospheric and welcoming environment, somewhat diminished by the proximity of the busy traffic roundabout.

❑ **Other accommodation**: *Albergue* ❷ A Casa da Herba *Priv.[24÷3]* €12 ℂ 639 757 684 Praza de Alfóndiga occupying one side of this tiny square 100m from Casa da Torre. Just beyond the Santiago church square we find: ❸ El Camino *Priv.[24÷3]* €10-12 ℂ 650 963 676 m: 986 639 804 c/ Telmo Bernádez 11. *Hs Rosa D'Abreu* ℂ 688 422 701 Rúa Isidoro Queimaliños 33. Alvear Suites €60+ ℂ 986 400 637 Pai Crespo 30. There are no hotels in the town but limited hotels on the outskirts include: *Hs* Brasil 2 €27 ℂ 986 402 251 Quintela 61 / N-550 (–1.9 km) and several alternatives directly on the camino (+3.1 km) out of town including a new hostel at Cesantes (see next stage).

Redondela Town: built at the top end of the ría de Vigo but not visible from the town itself. The albergue is located in the centre 100m from lively *cafés bars* and *restaurants* lining the paseo while adjoining the albergue is restaurant *O Migas*. The 15th century *Iglesia de Santiago* is located up the cobbled rua do Adro only 200m from the albergue and just off the waymarked route (adj. albergue 2). The church is very emblematic of the camino with a statue of Santiago Matamoros above the fine rose

window circled with shells and other Santiago motifs. There is a regular pilgrim mass at 8.30 p.m. (times may vary; check at the hostel).

❏ **Words are but symbols of symbols and therefore twice removed from reality.** *A.C.I.M.*

20 *84.3 km (52.4 miles) – Santiago*

REDONDELA – PONTEVEDRA

⫿⫿⫿⫿⫿ --- ---	5.7	--- ---	29%
▬▬ --- ---	11.7	--- ---	59%
▬▬ --- ---	2.3	--- ---	12%
Total km	**19.7 km** (12.2 ml)		

◣▬ 21.5 km (+^ 360 m = 1.8 km)
Alto(m)▲ Alto da Lomba 153 m (502 ft)
< Ⓐ Ⓗ > Cesantes (Jumbolí) **3.1** km / Arcade **6.9** km

The Practical Path: We now encounter an interesting stage along the coastal inlet of Ría de Pontevedra. We start at sea level then climb up through mixed forest around the Alto de Lomba before dropping down again to the sea at Arcade both offer the opportunity for safe swimming (with beach showers). We then start the 2nd uphill stretch of the day to climb the ancient stone paths of the Verea Vella da Canicouva to the next high point around the Cruceiro Cacheiro before descending finally to the provincial capital of Pontevedra. The route is varied with several drinking fonts and cafés. If you take the river option into Pontevedra 48% is via woodland paths offering shade and tranquillity. The remainder is largely along quiet country lanes, apart from a brief but dangerous uphill stretch of the N-550 into Arcade and city pavements. Note that the modern and well-equipped pilgrim hostels are 1½ kilometres *this* side of the town centre in Pontevedra.

❏ **The Mystical Path:** 'Words will mean little now ... we seek direct experience of truth alone. For we wait in quiet expectation of our God and Father. We have come far along the road, and now we wait for Him. We look ahead, and fix our eyes upon the journey's end.' A Course In Miracles. *Workbook Part II Intro.*

❏ **Personal Reflections:** "I surround myself in the silence of nature endeavouring to empty my mind of its constant stream of thought. To write these reflections I must engage my mind. I will close this notebook and I will wait… and see."

0.0 km **Albergue** Leaving the hostel in Redondela head into rua Isidoro Quemalinos past the narrow connecting street (right – which leads to rua do Adro and the Church of Santiago) pass under the rail viaduct and over the **N-550 [0.7** km] by the 18th century Capela de Santa Mariña / Capela das Angustias (right). We now follow a narrow asphalt road into Cesantes veering right> up into **rua de Torre [1.4** km] and shortly after turn <left onto path just over rail line. We now make our way up to the **N-550 [1.0** km] at Cesantes:

3.1 km N-551 *Cesantes Hs* Jumbolí €25 © 986 495 066 and *café* Carballiño.

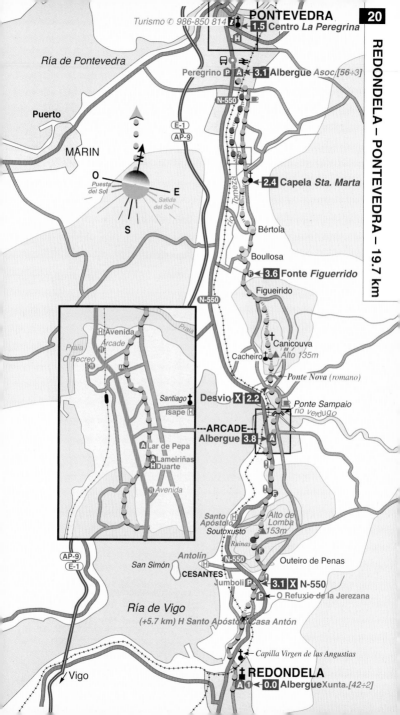

PONTEVEDRA

Turismo © 986-850 814

1.5 ← Centro *La Peregrina*

Peregrino P **3.1** ← Albergue *Asoc.[56÷3]*

N-550

2.4 ← Capela *Sta. Marta*

Bértola

Boullosa

3.6 ← Fonte *Figuerrido*

Figueirido

Canicouva
Alto 135m

Cacheiro

Ponte Nova (romano)

Santiago

Desvio X **2.2**

Isape H

*Ponte Sampaio
rio verdugo*

Lar de Pepa

Lameiriñas
Duarte

---**ARCADE**---
Albergue 3.8 →

Avenida

Avenida
Arcade

Praia
O Recreo

Praia

Santo
Apóstolo
Soutoxusto

Alto de
Lomba
153m

Ruinas

Antolín

Outeiro de Penas

San Simón

N-550

CESANTES

Jumboli P **3.1** X N-550

P ← O Refuxio de la Jerezana

Ría de Vigo
(+5.7 km) H Santo Apóstolo / Casa Antón

Capilla Virgen de las Angustias

Vigo

REDONDELA

A 1 ← **0.0** Albergue Xunta.*[42÷2]*

Ría de Pontevedra

Puerto

MARIN

E-1
AP-9

O
*Puesta
del Sol*

E
*Salida
del Sol*

S

AP-9
E-1

Welcoming hostel 200m down right along the N-550 *Albergue* **O Refuxio de la Jerezana** *Priv. [24÷1]* €12 incl. ℂ 601 165 977 Estrada do Pereiro 43-45. *Detour Cesantes (+2.5 km):* ● ● ● ● quaint seaside resort *H* **Antolín** €30+ ℂ 986 459 409 Paseo da Praia. *Camping* **Cesantes** ℂ 656 323 657. *Soutoxusto (+5.7 km):* *H* **Santo Apóstolo** *(Antón)* €40+ ℂ 986 495 136 Ctra. N-550, Km 34.

Cross the busy N-550 [!] and turn up steeply <left **[0.4** km] to *[F.]* **[0.2** km] with pilgrim motifs and cool water to refresh after the steep climb. Just above the drinking font turn off <left onto forest track through the eucalyptus woods around *Outeiro de Penas* passing the ruins of an ancient wayside Inn **[0.7** km] *Hostal da Malaposta* to reach the high point of this stage Alto de Lomba (155m). The otherwise peaceful surroundings disturbed by occasional air traffic on the flight path to Vigo. Views over the distant ría de Vigo and its iconic bridge now open up as we descend back to the **main road [1.3** km] *[F.]* (right). We now join

the N-550 for a noisy and dangerous [!] 700m stretch (take care as the verge is narrow, unprotected and on a bend) to arrive at Arcade with tourist kiosk in the park *turismo* **[0.7** km] (summer only). The waymarked route turns <left off the main road for a short circuitous detour past *Fonte do Lavandeira* (*not* drinking water) and back to the main road, which we cross over again **[0.5** km] to:

3.8 km Arcade *albergue* We now make our way down the narrow rua Barronoas through Cimadevila to crossroads with *rua Rosalia de Castro* **[0.7** km] ❖ *Café Flora* and *mini-mercado* at this point the waymarked route proceeds s/o and we have various options in this seaside town with its cafés, restaurants... and beaches. ❐ **Arcade accommodation** *(see map):* *Alb.*❶ **Lameiriñas** *Priv. [28÷2]* €10-12 ℂ 616 107 820 Rua Lameiriñas 8 (adj. Hotel Duarte). ❷ **O Lar de Pepa** *Priv. [10÷4]* €10 ℂ 986 678 006 m: 649 714 950 camino Ribeiro 1. *H"* **Duarte** €25 ℂ 986 670 057 c/Lameriñas 8. *H"* **Isape** €25 ℂ 986 700 721 via rua Escalinata de Soutomaior opp. *Iglesia de Santiago de Arcade* (+ 0.8km). *H"""* **Avenida** €30 ℂ 986 670 100 N-550 (+ 0.4 km).
    To access the beach for safe swimming (600m *off* route) proceed over main road at traffic lights past taxi rank and over rail line to roundabout with statue *Mariscadora* past the popular bar and restaurant *O Recreo* (*mariscos*) to the sandy beach *Praia do Peirao* with beach showers. Along the main street in Arcade are several seafood restaurants including the Michelin recommended *Restaurant Arcadia* and *Marisqueria Avenida* both located on the main road.

❖ Continue s/o past library *biblioteca* and make your way through *A Calle* to **Pontesampaio [0.4** km] the handsome stone bridge over the río Verdugo built in 1795 over earlier foundations *[it was here that local militia inflicted a significant rout on Napoleon's troops during the War of Independence, witnessed by a memorial at the far side]*. A delightful spot for a rest with a fine sandy beach for swimming (beach and showers over the bridge right).

(*Detour:* ● ● ● ● *to view the 13th century Romanesque Igrexa Santa María de Pontesampaio continue up the main road for 300m*). The waymarked route now branches off steeply up <left just past the memorial and *café-bar* to take a detour away from the main road passing the *cruceiro de Ballota* and winding its way up and down again before crossing back over the main road **[1.1 km]**.

2.2 km Cruce *desvio [a 500m detour over road bridge may still be in operation here to avoid the original footbridge which was destroyed in recent floods].* However, unless the river is in spate it easy to follow the original route and cross the rio Ulló by the remains of the medieval bridge **A Ponte Nova** (*built on Roman remains as this was part of the calzada Romana XIX*) and continue up the far side by picnic area in the woodland glade to wind back up to the side of a fish farm **[0.5 km]** where the  temporary detour joins from the left. Continue up the ancient stone paved pilgrim way *Verea Vella da Canicouva* up to the crossroads and wayside cross *cruxeiro Cacheiro*. This section alternates between paths and quiet country lanes and just past the hamlet of Boullosa we begin to descend towards Bértola and Pontevedra and here on our right we can refresh ourselves at a *[F.]* **[3.1 km]**:

3.6 km Fonte de Montes de Figueirido. Drinking font and picnic area by side of the road. We alternate again between quiet asphalt roads and green pathways until we enter the municipal area of Pontevedra *Concello de Pontevedra* at Capela da Sta. Marta **[2.2 km]** and proceed up to the main road where we turn left over rio Pobo towards Pontevedra and option for riverside walk **[0.2 km]**.

2.4 km Río Tomeza *Option* ▲ From here the waymarked route is all by the side of the busy main road into Pontevedra. However there is a wonderful alternative route (adding 600m yellow and white signs) along tree lined river valley all the way to the outskirts of the city 200m from the pilgrim hostel. This alternative is highly recommended where bird song replaces the noise of traffic.

Alternative River Route 3.7 km: ● ● ● ● *Senda Fluvia do río dos Gafos.* Turn <left at sign for Ponte Rebón s/o over bridge and turn <left onto path into woodland and right> over the river **[0.5 km]** which we now follow north all the way into Pontevedra. This shaded river route crosses several small tributaries and is well maintained with panels explaining the names of the trees and areas we pass through. Continue over lane (new rail ink under construction) by the ***Ponte da Condesa*** **[1.3 km]** passing the Poza da Moura (mill race) and the romantic Valentine's bridge ***Ponte Valentín*** **[0.8 km]** up to (but not over) railway and under road bridge **tunnel** **[0.7 km]** (see photo right) and then under rail bridge tunnel **[0.2 km]** to rejoin the waymarked route on the main road where we turn left up to the Albergue in Pontevedra **[0.2 km]**.

▲ For the waymarked route continue s/o along the main road to *Casa Mella café* **[2.5 km]** and s/o over Av. de Marco at traffic lights. The traffic now intensifies as we enter the suburbs of Pontevedra turning up <left at roundabout to *Hs Peregrino* ℗ 986 858 409 rúa Otero Pedrayo, 8 directly opp. albergue ramp.

3.1 km **Pontevedra Sur** *(South)* *Alb.*
❶ **La Virgen Peregrina** *Asoc.[56÷3]* €6 ℗ 986 844 045 rúa Otero Pedrayo (adj' Estación de tren) opens 13:00. Modern hostel between road and rail line by the main station and bus depot. What it lacks in romantic ambience it makes up for in excellent facilities and warm welcome. Close by *opp.* the entrance to the station:

❷ *Hs* **Aloxa** Priv.*[50÷2]* €10-30 ℗ 986 896 453 m: 663 438 770 rua Gorgullón (by Nº 68) opens at 10:00. Also close by on the main road is *H** **La Peregrina Residencia** Rúa Eduardo Pondal, 76 ℗ 986 850 145.

Note: These hostels are located 1½ kilometres *south* of the medieval city centre. Depending on your arrival time you can visit the city centre after a rest and shower or spend time in the centre on the way through in the morning. Another option is to continue to the city centre and find a more central hotel or pension. Allow a leisurely 30-minute walk to the Praza da Peregrina at the start of the old town; alternatively, there are buses or taxis from the rail station or the main bus station opposite. Whatever you do, don't miss savouring this wonderful city with its many fascinating monuments and historic buildings, many of them directly associated with the pilgrimage.

Continue over the roundabout in front of the rail station and take the secondary road *rua do Gorgullón* parallel and below the main road *Avenida Eduardo Pombal* which we cross later into *rua Virxen do Camiño* (Galician spelling) past the hotel Virgen del Camino s/o past the *Glorieta de Compostela* into rua de Peregrina to:

1.5 km **Pontevedra Centro** *Praza Peregrina Santuario da Peregrina.*
❏ *Turismo de Pontevedra* Casa da Luz, Praza da Verdura 986 090 890. *Alb.* ❸ **Slow City Hostel** *Priv.[6÷1]* €17-40 ℗ 631 062 896 (Jorge) rúa da Amargura 5.
❏ **Hostels** *central*: The following are all located in or adjoining the old quarter. Adj. praza España. *Fonda* **Chiquito** ℗ 986 862 192 rua Charino 23. **Casa O Fidel** ℗ 986 851 234 pulpería Fidel, rua San Nicolás 7. **Casa Alicia** ℗ 986 857 079 Av. Santa Mariá 5, **Casa Maruja** ℗ 986 854 901 rua Alta. *Hospedaje* **Penelas** ℗ 986 855 705 rua Alta 17. *(€30-50)* *H**la Peregrina* ℗ 986 866 249 rua Eduardo Pondal,1. *H***Avenida* Eduardo Pondal, 46. *H** **Room** *(Vedra)* ℗ 986 869 550 c/ Filgueira Valverde, 10. **Hotel Virgen del Camino** ℗ 986 855 900 c/ de la Virgen del Camino, 55. *H**Madrid* ℗ 986 865 180 Rúa Andrés Mellado, 5. *H*** **Rias Bajas** ℗ 986 855 100 c/ Daniel de la Sota Valdecilla, 7. *H** **Ruas** ℗ 986 846 416 rua Sarmiento, 20. *H** **Boa Vila** rua Real, 4 986 10 52 65. *(€100+)* **Parador Casa del Barón** ℗ 986 855 800 c/ Barón, 19 baronial house close to exit.

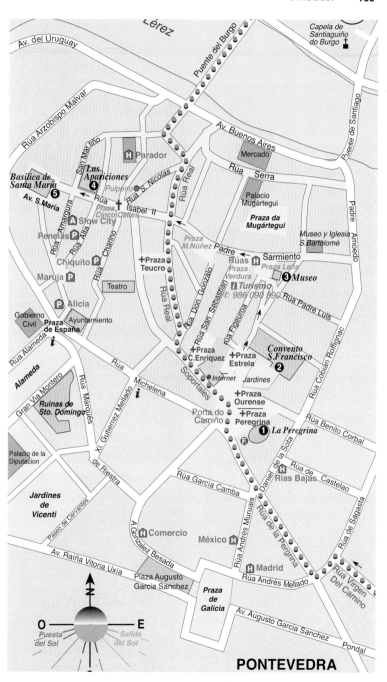

Lérez

Av. del Uruguay

Capela de
Santiaguiño
do Burgo

Puente del Burgo

Puente de Santiago

Av. Buenos Aires

Rúa Arzobispo Malvar

San Martiño

Parador

Mercado

Rúa
Serra

Las
Apariciones **4**

Pulpeiro

Rúa S. Nicolas

Rúa Real

Palacio
Mugártegui

Basílica de
Santa María **5**

Amargura

Rúa
Isabel II

Praza
Cinco Calles

*Praza da
Mugártegui*

Av. S.María

Slow City **A**

Rúa Alta

Rúa Charino

*Praza
M.Núñez*

Padre

Museo y Iglesia
S.Bartolomé

Penelas **P**

Sarmiento

Chíquito **P**

Rúas
Verdura

Praza Leña

Museo **3**

Maruja **P**

*Praza
Verdura*

**+Praza
Teucro**

i Turismo
© 986 090 890

Rúa Padre Luís

Teatro

Rúa Real

Rúa Don Gonzalo

Alicia **P**

Rúa San Sebastián

Gobierno
Civil

Ayuntamiento

i

Rúa Figueroa

Convento
S.Francisco **2**

Praza
de España

Rúa Cobián Roffignac

Rúa Alameda

**+Praza
C.Enríquez**

**+Praza
Estrela**

Alameda

Rúa

Michelena

Internet

Jardines

Gran Vía Montero

Rúa Marqués

i

Soportales

**+Praza
Ourense**

*Ruinas de
Sto. Domingo*

**+Praza
Peregrina**

X. Gutierrez Mellado

Porta do
Camiño

1 La Peregrina

*Palacio de la
Diputacion*

de Riestra

Daniel de la Sota

Rúa Benito Corbal

Rúa de Castelao

Rías Bajas

Rúa García Camba

Rúa de la Pergrina

Rúa de Sagasta

*Jardines
de
Vicenti*

Paseo de Cervantes

A. Gonzalez Besada

Comercio

México

Rúa Andrés Muruais

Madrid

Av. Raiña Vitoria Uxía

Plaza Augusto
García Sánchez

Rúa Andrés Mellado

Rúa Virgen
Del Camino

*Praza
de
Galicia*

Av. Augusto García Sánchez

Pondal

O ——— E

N

*Puesta
del Sol*

*Salida
del Sol*

PONTEVEDRA

Pontevedra. Regional capital & lively commercial and tourist city with a population of 75,000. At the heart of its modern suburbs is a delightful medieval core *zona monumental / barrio Antigo*. The waymarked route follows the original camino *Rua Real* that goes right through the centre of the ancient quarter but the following walking tour takes in most of the historic sites: We approach the centre via ruas Virgen del Camino and Peregrina and the *Porta do Camiño* into 4 interconnecting squares, the first (highest) of which is ✣ *Praza de la Peregrina* and location for the unequalled elegance of the pilgrim chapel ❶ **Santuario da Peregrina** (see photo above). This beautiful 18th century chapel was conceived by the architect Arturo Souto and built in the Baroque style to a floor plan in the shape of... a scallop shell! One of the great treasures of the camino. The route leads into ✣ *Praza de Ourense* with its delightful gardens *Xardíns de Castro San Pedro* and cheerful cafés and bars forming part of the nightly *paseo* with the imposing edifice of the 14th century ❷ **Convento de San Francisco** in the background. The lower section of this extensive open area is known as ✣ *Praza da Herrería* and ✣ *Praza de Estrela* which provide an option (recommended) to take a short 100m detour to one of the city's most emblematic squares and best museums:

✣ *Praza de Leña* ● ● ● ●

Continue past Convento San Francisco s/o 'out' the far side of Praza Estrela and turn left directly to this intimate square with its squat granite arcades and central *cruceiro* so typical of Galicia. Several cafés and the hotel Ruas give it a lively atmosphere and here we also find the excellent provincial museum ❹ **Museo de Pontevedra** housed in several adjacent historic buildings with a connecting stone bridge. Casa García Flórez houses exhibits of the famous jet-black jewellery from Santiago and an interesting collection of images of St. James dating from as early as 12th century. There is also an entire floor dedicated to the famous Galician writer and philosopher Alfonso Castelao who, along with Rosalía de Castro, did so much to preserve the unique Galician culture that we can enjoy today.

Return to Praza da Herrería or continue into rua Padre Sarmiento passing ✣ *Praza da Verdura* **Turismo** and ✣ *Praza Méndez Núñez* (accessible via the colourful rua de Don Gonzálo (see photo right) either of which leads back to the camino in rua Real.

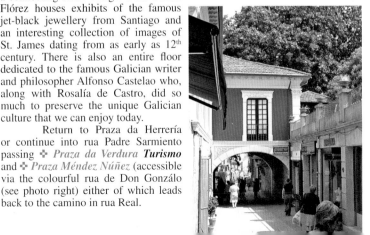

From *Santuario da Peregrina* continue along the waymarked route via the ancient arcaded street *rua dos Soportais* that leads into ✤ *Praza Curros Enríquez* and thence along the ancient Royal Road *Rua Real* passing through ✤ *Praza do Teucro* to its junction with rua Padre Sarmiento (from the museo) which provides another detour (recommended) to visit the cathedral ● ● ● ● as follows: turn left up rua de Isabel II to ✤ *Praza y Cruceiro das Cinco Ruas* the meeting point of five of the timeworn cobbled laneways. A magical spot with an intriguing *cruceiro* depicting the temptation of man with a snake coiled around the shaft watching a naked Eve offering the apple to Adam. Continuing up rua de Isabel II we pass ❹ **Santuario da Aparicións** where the Blessed Virgin also appeared to sister Lucía and just beyond we arrive at ❺ **Basílica de Santa María A Grande** the celebrated 16th century Basilica dedicated in her name. Either side of the main entrance are statues of the founding fathers of the church, St. Peter and St. Paul, while the rose window portrays the Assumption and Coronation of the Virgin Mary. But the real celebration is the southern façade and the mystery and mastery of Flemish sculptor *Cornielles de Holanda* and the Portuguese artist *João Nobre* together with the stonemasons who created this 'storybook in stone' displaying the unfolding drama of the church ending with the Passion of Christ and the promise of redemption – reminiscent of the craftsmanship that created the Pórtico da Gloria in Santiago cathedral.

If you have followed this itinerary you are probably in need of refreshment. Help is at hand as the cobbled lanes of the old quarter are bursting with *tapas* bars and cafés. Immediately behind the Basilica on the narrow rua Isabel is the atmospheric *O Cortello* with a selection of smoked hams hanging from the ceiling – a reference, perhaps, to its Galician name that translates as pigsty! If you head back towards Praza España along Avenida de Santa María you come to a shaded triangular Praza, site of a medieval Jewish cemetery Lampán dos Xudeus around which are several cafés and pensions and the *Meson Santa María*. S/o is ✤ *Praza de España* the main square that divides the modern city from its ancient heart. Here we find the main government buildings, town hall and Alameda with its array of statues to modern and ancient heroes of España. Here also we find the ruins of the 13th century Igrexa de Santo Domingo – now a national monument. Head back towards the old centre down any of the myriad narrow paved streets back to the Praza das Cinco Ruas with its tempting Taperías offering a local speciality *Zamburiñas* (scallops in garlic) and all watched over, in case you had forgotten, by the cross of temptation and a direct route to the heavenly Parador down rua do Barón *or* turn right and pick up the waymarks to the camino down rua Isabel.

REFLECTIONS:

> If you want to become full, let yourself be empty.
> If you want to be reborn, let yourself die. *Lao Tzu*

21 *64.6 km (40.1 miles) – Santiago*

PONTEVEDRA – CALDAS DE REIS

ιιιιιιιιιιιιι	--- ---	7.6	--- ---	35%
▬▬▬▬▬	--- ---	13.1	--- ---	61%
▬▬▬▬	--- ---	0.9	--- ---	4%
Total km		**21.6 km** (13.4 ml)		

◣◣ 22.4 km (+^ 160 m = 0.8 km)
Alto*(m)*▲ San Amaro 135 m (443 ft)
<🅰 🅗> Barro/Portela **10.0** km (+ 0.5) – Briallos **16.5** km (+ 0.7)

The Practical Path: One third of this stage is along natural pathways through woodland along gentle river valleys which we share with the rail line. We have good shade and several drinking fonts to quench our thirst. Approaching Caldas de Reis we hop on and off the N-550 but the stretches are short and level with good sight lines. However, there are only a few small bars or cafés so it is well to buy some food in Pontevedra to fuel the body through the day and to make a meal if you intend to stay in either of the 2 remote albergues *off* route.

0.0 km **Pontevedra Centro** *Praza Peregrina* The camino now continues through the *praza de Ourense* down the arcaded *rua dos Soportais* into the evocative *rua Real* passing the *praza do Teucro* to veer left into the *rua da Ponte* and emerging from the old quarter at the **río Lérez [0.6 km]**. *Here we can see the excavations of the foundations of the original Roman bridge and a replica miliário.* Cross over the busy city ring road [!] over the río Lérez across the Ponte do Burgo into Av. do Coruña and turn <left at the **Banco de Galicia [0.2 km]** into rua Da Santiña, winding our way through the city suburbs and Pontecabras past a welcome *[F.]* erected by the *Communidades Montes* onto a **track [1.7 km]** *Via Romana XIX* and under rail **bridge [0.6 km]**. The route now runs parallel to the rail line through the hamlet of Pontecabras for **[0.6 km]** to:

3.7 km **Alba / San Caetano** *[F.] Iglesia Santa de María de Alba* and pilgrim monument. Continue up past wayside cross and turn <left onto the busy main **road [0.4 km]** [!] *narrow verge [!]* under rail bridge and through Caetano with *Capela San Caetano (right)* veering right> off main road by factory **[0.6 km]** onto country lane turning <left just before railway to pick up the **path [1.2 km]** for a lovely stretch that runs alongside the rail line through eucalyptus woods. In the low-lying sections the path can be wet and the otherwise tranquil setting is somewhat disturbed by the proximity of the AP-9 / E-1 motorway, thankfully out of sight over to our left. We now cross over **rail line** [!] **[2.3 km]** and up into **San Amaro [0.6 km]**:

5.1 km **San Amaro** *Café-Meson Pulpo* small hamlet in the concello de Barro.

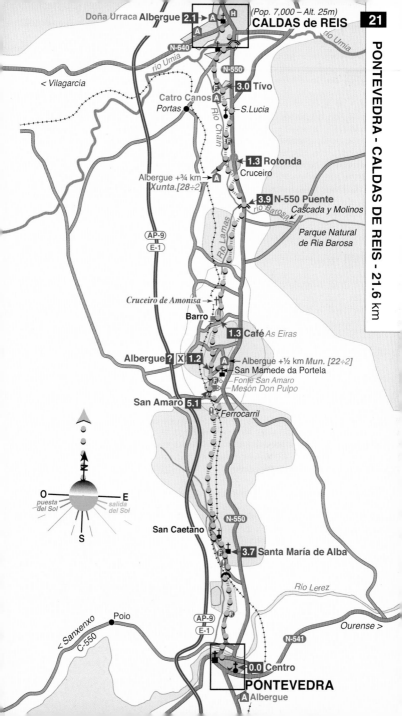

Doña Urraca **Albergue** **2.1** → A H
(Pop. 7,000 – Alt. 25m)
CALDAS de REIS

rio Umia

N-640
A
rio Umia
N-550

3.0 Tívo

< Vilagarcía

Catro Canos
A
Portas ● — S.Lucia
Rio Chain

F

1.3 Rotonda
Cruceiro

Albergue +¾ km →
Xunta.[28÷2]
A

3.9 N-550 Puente
Cascada y Molinos
rio Barosa

Parque Natural
de Ria Barosa

AP-9
E-1

Río Lamas

Cruceiro de Amonisa →

Barro

1.3 Café *As Eiras*

Albergue ? X **1.2**
A → *Albergue* +½ km *Mun. [22÷2]*
■ — San Mamede da Portela
F — *Fonte San Amaro*
— *Mesón Don Pulpo*

San Amaro **5.1**
ū *Ferrocarril*

N-550

San Caetano
† †
F ■ **3.7** Santa María de Alba

Río Lerez

AP-9
E-1

< *Sanxenxo*
C-550
● *Poio*
F

Ourense >
N-541

0.0 Centro

PONTEVEDRA
A Albergue

O E
puesta *salida*
del Sol *del Sol*
S

Just behind the cafe we pass a rest area and *[F.]* **[0.1** km] s/o passing cruceiro de Parada **[0.6** km] to junction and option **[0.5 km].**

1.2 km **Barro / Portela / Option** (½ km detour to albergue).

Detour ● ● ● ● turn up right> and
<left at the Iglesia de San Mamede da
Portela and continue to *Albergue* **Portela**
Par.[32÷2] €6 ℂ 655 952 805 **[0.6** km]
renovated school building in quiet
location with no shops or other facilities
– the nearest place for food is back at
Meson Pulpo in San Amaro (1.2 km) or
Restaurant As Eiras in Barro (1.3 km).

From the detour junction continue s/o and turn <left on road **[0.5** km] and right>
onto track through woodland and up to road turn right to A Eira **[0.8 km].**

1.3 km **Barro** *Meson As Eiras* cafe.
*[Also Pensión Meli on N-550 – 1 km off
route].* The camino continues past the
ancient Cruceiro de Amonisa set at a
jaunty angle with St. James replete with
staff looking towards Compostela. Veer
<left by granite blocks and <left again to
follow the new railway and turn right> at
T-**junction [1.9** km] over river and <left

onto path **[0.3** km] before emerging onto the **main road [1.7** km]:

3.9 km N-550 / Option *[**Detour** ½ km ● ● ● ● Parque Natural de Río
Barossa. To visit the impressive cascades and mill buildings cross the main road
and head up directly for ½ km to viewpoint].* To continue along the camino turn
<left along the N-550 over the river Barossa turning <left onto one of several
short (but welcome) sections of path through vineyards that run parallel to the
road. Continue to junction with signpost for detour to the albergue in Briallos just
short of the major road roundabout.

1.3 km **Rotonda / Option** (¾ km detour to albergue).

Detour 0.7 km ● ● ● ● *Albergue*
Briallos *Xunta.[27÷2]+* €6 ℂ 986 536
194 (Pilar) Lugar San Roque. Follow
the signs along a quiet country road to
this welcoming modern albergue with
extensive modern facilities and large
kitchen and dining area and upstairs
lounge. Note: Caldas de Reis is 5 km
further on and there are no shops or
restaurants in the immediate area.

Continue on a track (left) alongside the main road, past *[F.]* to join the main
road again for a short but busy stretch before turning off <left onto a path by the
capela Santa Lucia [0.6 km] the path meanders into the río Chaín valley into the
delightful hamlet of **Tívo [2.2** km] where we can refresh at:

3.0 km **Tívo** *Alb.* **Catro Canos** *Priv.* *[16÷6]* €10 ℂ 696 582 014 / 600 345 181 *(José Manuel y Lorena). Bar* (+50m right). At the far end of this peaceful hamlet we find a handsome drinking font *[F.]* by wayside cross. Continue on quiet country lane onto asphalt path to rejoin the main road veering off <left imm. beyond the roadside church Iglesia de Santa Maria into rua Santa Marta to rejoin the N-550 to the **bridge [1.6 km]** [!] *narrow* over the río Umia into Caldas de Reis with hotel and spa *balneario* **Acuña** (left) opp. the Ayuntamiento and Policía Local. Cross the stone bridge with the entrance to the renowned *Taberna O Muiño* (right).

The waymarked camino now turns <left at Banco Pastor into rua Laureano Salgado to the *balneario* **Hotel Dávila** with public fountain **fonte caldas [0.1** km] where the famous hot waters pour out so you can soothe your feet for free (beware slippery surface–see photo) and the extensive park overlooked by the impressive parish church of St. Thomas à Becket *Iglesia parroquial de Santo Tomás de Canterbury!* which marks the historic and commercial ● **centre of town**. To continue to the pilgrim hostel proceed along the principal pedestrian street with its granite colonnades (part of the original camino) *rua Real* to cross [!] the busy calle de Juan Fuentes Echvarria **[0.2** km] and cross the emblematic medieval stone bridge *[F.]* over the rio Bermaña with several pleasant *cafés* and bars overlooking the river and surrounding the square to the adjacent pilgrim hostel (left) **[0.2** km]:

2.1 km **Caldas de Reis ❶ Posada Dona Urraca** *Muni.[44÷1]* €5 ℂ 986 541 310 m: 669 822 529 adjoining the Puente y Rua Real immediately over Bermaña bridge (back left) close to all amenities.

Caldas de Reis (Reyes) with a population of 10,000 is neatly contained between the ríos Umia and Bermaña. The history of Caldas is inextricably linked to its thermal waters that have gushed from its ground source at a constant 40 degrees for millennia. Inhabited by early Celtic tribes it became a major spa *Aquae Celenae* on the Via Romana XIX. Under Christian authority it became the bishopric of Celenis, transforming itself into Rex Calda during the *Reconquista*. King Alfonso VII, son of Queen Doña Urraca was born here – it was later to become the birthplace of hydro electricity in Galicia during the industrial era.

Today Caldas de Reis continues to benefit from its waters as a major health spa. It also has delightful botanical gardens *xardín botánicas* planted along the shaded banks of the river Umia located just beyond the Library *Turismo* off Av. Román López. The parish church *igrexa parroquial Sto.Tomás* commands a central position in town and was built in 1890 from the stone salvaged from the medieval castle where Alphonso VII was born. Rest your feet in the hot spring •*fonte* (see photo right) and drink the cool waters in the •*fonte* on the *Ponte Romano*.

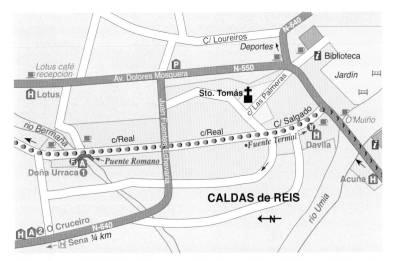

❏ *Turismo:* ℂ 986 539 025 (summer) Av. Román López / Dto. de Cultura del Ayuntamiento 09.00-15.00 986 540 110 Ferrería, 1.

❏ **Other Accommodation:** ❷ **O' Cruceiro** *Priv.[44÷4]* €10-15 ℂ 986 540 165 Juan Fuentes Echevarría, 44 adjoining (and part of) *H*°° **O' Cruceiro** €25+ ℂ 986 53 00 22. *H*°° **Sena** c.€25 ℂ 986 540 596 further out along c/ de Juan Fuentes, 99. *H*°° **Lotus** Av. Dolores Mosquera, 27 (the main street / N-550) ℂ 986 54 06 02 popular with pilgrims due to its central location; rooms at the rear have balconies overlooking the Ponte Romano (reception in Café Lotus). Amongst the centrally located spa hotels *balneario* are: *H*°° **Balneario Acuña** c/ de la Herrería, 2 €40 ℂ 986 540 010. *H*°°**Balneario Dávila** Rúa de Laureano Salgado,11 €40 ℂ 986 540 012 Founded in 1780 but recently modernised with gardens to the rear.

A wide choice of Bars, cafes and restaurants sprawl out along the town pavements and the riverbanks. For an authentic Galego Taberna try your luck in the *Taberna O'Muiño* by the bridge on the way in to town where you can eat inexpensively with the locals down by the river. The *camarero* is wont to wipe the sweat from his brow with the self-same cloth that wipes the glasses, but if  you've made it this far you should survive and even enjoy the experience.

REFLECTIONS:

❏ **Emptiness, which is conceptually liable to be mistaken for nothingness, is in fact the reservoir of infinite possibilities.** *Daisetz Teitaro Suzuki*

22 *43.0 km (26.7 miles) – Santiago*

CALDAS DE REIS – PADRÓN

▥▥▥▥▥	--- ---	9.1	--- ---	49%	
▬▬▬▬	--- ---	8.7	--- ---	49%	
▬▬▬▬	--- ---	0.3	--- ---	2%	
Total km		**18.1 km** (11.2 ml)			

◣◢ 19.4 km (+^ 260 m = 1.3 km)
Alto(m)▲ Cortiñas 160 m (525 ft)
< 🅰 🏠 > Carracedo 4.9 km / Valga 9.2 km / Pontecesures 15.6 km

The Practical Path: Half this stage is on natural pathways through mature woodland. Facilities are limited on this relatively short stage but there is a choice of hostals and cafes just *off* route – fill up with water as you pass the few drinking fonts. The route takes us along two river valleys, firstly the Bermaña and then a gentle climb up Cortiñas (the high point of this stage) before dropping down sharply into the Valga valley. From there we have another gentle climb up to a viewing point above the industrial suburbs of Pontecesures before dropping down finally to cross the río Ulla to pick up its small tributary the río Sar into Padrón. There are only two short stretches of main road, firstly leaving Caldas de Reis and as we enter Padrón over the bridge at Pontecesures. Otherwise the route is split between natural pathways and quiet country roads – buen camino...

0.0 km Caldas de Reis *Centro* Leaving the albergue in the centre of town pass *Capilla de San Roque* and turn up <left on the main road and down right> onto path where we head along the gentle Bermaña river valley under viaduct [**1.0 km**] through woodland to crossroads on the busy [!] N-550 in *Carracedo* [**3.9 km**].

4.9 km Cruce N-550 *Café Esperon*
with *Hs* **Parrillada Antonio** €25 Ⓒ 986
534 260 N-550 Cruceiro-carracedo up to
the left (+100m). S/o over the N-550 [!]
along laneway to iglesia Santa Mariña de
Carrecedo with adj. cruceiro (see photo)
and extensive plaza with bandstand [**0.5
km**] and •*fonte* (often dry in summer).
Continue up through *As Cortiñas* and over
[!] **N-550** [**1.3 km**] onto pathway running
alongside the motorway, which we cross
after [**1.2 km**]:

3.0 km AP-9 Puente *Café Pardal (s/o +70m)* turn right> immediately over motorway down path between N-550 and AP-9 through woodland and up to

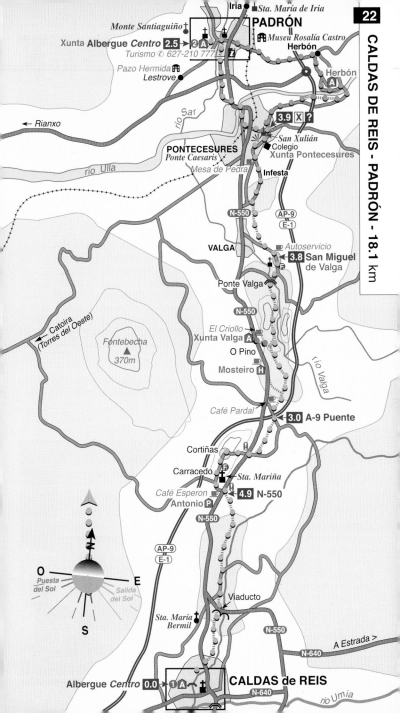

Iria ■ *Sta. María de Iria*

Monte Santiaguiño †

PADRÓN

■ *Museu Rosalía Castro*
Herbón

Xunta Albergue *Centro* 2.5 → 2 A i

Turismo © 627-210 777

Pazo Hermida 🏠
Lestrove ●

Herbón
A

← *Rianxo*

río Sar

3.9 X ?

San Xulián
Colegio

río Ulla

PONTECESURES
Ponte Caesaris

Xunta Pontecesures

Mesa de Pedra

→ **Infesta**

N-550

AP-9
E-1

VALGA

Autoservicio

3.8 **San Miguel**
de Valga

Ponte Valga

N-550

Catoira
(Torres del Oeste)

Fontebecha
▲ *370m*

El Criollo →
Xunta Valga A

O Pino

río Valga

Mosteiro H

Café Pardal

3.0 **A-9 Puente**

Cortiñas

Carracedo
Sta. Mariña

Café Esperon
Antonio P

4.9 **N-550**

N-550

AP-9
E-1

O
Puesta
del Sol

E
Salida
del Sol

S

Viaducto

Sta. María
Bermil †

A *Estrada* >

N-550

N-640

Albergue *Centro* 0.0 → 1 A †

CALDAS de REIS

N-640

río Umia

Carracedo *Hs⁺* Mosteiro €30 ℂ 986
559 120 m: 619 905 200 *Cernadas, O
Pino* on the **N-550 [1.3** km]. Here also
we find truckers bar *Los Camioneros*
(with an occasional pilgrim visitor)
and nearby the sign for *Albergue* Valga
Xunta.[80÷4] €6 ℂ 638 943 271 (Maria
Teresa) Lugar de O Pino N-550 (+200m)
purpose built hostel (see photo) located
opp. *El Criollo* with *menú peregrino*.
This is the high point of this stage at
160m and the camino now descends a

steep path past pond **[0.4** km] through woodland to the río Valga and **bridge [1.4**
km] with viewpoint over the river to join the country lane into the village of *San
Miguel [F.] (right)* **[0.5** km] passing the parish church of San Miguel and up to
shop and bar **[0.2** km]**.

3.8 km San Miguel de Valga *Café-Autoservicio* (right) and turn off <left onto
path after which we cross and re-cross a series of country lanes through the
hamlets of *Pedreira*, *Cimadevila [F.]* **[0.6** km] and *Fontela* but the camino is well
signposted to viewpoint (view over Pontecesures port on the río Ulla with Padrón
on the río Sar (tributary of the Ulla) behind. Here at school and sports hall *escuela
y polideportiva* **[2.7** km] we find *Albergue* Pontecesures *Xunta.[54÷2]* €5 ℂ 699
832 730 Estrada das Escolas, Lugar de Infesta purpose built hostel. *200m off
route down rua Infesta is Mesa de Pedra with menú peregrino*. Continue down
rua Coengos to pass the 12th century Romanesque church of San Xulián *[F.]* to
T-junction **[0.6** km]**.

3.9 km Cruce Opción Turn <left for the main waymarked route directly to
Padrón or turn right> for the alternative route to the monastery in Herbón.

Detour Herbón 3.1 km: Albergue Herbón *Conv.[22÷1]* €-donativo (AGACS)
Monasterio Franciscano de Herbón in the ancient and peaceful surroundings of
the Convento de Herbón for individual
pilgrims seeking a more contemplative
time under the care and hospitality of
this Franciscan monastery. Communal
dinner following mass at 20:00. Breakfast
at 07:30 with mass at 08:00. The hostel
is run by volunteers from the Galician
pilgrim association (AGACS) and is
temporarily housed in a block at the rear
with entrance from a discreet door in the
top terrace. 22 individual bunk spaces
(no groups) in one dormitory with basic
facilities. *Directions*: Follow *red* arrows
to Cortiñas and turn back sharp left **[1.0**
km] onto overgrown path down to and
along the river and cross over bridge
[1.4 km] back along far side of river up
to monastery **[0.7** km] *(Total 3.1 km)*.
Note: Yellow arrows mark the way back
to *Padrón* by road to the town centre a
distance of *2.6 km.*

To continue turn <left cross railway and take tunnel under N-550 and proceed to the bridge with statue of Santiago leaning on his staff (left) *Café la Marina* and to the rear (200m) hotel **A Casa do Rio** €40+ ℂ 986 557 575 c/Dr. Victor García. Cross the río Ulla in Pontecesures and at the far end of the **bridge [0.4 km]** veer <left (don't stay on the main road which is narrow and busy). We now make our way up a quiet country lane turning right> along the banks of the **río Sar [0.6 km]** under C-550 ring road and into the outskirts of Padrón at the main market square **[0.9** km] public toilets (left) and Option: To our right *Alb.* ❶ **Flavia** *Priv.[22÷5]*+ €10 ℂ 981 810 455 *(Isabel)* Campo da Feira, 13 + *Pensión & Parrillada Flavia.*

or continue s/o along the river Sar (replica Padron on the far bank) by shaded *paseo* lined with plane trees to the heart of Padrón with the statue of her most famous daughter and illustrious poetess, Rosalía de Castro with the church of St. James behind *Igrexa de Santiago* **[0.4** km]. For the original Xunta hostel turn <left over the bridge [!] (narrow medieval bridge also used by traffic) and cross over the road [!] (blind bend) and the hostel is just behind the *fuente del Carmen* below the Convento do Carmen perched on the rocky promontory above **[0.2 km]**

2.5 km Padrón ❷ **Padrón** *Xunta.* *[46÷1]* €6 ℂ 666 202 863 Costiña da Carmen. small kitchen area with patio off. The impressive edifice of the adjacent 18th century Carmelite monastery lie above and the climb up offers good views over the river Sar and town beyond. Close by, just beyond *fuente del Carmen* are the access steps to Monte Santiaguiño. Back in the historic town centre is the latest albergue (2015) ❸ **Corredoiras** *Priv.[26÷1]* €16 ℂ 981 817 266 on Corredoira da Barca 10.

❑ **Padrón:** *Turismo:* ℂ 981 811 550 Av. Compostela.
❑ **Hoteles:** *P** **Flavia** ℂ 981 810 455 Campo da Feira. *Hs*** **Chef Rivera** ℂ 981 810 413 Travesía del Enlace al Parque also restaurant (opp. turismo). *Hs*** **Casa Cuco** ℂ 981 810 511 Av de Compostela (modern building opp. Jardín Botanico). *P*** **Jardín** ℂ 981 812 490 period town house on the corner of rúa Franco Salgado Araujo and Av. da Estación adj. Jardín Botanico. *H*** **Rosalia** ℂ 981 81 24 90 modern hotel on rua Maruxa Villanueva (adj. estación de tren and museo de Rosalia de Castro). *Hs* **Grilo** ℂ 981 810 607 Av. Camilo José Cela (the main road). Beyond Iria Flavia in Pazos **Hotel Scala** (see next stage).
❑ **Restaurantes:** *O Pementeiro* Praza do Castro (specialising in *Pimientos de Padrón*). *O Santiaguiño* Praza de Macias *(pulpo and mariscos).* Wide selection of cafés and snack bars.

Padrón Town: 20 kilometres South of Santiago is where we find the legendary starting point of James ministry in Spain and also the subsequent return of his mortal remains following his martyrdom in Jerusalem that lie in the reliquary at the heart of Santiago cathedral. Padrón is built along the banks of the rivers Sar and Ulla and essentially an 'extension' of Iria Flavia. The latter being the original

seat of the bishops of Galicia before it was transferred to Santiago de Compostela. The varied attractions of this historical town include: ❶ **Igrexa de Santiago.** This Romanesque church dates back to the time of Bishop Xelmírez but has been extended many times since and the present structure is rather sombre in appearance. Inside is one of the great Jacobean treasures for here, below the altar, is the original stone *O Pedrón* from which the town takes its name. You may need to ask for the partition to be rolled back and the light switched on for you to see the stone itself.

While legends abound, the most consistent is that this is the mooring post to which the boat carrying James the Apostle tied up to the quayside along the river bank here. And, just as St. James relics in Santiago were covered over with the basilica church, so too this sacred spot is covered over with the present church. The stone was, allegedly, also a Roman altar dedicated to Neptune. A handsome replica is built alongside the river on the opposite side of the bridge and may evoke a somewhat more authentic response to the legend. It is certainly easier to imagine a boat coming alongside here to tie up with its sacred cargo. Inside the church we find a fine 16th century Gothic pulpit with an image of Santiago Peregrino, while a glass case houses the image of Santiago Matamoros, slaying the Moors as the spearhead of the Reconquista. A recently restored 18th century oil painting has a more peaceful image of St. James body being carried across the sea accompanied by his faithful disciples.

Immediately over the bridge on the western bank (on the way to the pilgrim hostel) we pass the emblematic drinking font and roadside monument ❷ **Fonte do Carme** *XVI* displaying the arrival of the sarcophagus of St. James with his disciples Theodore and Athanasius and the scene of the conversion and baptism of the pagan Queen Lupa. And standing prominently above is the imposing facade of ❸ **Convento do Carme** *XVIII* with its extensive balcony in front with fine views over the town. Nearby is one of the best kept Santiago secrets and little visited ❹ **Monte Santiaguiño** here, legend tells us, is where St. James first preached the gospel message. Standing imposingly above the river it is not difficult to envisage

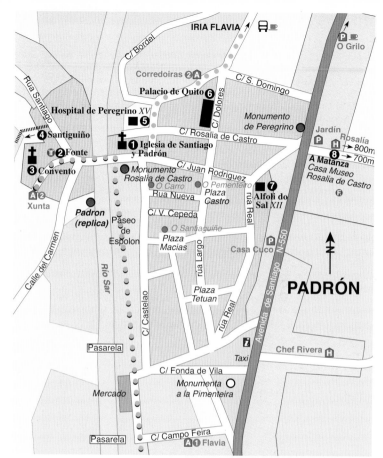

him delivering Christ's message of unconditional love and forgiveness from this remote and peaceful place. It is accessed, somewhat inconspicuously, between two houses on the road to Noia (just beyond the Fonte do Carme). Adjoining Santiaguiño Mount is the small chapel of Santiaguiño with a stone motif of the apostle baptising a pilgrim with water poured from a scallop shell. While it is located less than a kilometre from the town centre it is a very steep climb up the stone steps along the Stations of the Cross but well worth the effort to this most significant of Jacobean sites that forms the front cover of this guide. Just as the vast majority of pilgrims (as well as the population at large) believe there is only one camino de Santiago they also mistakenly believe that St. James arrived in Spain dead – not alive. They therefore miss, perhaps, the most important part of the Santiago story – his life and teaching rather than his death and burial.

❺ **Hospital de Peregrinos** *XV*. The medieval pilgrim hostal adjoining the church of St. James. ❻ **Palacio de Quito** *XVIII* century Palace of the Bishop of Quito. *(see next stage for* **Colegiata de Santa María de Iria Flavia** *and* **Museo de Cela***).* ❼ **Alfoli do Sal** *XII* century former salt depot and one of the oldest extant building in Padrón (now a café). While not connected directly with the Santiago story, don't miss the most visited museum in Galicia ❽ **A Matanza** – Casa Museo *Rosalía de Castro* (1837 – 1885) is the house where she lived, wrote some of her exceptionally beautiful prose and died (see photo next page). It is lovingly maintained in its original condition and set in peaceful and delightfully shaded gardens. Some of her works are available from the museum shop (with translations from Gallego into Castellano and English). The house is situated just outside the town centre 700 meters from the main road. *Directions:* Take the Calle Salgado Araujo between the Botanical Gardens and the Pensión Jardín, continue over the river cutting (connecting the río Sar and río Ulla) and immediately over the railway turn left and the museum is on your right after 100 meters.

And don't miss sampling a plate of the famous Padrón Peppers *Pemento de Padrón* cultivated exclusively in nearby Herbón a delicious combination of sweet and piquant flesh with only one in every 30 or so being chilli-hot – The added fun is you never know which one! *Restaurante O'Pementeiro* in Plaza do Castro specialises in them and you can order as a *tapas* from the bar without having to wait for the excellent restaurant (upstairs) to open. Many cafés and restaurants in the area offer this local speciality. The seeds were imported by the Franciscan monks of Herbón during their missionary work in Central and South America which adapted to the soil conditions found locally.

REFLECTIONS:

❏ **The eye with which I see God, is the same eye with which God sees me.**
Meister Eckhart.

23 *24.9 km (15.5 miles) – Santiago*

PADRÓN – SANTIAGO

ⅢⅢⅢⅢⅢⅢ --- ---	7.5	--- ---	30%
▭▭▭ --- ---	13.8	--- ---	55%
▬▬▬ --- ---	3.6	--- ---	15%
Total km	**24.9 km** (15.5 ml)		

◣▬◢ 26.6 km (+^340m=1.7 km)
Alto(*m*)▲ Monte Agro 260m (853 ft)
< Ⓐ Ⓗ > Areal **8.5** km / Teo **10.4** km

The Practical Path: This final stage into Santiago provides us with a varied day's walking and the inevitable stretches of main road that gets increasingly busy as we near the city. However, we still manage 30% on natural pathways through oak, pine and eucalyptus woodlands offering shade and respite from the traffic. There are also several cafés and alternative accommodation along the N-550, and drinking fonts at regular intervals. This stage also has the detour to Castro Lupario, so if you want to push through the undergrowth and sit atop the pile of stones (all that remains of Lupa's hill fortress) allow yourself an extra two hours. Alternatively stay at one of the nearby pilgrim hostels in Teo or the casa rural in Parada de Francos and make your way into Santiago at a leisurely pace in the morning to make the pilgrim mass at noon.

0.0 km **Padrón Albergue** Leaving the Xunta hostel cross back over the river Sar via the medieval bridge turning <left past the church of Santiago **[0.2 km]** and make your way through the streets of the old quarter of Padrón along rua Dolores with the 18th century Palace of the Bishop of Quito *Palacio de Quito* (left) emerging onto open ground with the river on your (left) and the main road over to your (right). We pass the bus station **[0.4 km]** with regular services to Santiago throughout the day and *café* (opens early). Next we cross a channel connecting the rivers Sar and Ulla and cross [!] the main road **N-550 [0.4 km]** with several *cafés* on either side *(open early for breakfast)* and join the rail line before entering the ancient bishopric of Iria Flavia **[0.1 km]**.

1.1 km **Iria Flavia** Colegiate church of Santa María de Iria and the adjacent cemetery of Adina mentioned in Rosalía de Castro's melancholy poetry. It was here in 1885 that, as she had wished, Rosalía de Castro was buried. You can see her grave*stone* along the wall adjoining the main road. In a cruel twist of fate, her body was exhumed and moved to the Pantheon in Santo Domingo de Bonaval in Santiago. The medieval church was originally dedicated to Santa Eulalia and was ransacked by Almanzor in 997. It was later reconstructed and re-dedicated

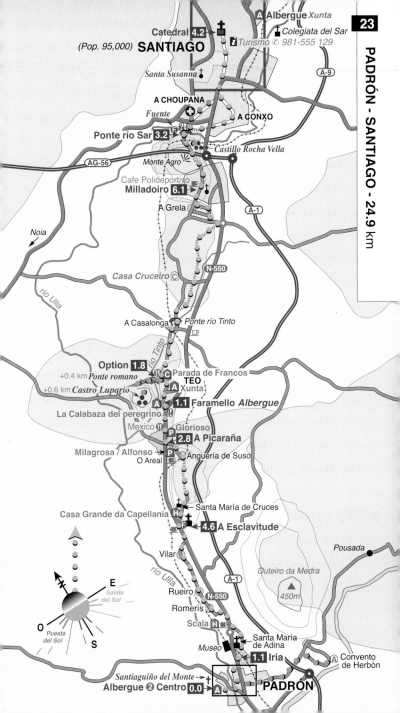

A **Albergue** *Xunta*

Catedral 4.2

Colegiata del Sar

(Pop. 95,000) **SANTIAGO**

i *Turismo* ☏ 981-555 129

Santa Susanna

A-9

A CHOUPANA

Fuente

A CONXO

Ponte río Sar 3.2

Castillo Rocha Vella

Monte Agro

AG-56

Cafe Polideportivo

Milladoiro 6.1

A-1

A Grela

Noia

N-550

Casa Cruceiro C

río Ulla

río Tinto

A Casalonga   *Ponte río Tinto*

Option 1.8

+0.4 km *Ponte romano*   **Parada de Francos**

+0.6 km *Castro Lupario*   **TEO**

A **Xunta**

A   1.1 **Faramello** *Albergue*

La Calabaza del peregrino

Mexico   P **Glorioso**

2.8 **A Picaraña**

Milagrosa / Alfonso   P   *Anguería de Suso*

O Areal

Santa María de Cruces

Casa Grande da Capellania H

4.6 **A Esclavitude**

Vilar

río Ulla

A-1

Outeiro da Medra

Pousada

N-550

Rueiro

450m

Romeris

Scala H

Museo   *Santa María de Adina*

1.1 **Iria**

A *Convento de Herbón*

E
Salida del Sol

O
Puesta del Sol
S

Santiaguiño del Monte →

Albergue ❷ **Centro** 0.0   A   **PADRÓN**

to the Virgin Mary, a sign of increasing Marian devotion along the Camino at this time. Xelmírez of Santiago further embellished the church in the Romanesque style in the 12th century and accorded it collegiate status. During the 13th century it was expanded along the lines of a basilica and was changed again during the Baroque period by the munificence of the Bishop of Quito (who was born in Padrón) and who commissioned the architect Melchor de Velasco to build the chapel of San Ildefonso.

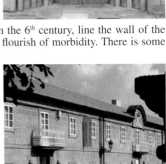

Open sarcophagi, reputedly from the 6th century, line the wall of the church and provides the whole with a final flourish of morbidity. There is some shade by the entrance with *[F.]*.

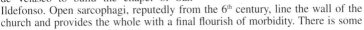

On the opposite side of the main road is the house of the cannons now principally the museum and office of the Camilo José Cela Foundation. Like Rosalía de Castro, he lived in Padrón and wrote some of his famous works here. He was awarded the Nobel Prize for Literature in 1989, *'for a rich and intensive prose, which with restrained compassion forms a challenging vision of man's vulnerability.'* He died in 2002. Adjoining is the Cela Railway Museum also housed in this fine 18th century terrace. Cela's maternal grandfather, John Trulock, was a Scot and built the first railway in Galicia.

We now pass to the rear of the church and make our way over the railway line [!] **[0.5 km]** emerging back onto the N-550 [!] passing the modern *H*⁺⁺⁺ **Scala** €40 *Ⓒ* 981 811 31 and *Café* **N-550 A Rua [1.0 km]** continue s/o and turn off <left by a small garage *Talleres Casal* **[0.3 km]** to take a quiet road *(that runs between the railway and N-550)* part of which has overhanging vines and granite horreos as we pass through a collection of small hamlets **Quintáns**, **Rueiro** over stream **[0.8 km]** and thence through **Cambela** and **Vilar**. We now take a short stretch of track by the rail line to emerge back onto the **N-550 [1.6 km]** [!] in **Loureiro** *Café Rianxeira* for a noisy but brief stretch to **A Escravitude [0.4 km]**:

4.6 km **A Escravitude** *[F.]* Another famous Marian shrine built in the early 18th century over a fountain, site of a miracle that took place in 1732. It is an enormous Baroque sanctuary, and like the church at Iria, has the N-550 built hard up against both the fountain and the church. Not a peaceful place to pray or slake the thirst but *Café-bar Anaga* nearby has refreshments. On the corner is *CR Grande da Capellanía* €40 incl. *Ⓒ* 981 509 854 also *Restaurante Pardal and off route [+200m] in Muiños casa rural CR da Meixida Ⓒ* 981 811 113 c/ Esclavitud *(from €50)*. Proceed around the small park at the side of the sanctuary and up a steep country lane past the Romanesque church of **Sta. María de Cruces [0.3 km]** and up along an asphalt road to turn off <left onto **path [0.7 km]** through peaceful pine woods over rail line at **Picaraña Abaixo [0.8 km]** and through the village of **Anguería de Suso** and back down to the N-550 at **Areal [1.0 km]**.

2.8 km **Picaraña** *(Areal / A Gandaría)* choice of Pensiónes (from €20) and restaurants along the main road opposite the industrial estate. *P* **Milagrosa** *Ⓒ*

668 862 874 and *P Glorioso* Ⓒ 981 803 181 above restaurant of the same name. We have another one kilometre stretch of main road up to a steep bend where we need to cross over [!] at sign for ***Faramello*** [**1.0** km] passing the ancient Pazo do Faramello (left) to Lugar del Faramello [**0.1** km] *Concelho de Teo:*

1.1 km **Faramello** *Alb.* ❶ La Calabaza Del Peregrino *Priv.[40÷4]*+ €10-12 Ⓒ 981 194 244 *(María Rodriguez)* Lg Faramello 5. Renovated stone house with café (expensive). Continue s/o past *[F.]* (right) to fork in the road ❖ and ***albergue sign Teo*** [**0.8** km] 100m *off* route up to the right. *Alb.* ❷ Teo *Xunta.[24÷2]*+ €6. I km further up on the main road (past Casa Tonceda) is *Café Casa Javier* and several other restaurants along the noisy main road.

At the fork ❖ the camino continues down left to the río Tinto and up sharply to the ermita de San Martiño and cruceiro do Francos [**0.6** km] one of the oldest wayside crosses in Galicia (see photo right). It is here we also join the ancient pilgrim way, which still retains its original name *rua de Francos* and leads us to the shaded village green with casa rural and optional detour in ***Parada de Francos*** [**0.4** km].

1.8 km **Parada de Francos** *Option* ❖ *CR* Casa Parada de Francos €45+ Ⓒ 981 538 004 Rúa de Francos opp. *Restaurante Carboeiro* tranquil location amongst the ancient oaks directly on the camino. Detour here to *Castro Lupario:*

Castro Lupario

Detour 1.1 km Castro Lupario (one of the sites associated with legendary queen Lupa central to the Santiago story): Round trip 2.2 km (ruins only – no standing buildings). Access has recently been improved but you may have to push through the undergrowth. Allow around 2 hours to give yourself some time for reflection amongst the ancient stones and to admire the view. This route is not waymarked but a sign on the road now points to the start of the track and indicates the hillfort. ***Directions***: make your way diagonally over to the far side of the square and take the asphalt road by the modern house (no. 56). As you turn the corner, a distant view of Castro Lupario opens up in front of you (see photo). Proceed down to the río Tinto (a tributary of the Sar which in turn flows into the Ulla at Padrón) and cross over on the original and beautifully preserved ***Roman bridge [400m]***. Continue up the asphalt road into the Concello de Brión and proceed to the top of the short incline and just where the road begins to drop down again over on the left hand side of the road is a rough ***lay-by [200m]***. Proceed along the track and after *[150m]* ***turn up right*** onto the ancient stone access route that winds its way up around the ***hill for [350m]***. The fort extends over the entire hilltop which is surprisingly level with a diameter of 100m. Make your way to the stand of stunted oak trees that struggle for a root hold amidst the ruins and let your imagination loose. It certainly evokes a greater sense of mystery than the alternative sites at Castro de Lobeira overlooking the ria Arousa and the Pico Santo. From the ancient ruins here it is not difficult to imagine the pagan rituals, wild bulls and wolves which are all intimately connected with the fabled story of Queen Lupa and Sant Iago's faithful disciples searching for a site in which to bury his mortal remains.

❖ From the option point in the Village square take the road between the casa rural and restaurant and head down the narrow track to short stretch of path before turning right> over **rail bridge [0.9** km] into *Osebe (O Seve)* turning right> and then <left *(just before the N-550 with café 200m off route)* past **Casalonga** school to cross medieval bridge over the río Tinto **[1.1 km]** where you can (perhaps) observe the red rocks providing us with the key to its name *[F.]*. Continue s/o over crossroads onto delightful **woodland path [0.3 km]** crossing **road [1.0 km]** *[Biduido: Casa do Cruceiro €45+ [+400m] © 981 548 596 aldea Raices]*. Continue s/o onto wide forest track before emerging onto road by factory and continue to new roundabout on the N-550 in **A Grela [1.3 km]**. Take the pilgrim track to join a quiet lane and take the 2nd turn <left up to the **main road [0.6 km]** and turn right> to climb steeply up to *Novo Milladoiro* **[0.7 km]** (the tiny chapel *Capela de María Magdalena* looks somewhat out of place amongst the towering modern luxury apartment blocks right). Continue along the main road for **[0.2 km]** to:

6.1 km Milladoiro *Polideportivo café* modern sports complex with café (left). *(Milladoiro is an exclusive new residential suburb of Santiago)*. S/o to the junction at the far end (radio mast) onto narrow asphalt track through eucalyptus passing the gates of the electricity utility *Union Fenosa* **[1.1 km]** to the high point of the day *Agro dos Monteiros* 260m and the Camino Portugués version of *Monte Gozo* with the spires of Santiago cathedral now visible just below the north / east horizon. Take the bridge over the AG-56 motorway turning <left onto woodland path that winds its way down to emerge between 2 houses in *A Rocha Vella*. Turn right> along the railway to bridge **[1.6 km]**. ❖

Detour 200m *Castelo de Rocha Vella* ● ● ● ● on the far side of the crash barrier is a path alongside the railway leading to Castelo de Rocha Vella site of the city's ancient fortified bishops residence. *Directions*: Head towards the electric pylon in the centre of the ruins. This historical area is presently undergoing excavation but the site is very accessible and has not (yet) been closed off to the public. If you visit be aware this is private land and take care not to disturb the ruins or fall into any of the open stone stairwells.

Proceed over the railway bridge at ❖ down steep lane turning right> at **junction [0.2 km]**. *[Detour 100m (left) to medieval fonte in shady dell above the banks of the river Sarela]*. continue on down to bridge over río Sarela **[0.3 km]**:

3.2 km Ponte río Sarela Note: a new route now enters Santiago via *Conxo*. This adds 0.7 km to the original road route but is quieter and well waymarked.

For the original road route proceed up (left) under city bypass past Universitario/ Hospital and down to a small park in *A Choupana*. Continue up to a modern block of apartments at Campo and turn <left along the main road into the city (church of Santa Marta opposite) merging into rua Rosalía de Castro to rejoin the alternative route as follows:

For the quieter alternative take the path up right> under bridge **[0.7 km]** taking a series of turns into rua da benéfica de Conxo up past Televés over roundabout into rua de Sanchez Freiré crossing the busy Av. Romero Donallo and rejoining the road route in rua Rosalía de Castro **[2.4 km]** Here we turn up right over Av. Coruña into Av. Xoán Carlos I turning <left up into the city park *Alameda* by Capilla del Pilar through the park passing over the busy ring road and the traditional Portuguese entrance *Porta Faxeira* **[0.7 km]** (The historic gate no longer exists). We now take our final steps towards the fabled cathedral down the narrow rua Franco, lined with bars and restaurants and pause, perhaps, at another of the little known gems of the caminos and one of the most historic of all the buildings in Santiago associated with St. James *Capela de Santiago (this tiny chapel is the place where, by tradition, the cart carrying the body of St. James from Finisterre came to a halt and the body was laid out awaiting its final resting place. The discreet shell above the door adjoining No.5 is easily bypassed).* We have taken our weary body on the self-same road and now we take our last few steps towards the cathedral. By tradition the pilgrim from Portugal turns up right into rua Fonseca into the *Praza das Praterías* to enter the cathedral by the south door. This was the particular entrance used by the medieval pilgrim travelling the Camino Portugués and remains the oldest doorway to the Cathedral dating back to the 11th century (1078). The magnificent stone carvings

surrounding this portal show hardly a hint of the intervening 900 years. St. James is represented in the centre between 2 cypress tress next to Christ **[0.4 km]**.

4.2 km **Santiago Cathedral**. Take time to just 'arrive'. We each feel different emotions on arriving at our destination after weeks of physical, emotional and spiritual challenges. Entering the cathedral can bring tears of joy… or disappointment. Whatever our individual reaction it is absolutely valid in that moment so honour it. Gratitude for our safe arrival is a universally appropriate response. However, if you are overwhelmed by the crowds why not return later when you might feel more composed and the cathedral is, perhaps, quieter. Whether now or later and whichever door you entered by, you might like to follow the timeworn pilgrim ritual as follows:

[1] Stand before the Tree of Jesse, the central column of Master Mateo's masterpiece: the Entrance of Glory *Pórtico da Gloria*. Millions of pilgrims, over the millennia, have worn finger holes in the solid marble as they placed their hands there as a mark of gratitude for their safe arrival (a barrier was placed here in 2007 to prevent further wear) but we can breathe in the beauty of this inner portico fashioned by Mateo in the 12th century (the outer porch was added in 1750). The Bible and its main characters come alive in this remarkable marble façade. The central column has Christ in Glory, flanked by the apostles and, directly underneath, St. James sits as intercessor between Christ and the pilgrim.

Proceed to the other side and [2] touch your brow to that of Maestro Mateo, whose kneeling figure is carved into the back of the central column (facing the altar), and receive some of his artistic genius in the ritual known as the head-butting saint *santo dos croques*. Proceed to the High Altar (right hand side) to ascend the stairs and [3] hug the Apostle. Perhaps lay your forehead on his broad shoulders and say what you came here to say. Whatever your motivation and beliefs you have arrived here in one piece because, on some level, of the call of St. James. Proceed down the steps to the far side to the crypt and the reliquary chapel under the altar. [4] Here, you can kneel before the casket containing the relics of the great Saint and offer your prayer. A Pilgrim mass takes place every day at 12-noon. The swinging of the giant incense burner *Botafumeiro* was originally used to fumigate the sweaty (and possibly disease ridden) pilgrims. Requiring half a dozen assistants known as *Tiraboleiros* it became a rare occurrence, but it is used increasingly during mass these days. It is certainly a very moving and unique experience despite the constant sound and sight of flashlights. Perhaps the photo in this guide will suffice for your own memories so you can enter the whole experience more fully without having to think of composing your own shot.

REFLECTIONS:

_____
_____
_____
_____
_____
_____
_____
_____
_____
_____
_____
_____
_____
_____
_____
_____
_____
_____

Before a new chapter is begun, the old one has to be finished. Stop being who you were and change into who You are. *Paulo Coelho*

4 squares surround the cathedral, as follows:

■ **Praza do Obradoiro**. The 'golden' square of Santiago is usually thronged with pilgrims and tourists admiring the dramatic west facing façade of the Cathedral, universal symbol of Santiago, with St. James looking down on all the activity from his niche in the central tower. This provides the main entrance to the Cathedral and the Portico de Gloria. To the right of the steps is the discrete entrance to the museum.
A combined ticket will provide access to all rooms including the crypt and the cloisters and also to the 12th century palace of one of Santiago's most famous individuals and first archbishop, Gelmírez *Pazo de Xelmírez* situated on the (left). In this square we also find the beautiful Renaissance façade of the Parador named after Ferdinand and Isabel *Hostal dos Reis Católicos* on whose orders it was built in 1492 as a pilgrim hospice. Opposite the Cathedral is the more austere neoclassical seat of the Galician government and town hall *Pazo de Raxoi* with its solid arcade. Finally, making up the fourth side of the square is the gable end of the *Colegio de S. Jerónimo* part of the university. Moving anti-clockwise around the cathedral – turn up into Rúa de Fonseca to:

■ **Praza das Praterías**. The most intimate of the squares with its lovely centrepiece, an ornate statue of horses leaping out of the water. On the corner of Rúa do Vilar we find the Dean's House *Casa do Deán* now the **pilgrim office.** Along the walls of the Cathedral itself are the silversmith's *prateros* that give the square its name. Up the steep flight of steps we come to the magnificent southern door to the Cathedral, the oldest extant doorway and traditionally the entrance taken by pilgrims coming from Portugal. The quality of the carvings and their arrangement is remarkable and amongst the many sculptured figures is one of St. James between two cypress trees. Continuing around to the right we come to:

■ **Praza da Quintana.** This wide square is identified by the broad sweep of steps separating the lower part *Quintana of the dead* from the upper *Quintana of the living*. Opp the Cathedral is the wall of the *Mosteiro de San Paio de Antealtares* (with museum of sacred art). The square provides the eastern entrance to the Cathedral via the Holy Gate *Porta Santa* sometime referred to as the Door of Pardon *El Perdón* only opened during Holy Years (the next in 2021). Adjoining it is the main entrance to the Cathedral shop that has several guidebooks (in various languages) with details of the Cathedral's many chapels and their interesting carvings and statuary and the priceless artefacts and treasures in the museum. Finally, we head up the broad flight of steps around the corner and back into:

■ **Praza da Inmaculada (Azabachería)** to the north facing Azabachería façade, with the least well-known doorway and the only one that *descends* to enter the Cathedral. It has the most weathered aspect, with moss and lichen covering its bleak exterior. Opposite the cathedral is the imposing southern edifice of *Mosteiro de San Martiño Pinario* the square in front gets any available sun and attracts street artists. The archbishop's arch *Arco Arzobispal* brings us back to the Praza do Obradoiro.

Check-in at the **Pilgrim Office** *Oficina del Peregrino* (formerly rua Vilar) now rua Carretas *below the parador* © 981 568 846 open daily 09:00-21:00 (10:00-20:00 winter). The office issues the *compostela* and welcomes pilgrims with teams of *Amigos* an initiative of the Irish Society and the CSJ in London who offer help with queries. Here we also find toilets and backpack storage to facilitate unencumbered exploration of the city and a notice board for pilgrim messages. Providing you have fulfilled the criteria of a bona-fide pilgrim and walked at least the last 100 km (200 km on bike or horseback) for religious / spiritual reasons and collected 2 stamps per day on your credencial you will be awarded a certificate of completion

Compostela. This may entitle you to certain privileges such as reduced entry fees to museums and a free meal at the Parador.

•**The Camino Chaplaincy** offers Mass in English in the Cathedral 10.30 & 18:00 daily May–Oct. •**Camino Companions** meet in the Pilgrims Office on rua Carretas 9:00 & 14:30 daily May–Oct for reflection and integration (see CC facebook for updates). •**Pilgrim House** rua Nova 19 also offers a place of welcome and reflection 11:00–20:00 (closed Wed & Sun) under the care of Terra Nova USA.

❏ **Turismo:** ❖ r/Vilar, 63 Ⓒ 981-555 129 *June-Sept 09-21 / Oct-May 10-15 & 17-20.* ❖ *Kiosco* Plaza do Galicia. ❖ *TurGalicia* r/do Vilar.43 Ⓒ 981 584 081.
❏ **Luggage storage** (Ivar Rekve) Ⓒ 603 466 490 Travesa Universidade 1.

❏*Albergues:* ❶ – ❾ (accessed from the camino francés). *€–depending on season)*
❾● La Salle *Priv.[84÷10]* €17-19 c/de Tras de Santa ClaraⒸ 981 584 611. 10●
Meiga Backpackers *Priv.[30÷5]* €10-13 c/Basquiños, 67 with garden. Ⓒ 981 570
846. 11● O Fogar de Teodomiro *Priv.[20÷5]* €15+ Plaza Algalia de Arriba,3
Ⓒ 981 582 920. 12● The Last Stamp *Priv.[62÷10]* €12-18 r/Preguntorio,10. Ⓒ
981 563 525. 13● Azabache *Priv.[20÷5]* €13-18 c/Azabachería,15 Ⓒ 981 071
254. 14● Mundoalbergue *Priv.[34÷1]* €12-€17 c/San Clemente, 26 Ⓒ 981 588
625. 15● Roots & Boots *Priv.[48÷8]* €12-18 r/Campo Cruceiro do Galo Ⓒ 699
631 594. 16● La Estación *Priv.[24÷2]* €12 r/Xoana Nogueira, 14 Ⓒ 981 594
624 (½ km *far* side of railway station). *Alb.* ❸ Compostela Inn *Priv.[120÷30]*+
€12-15 Ⓒ 981 819 030 Carretera de A Estrada Km 3.
❏ *Hotels:* ■ *€30 – €60:* Hs Moure Ⓒ 981 583 637 r/dos Loureiros. *Hs* Moure-II
r/Laureles 12. *H* Fonte de San Roque Ⓒ 981 554 447 r/do Hospitalillo, 8. *Hs* La
Campana Ⓒ 981 584 850 Campanas de San Juan, 4. *Hs* Estrela Ⓒ 981 576 924
Plaza de San Martín Pinario, 5-2° *Hospedería* San Martín Pinario Ⓒ 981 560
282 Praza da Inmaculada. Pico Sacro r/San Francisco, 22 y Pico Sacro II Ⓒ 981
584 466. La Estela Ⓒ 981 582 796 rua Raxoi, 1. *Hs* Barbantes Ⓒ 981581 077 r/
do Franco, 3. Santa Cruz Ⓒ 981 582 362 r/do Vilar, 42. *Hs* Suso Ⓒ 981 586 611
r/do Vilar, 65. San Jaime Ⓒ 981 583 134 r/do Vilar, 12-2°. A Nosa Casa Ⓒ 981
585 926 r/Entremuralles, 9. *Hs* Mapoula Ⓒ 981 580 124 r/Entremuralles, 10. *Hs*
Alameda Ⓒ 981 588 100 San Clemente, 32 ■ *€60+:* H Rua Vilar Ⓒ 981 557
102 r/Vilar, 12-2° *H* Airas Nunes Ⓒ 902 405 858 r/do Vilar, 17. Entrecercas Ⓒ
981 571 151 r/Entrecercas. Costa Vella Ⓒ 981 569 530 Porta de Pena, 17. MV
Algalia Ⓒ 981 558 111 Praziña da Algalia de Arriba, 5. ■ *€100+:* H**** San
Francisco Campillo de San Francisco ⒸⒸ981 581 634. H****Hostal de los Reyes
Católicos Plaza Obradoiro Ⓒ 981 582 200. *Malak Bistro* V. Rúa das Orfas 27.
❏ *Centro Histórico:* ❶ Convento de Santo Domingo de Bonaval XIIIth *(panteón
de Castelao, Rosalía de Castro y museo do Pobo Galego).* ❷ Casa Gótica XIVth
museo das Peregrinaciónes-1. ❸ Mosteiro de San Martín Pinario XVIth *y museo*
■ *Prazo Obradoiro* ❹ Pazo de Xelmirez XIIth ❺ Catedral XIIth –XVIIIth *Portica
de Gloria, claustro, museo e tesouro da catedral* ❻ Hostal dos Reis Católicos
XVth *Parador* ❼ Pazo de Raxoi XVIIIth *Presendencia da Xunta* ❽ Colexio de
Fonseca XVIth *universidade y claustro.* ❾ Casa do Deán XVIIIth *Oficina do
Peregrino.* 10● Casa Canónica *museo Peregrinaciónes-2.* 11● Mosteiro de San
Paio de Antealtares XVth *Museo de Arte Sacra.* 12● S.Maria Salomé XIIth.

Santiago is a wonderful destination, full of vibrancy and colour. Pilgrims, street artists, musicians, dancers, tourists... all come and add to the life and soul of this fabled city. Stay awhile and visit her museums and markets. Soak up some of her culture or relax in the delightful shaded park *Alameda* and climb to the *capela de Santa Susanna* hidden in the trees or stroll up the Avenue of the Lions *Paseo dos Leónes* to the statue of Rosalia de Castro and look out west over her belovéd Galicia and... *Finis terre.*

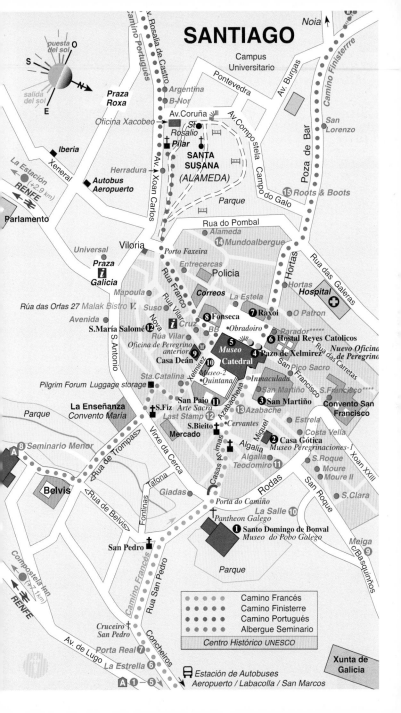

15a　*24.9 km – Santiago de Compostela*

VILA do CONDE – MARINHAS
Póvoa de Varzim　　*Esposende*

....	--- --- 3.7	--- ---	13%
▬▬▬	--- ---24.8	--- ---	87%
▬▬▬	--- --- 0.0	--- ---	00%
Total km	**28.5 km** (17.7 ml)		

▲ --- ---29.0 km (^100m+ 0.5km)
Alto ▲　Vila do Conde 8 m (853 ft)

< 🅐 🅗 >　Póvoa Varzim **3.9** km – Praia Santo Andrés **9.2** – *Praia Estela* **14.8** *(+0.5)* – Apulia **17.8** *(+0.6)* – *Fão* **21.5** *(+0.2)* – Esposende **24.2** km.

Campos de Masseira

■ Póvoa de Varzim: Turismo: Praça Marquês de Pombal ✆ 252 298 120. *Alb.* **São José de Ribamar** S. Miguel *Mun.[16÷1]* €-donativo ✆ 252 622 314 (paróquia) Av. Mouzinho de Albuquerque 11. *Hs* **Sardines and Friends** €35± ✆ 962 083 329 Rua da Ponte 4 *(Praça Republica)*. *H** **Luso Brasileiro** €45± 252 690 710 Rua Dos Cafés, 16. *H*** **Grande Hotel** €55± ✆ 252 290 400 Largo do Passeio Alegre, nº 20. **■ Estalagem de Santo Andre** Av. de S. André €55± ✆ 252 615 666. **■ Praia Estela:** *Rio Alto (Orbitur)* €8-16+ ✆ 252 615 699 Parque de Campismo Orbitur Rio Alto. **■ Apulia:** *Apulia Praia Hotel* €40± ✆ 253 989 290 Av. da Praia 45. **■ Fão:** *Pousada da Juventude Foz do Cavado* €20± ✆ 253 982 045 Alameda do Bom Jesus Fão. *H****Parque do Rio* €40± ✆ 253 981 521 Caminho Padre Manuel Sá Pereira, Ofir. **■ Esposende: Turismo:** Rua Sra. da Saúde,40 ✆ 253 960 100 *H**Mira Rio* €40± ✆ 253 964 430 Rua da Ponte D. Luis Filipe 113. **Clube Pinhal da Foz** €55± ✆ 253 961 098 R. Pinhal da Foz. *H***Zende* €40± ✆ 253 969 090 Av. Dr. Henrique. *H***Suave Mar* €50± ✆ 253 969 400 Av. Eng. Eduardo Arantes e Oliveira. **■ Marinhas:** *Alb.*S. Miguel *Mun.[34÷2]* €-donativo ✆ 967 611 200 Cruz Vermelha. *(Via Veteris: Associação Jacobeia de Esposende: Manuel Miranda* ✆ 962 748 657 *e José Costa* 933 561 896)*.
● ● ● ● **Rates – Esposende** *alternativo:*

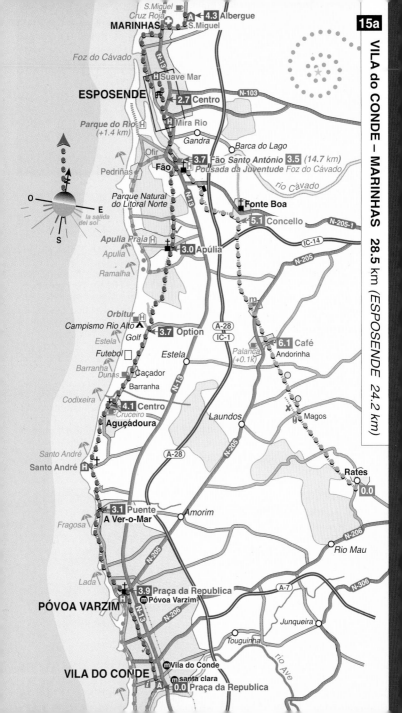

S.Miguel
Cruz Roja
A ◄ 4.3 Albergue
MARINHAS
S.Miguel

N-13

Foz do Cávado

H Suave Mar

ESPOSENDE
2.7 Centro
N-103

H Mira Rio
Gandra

Parque do Rio
(+1.4 km)

Barca do Lago
Ofir
3.7 Fão Santo António 3.5 (14.7 km)
Fão
Pousada da Juventude Foz do Cávado
Pedriñas
rio Cávado

Parque Natural
do Litoral Norte
Fonte Boa

N-13
5.1 Concello
N-205-1

Apulia Praia H
3.0 Apúlia
IC-14
Apulia
N-205
Ramalha

Orbitur
Campismo Rio Alto
3.7 Option
A-28
IC-1
m
6.1 Café
Estela Golf
Palanca
(+0.1k) Andorinha
Futebol
Estela

Barranha
Dunas Caçador
Barranha
Codixeira
Laundos Magos

4.1 Centro
Cruceiro
Aguçádoura
A-28
N-209

Santo André
Santo André H
Rates
0.0

3.1 Puente
A Ver-o-Mar
Amorim
N-206
Fragosa

N-205
Rio Mau

Lada
3.9 Praça da Republica
m Póvoa Varzim
A-7
N-306
PÓVOA VARZIM
N-13 N-206
Junqueira

Touguinha

m Vila do Conde
VILA DO CONDE
m santa clara
rio Ave
A 0.0 Praça da Republica

O ← → E

S

la salida
del sol

16a *24.9 km – Santiago de Compostela*

MARINHAS – VIANA do CASTELO
Esposende

┅┅┅┅	--- --- 6.5 --- ---	*31%*
▬▬▬	--- ---14.8 --- ---	*69%*
▬▬▬	--- --- 0.0 --- ---	*00%*
Total km	**21.3 km** (13.2 ml)	

◢◣ ---22.8 km (^300m+ 1.5km)

Alto ▲ Vila do Conde 8 m (853 ft)

< 🅐 🅗 > Chafé **12.7** km – Darque **18.6** km.

Río Nieve

[Elevation profile: 100m Esposende — MARINHAS (A) 0 km — Bolinho 5 km — Alto 140m▲ — rio Nieve — Chafé (C) — Anha 10 km — Monumento 110m▲ — 15 km — VIANA do CASTELO / Darque (H) 20 — rio Cávado — rio Lima]

Camino da Costa: ● ● ● ● ▮ **Chafé** *CR* Casa da Reina €60+ ✆ 258 351 882 Caminho do Pardinheiro, 122. ▮ **Darque:** *H°°* Club Postilhão €55+ ✆ 258 331 031 Rua das flores, 115 (N-13). *Hs* Don Augusto ✆ 258 322 491 Restaurante Residencial Tr. Antúrios, 60 (N-13). ▮ **VIANA DO CASTELO: Turismo:** Praça da Liberdade (rotunda) ✆ 258 098 415 / 913 348 813 > *Alb.* São João da Cruz dos Caminhos *[20-60÷2]* €5-15 ✆ 258 822 264 (Padres Carmelitas Descalços) Convento do Carmo, 1. **Pousada de Juventude** €11-13 ✆ 258 838 458 Rua de Limia. *H°°°* Do Parque €40 ✆ 258 828 605 Praça da Galiza. *H°°* Calatrava €35 ✆ 258 828 911 R. Manuel Fiúza Júnior 157. < *H°°°°* Fábrica do Chocolate €90 ✆ 258 244 000 R. do Gontim 60. *Hs* Zimborio €35 ✆ 938 354 863 Rua Gago Coutinho, 26. *P* Laranjeira €35 ✆ 258 822 258 R. Manuel Espregueira 24. *H°°* Laranjeira €55 ✆ 258 822 261 R. Cândido dos Reis 45. *Hs* Senhora do Carmo Rua Grande,72 ou Viela da Cega,44. *H°°* Jardim €40 ✆ 258 828 915 Largo 5 de Outubro 68. *P* Margarida Da Praca €38 ✆ 965 526 692 Largo 5 de Outubro 58. **Senda Litoral:** ● ● ● ● ▮ **Belinho** *Camping* Os Belinhenses ✆ 933 612 546. ▮ **Amorosa** *H°°* Areias Claras €40 ✆ 258 351 014 Rua da Praia. ▮ **Cabedelo** *Darque Camping* Orbitur INATEL ✆ 258 322 042. Av. dos Trabalhadores.

[Map: VIANA do CASTELO — rua Dr. Moisés Alves Pinho, S.Luzia, N-202, Elevador Santa Luzia, rua Portela de Cima, Pasarela, Túnel, estação, Taxi, N-13, Largo 9 Abril, Cruz Vermelha, Câmara, Santiago, Laranjeira, r/Nova Santana, r/do Aveiro, M.F.Júnior, Calatrava, r/Bandeira, Fonte, Concello, S.João da Cruz, Zimborio, Catedral, Chocolate, r/Gontim, Parque, Carmo, t/S.Pedro, r/M.Barbosa, Av.Luís de Camões, Av.Atlântico, Margarida da Praça, Jardim, Alves Cerqueira, Turismo, Limia, Ferry – Cabedelo, rio Lima]

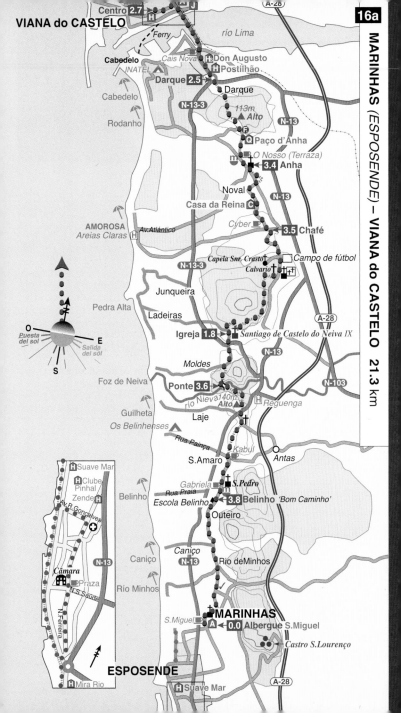

VIANA do CASTELO

16a

MARINHAS (ESPOSENDE) – VIANA do CASTELO 21.3 km

Centro 2.7

H J

río Lima

Ferry

Cabedelo

Cais Nova

H Don Augusto

INATEL

H Postilhão

Darque 2.5

Cabedelo

Darque

Rodanho

N-13-3

113m

▲ *Alto*

N-13

Q Paço d'Anha

F

🍴 *O Nosso (Terráza)*

m ✚ **3.4 Anha**

Noval

N-13

Casa da Reina C

Cyber ✚ **3.5 Chafé**

AMOROSA
Areias Claras H

Av.Atlántico

Capela Snr. Crasto ✝ ☐ *Campo de fútbol*

Calvario ✝ ✝✝✝

Junqueira

N-13-3

Pedra Alta

Ladeiras

A-28

Igreja 1.8 ✚ *Santiago de Castelo do Neiva IX*

Moldes

N-13

Ponte 3.6

Foz de Neiva

río Nieva *140m*

▲ *Alto*

H *Reguenga*

N-103

Guilheta

Os Belinhenses ▲

Laje ✝

Rua Painça

Kabul

S.Amaro

○ *Antas*

Gabriela ✝ **S.Pedro**

Belinho

H

Rua Praia

Escola Belinho ▲ **3.8 Belinho** *'Bom Caminho'*

Outeiro

Caniço

Caniço

N-13

Rio deMinhos

Río Minhos

✓

✝ **MARINHAS**

S.Miguel A **0.0 Albergue** S.Miguel

Castro S.Lourenço

ESPOSENDE (inset)

H Suave Mar

Clube
Pinhal
Zende H

H

Av.R.Gonçalves

✚

N-13

Câmara
🏛 ☐ Praza

N.S.Saúde

N.Ferreira

H Mira Rio

ESPOSENDE

H Suave Mar

A-28

17a *24.9 km – Santiago de Compostela*

VIANA do CASTELO – CAMINHA

Monte Tecla

España
Río Minho

....	--- ---10.9	--- ---	40%
————	--- ---16.5	--- ---	60%
————	--- --- 0.0	--- ---	00%
Total km	**27.4 km** (17.0 ml)		

▰◣ --- ---29.2 km (^365m+ 1.8km)
Alto ▲ Cruceiro 150m (492 ft)
< 🏠 🏨 > Areosa **4.8** km – Afife **12.1** km – Âncora **18.7** km.

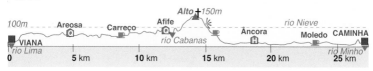

Alto +150m
100m   **Areosa**   **Afife**   *rio Nieve*
   Carreço   **Âncora**   **Moledo**   **CAMINHA**
VIANA   *rio Cabanas*   *rio Minho*
rio Lima
0   **5 km**   **10 km**   **15 km**   **20 km**   **25 km**

∎ **Areosa:** *Q* **Quinta da Boa Viagem** €70+ ℰ2 58 835 835 rua da Boa Viagem.
∎ **Carreço:** *CR* **Casa do Nato** €75+ x2 (2 nights/noches) ℰ 258 834 041 rua do Moreno, 130. *[P Restaurante* Compostela ℰ *258 981 465 Estrada Nacional 13].*
∎ **Afife:** *[Casa D' Joao Enes* €65+ x2 (2 nights/noches) *258 817 880 Afife + 1km].*
CR **Casa de Santa Ana** €75+ x2 (2 nights/noches) ℰ 258 981 774 Caminho do Barroso, 357 Largo de Cabanas. *[CR Casade Trajinha* €65 *Caminho da Tomenga, 438 +2 km].* ∎ **Âncora:** *H**** **Meira** *(restaurante Dona Belinha)* €65+ ℰ 258 911 111 rua 5 de Outubro 56. *H** **Albergaria Quim Barreiros** €40 ℰ 258 959 100 rua Dr. Ramos Pereira 115 Praia de Âncora. *P** *Restaurante /Alojomento* **Portinho** ℰ 258 911 577 Rua dos Pescadores 22. ∎ **Camarido / Caminha:** *Apt/H* **Aldeamento Turistico do Camarido** €45 ℰ 258 722 130 Lugar da Joaninha, Cristelo. ∎ **CAMINHA: Turismo:** ℰ 258 921 952 Praça Conselheiro Silva Torres. *Alb. Peregrinos de* **Caminha** *[32÷2]* €5 ℰ 914 290 431 Av Padre Pinheiro *(adj. Café Zarcus y piscina municipal). H**** **Design & Wine** €65+ ℰ 258 719 040 Praça do Conselheiro Silva Torres 8. *Residencial* **Galo D`ouro** €35+ ℰ 258 921 160 rua da Corredoura 15. *P** **Arca Nova** 35+ ℰ 935 390 402 Largo Sidónio Pais. *P** **Muralha de Caminha** €60 ℰ 258 728 199 rua Barão de S.Roque 69.

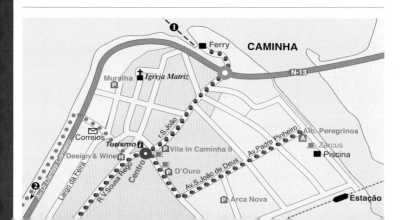

❶   ∎ Ferry   **CAMINHA**
N-13
Muralha   ✝ *Igreja Matriz*
✉ Correios
Turismo ℹ   r.S.João   Alb. Peregrinos
Design & Wine   P Vila in Caminha II   Av. Padre Pinheiro   🅰 Zarcus   ∎ Piscina
Centro   P D'Ouro   Av.S.João de Deus
R.V. Sousa Rego
Av. Dantes Carneiro
P Arca Nova   **Estação**
❷

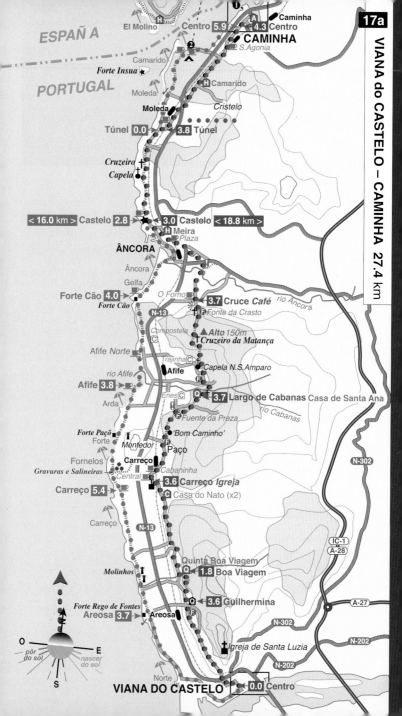

ESPAÑA A

El Molino

Centro 5.9   **A** **4.3 Centro**

Caminha

CAMINHA

S.Agonia

Camarido

2

PORTUGAL

Forte Insua ★

H Camarido

Moleda

Cristelo

Moleda

Túnel 0.0   **3.8 Túnel**

Cruzeira ✝

Capela ●

< 16.0 km > Castelo 2.8   ★   **3.0 Castelo < 18.8 km >**

H Meira

Plaza

ÂNCORA

Âncora

Gelfa

Forte Cão 4.0
Forte Cão   *O Forno*   **3.7 Cruce *Café***
N-13   ✝ F *Fonte da Crasto*   *río Ancora*

Compostela C   ▲ **Alto** *150m*
✝ *Cruzeiro da Matança*

Afife *Norte*   *Trajinha* C   ✝
Capela N.S.Amparo

río Afife   ● Afife   F

Afife 3.8   *Enes* C   Q F **3.7 Largo de Cabanas** Casa de Santa Ana
río Cabanas

Arda

F *Fuente da Preza*

Forte Paçõ   'Bom Caminho'
Forte   F
Montedor   **Paço**

Fornelos   Carreço
Gravuras e Salineiras   *Cabaninha*
Central   **3.6 Carreço *Igreja***

Carreço 5.4   C *Casa do Nato (x2)*

Carreço

N-13

N-302

Molinhos ✝   Quinta Boa Viagem
Q **1.8 Boa Viagem**

IC-1
A-28

Forte Rego de Fontes   Q **3.6 Guilhermina**
Areosa 3.7   ■ **Areosa**   F

A-27

✝ *Igreja de Santa Luzia*

N-302   N-202

O —   E
pôr   *nascer*
do sol   *do sol*

N-202

Norte

VIANA do CASTELO   **0.0 Centro**

S

18a *24.9 km – Santiago*

CAMINHA – MOUGÁS

▦▦▦▦	--- ---10.1	--- ---	44%
▬▬▬	--- ---13.1	--- ---	56%
▭▭▭	--- --- 0.0	--- ---	00%
Total km	**23.2 km** (14.4 ml)		

◣◣◣ --- ---24.4 km (^240m+ 1.2km)

Alto ▲ Monte Tecla 100m (328 ft)

< 🅐 🅗 > A Guarda **3.8** km – Oia **16.7** km – Viladesuso **20.3** km.

Ferry

```
100m  Alto
▲     A GUARDA                              Monasterio Oia   Viladesuso MOUGÁS
FERRY   🅐                                         🅗      🅗      🅐
0          5 km          10 km          15 km          20 km
```

▌ **A Guarda: Senda Litoral:** ● ● ● ● *H*** El Molino** €45 ☎ 986 627 233 Playa de Camposancos. ▌ **Turismo:** Oficina Municipal ☎ 986 614 546 Plaza Relo. *Alb.* **Peregrinos** *[36÷2]* €6 ☎ Concello da Guarda 986 610 025 m: 696 986 515 Rua Puerto Rico, 7. *H* **Celta** €60 ☎ 986 610 445 Calle Rua De Galicia, 53. *H**Vila da Guarda** €30 ☎ 986 61 11 21 Calle Tomiño, 8. *H**Bruselas** €25 ☎ 986 614 521 Rúa Ourense. *H** **Eli-Mar** €35 ☎ 986 613 000 Rúa Vicente Sobrino, 12. *H**** **Convento de San Benito** €60 ☎ 986 611 166 Plaza de San Benito. *H* **Brisamar** €35+ ☎ 986 613 901 Calle Donantes de Sangre, 72. *H** **Hostal Del Mar** €18+ ☎ 986 610 638 Irmáns Noia (Praia Area Grande). ▌ **Oia:** *CR* **Casa Puertas** €50+ ☎ 986 361 856 Vicente Lopez,7. *H* **A Raíña** €35+ ☎ 986 362 908 Rúa A Riña. **Real Monasterio de Oia** *(restauración hotel monumento c.2020).* ▌ **Viladesuso-Oia:** *H**** **Glasgow** €50+ ☎ 986 361 552. *H*** **Costa Verde** €40+ ☎ 986 361 561. *CR* **Budiño de Serraseca** €60+ ☎ 986 361 856 *A Serra Seca Viladesuso (+2 km).* ▌ **Mougás:** *Alb.* **Aguncheiro** *Priv.[20÷3]*+ €10-30 ☎ 665 840 774 (Javier y Jorge).

🏰 *Castillo de Sta. Cruz*

🛏 Albergue

✝ Santa María

🎨 Art Café

Praza Reló

Turismo ℹ

Ⓜ < Museo do Mar

< Paseo Marítimo

Rua Galicia

Taxi

🅗 Eli-Mar

Celta 🅗

Alameda

Rosalía de Castro

Ferry

Monte Tecla

🅗 Vila

A Coruña

🅗 Bruselas

Concepción Arenal

Manuel Alvarez

Tomiño

Tui

Ourense

Subida a Monte

Plaza Abastos

🅗 Convento de San Benito

A GUARDA

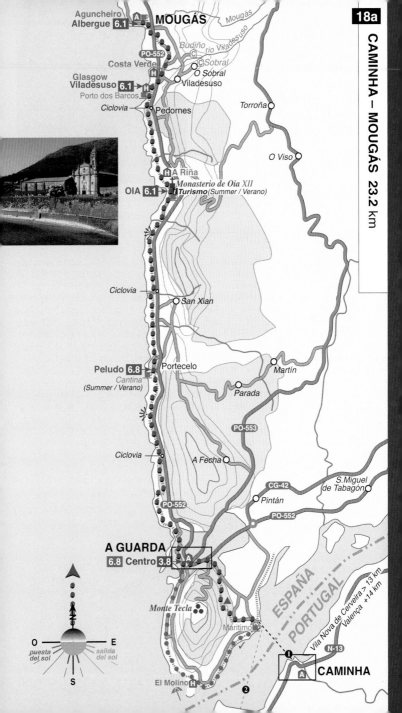

Aguncheiro
Albergue 6.1 Ⓐ Ⓗ **MOUGÁS**

Mougás

PO-552

Budiño
río Viladesuso
Ⓒ Ⓒ **Sobral**
Costa Verde Ⓗ Ⓒ *O Sobral*

Glasgow
Viladesuso 6.1 Ⓗ *Viladesuso*
Porto dos Barcos Ⓗ

Torroña

Ciclovia Pedornes

O Viso

Ⓗ **A Riña**
Monasterio de Oia XII
OIA 6.1 Ⓘ **Turismo** (Summer / Verano)

Ciclovia ○ *San Xian*

Peludo 6.8 Ⓗ **Portecelo**
Cantina
(Summer / Verano)

○ *Martín*

○ *Parada*

PO-553

Ciclovia ○ *A Fecha*

CG-42 ○ *S.Miguel*
de Tabagón

○ *Pintán*
PO-552

PO-552

A GUARDA Ⓐ
6.8 **Centro** 3.8 Ⓐ

Monte Tecla

ESPAÑA
PORTUGAL

Vila Nova de Cerveira > 13 km
Valença +14 km

Máritimo

❶
Ⓐ **CAMINHA**

N-13

O — E
puesta *salida*
del sol *del sol*
S

El Molino Ⓗ ❷

19a *24.9 km – Santiago de Compostela*

MOUGÁS – BAIONA – *NIGRÁN*
A RAMALLOSA

▒▒▒▒▒	--- --- 2.3	--- ---	14%
▬▬▬	--- ---14.0	--- ---	86%
▬▬▬	--- --- 0.0	--- ---	00%
Total km	**16.3 km**	(10.1 ml)	

▲ --- ---17.6 km (^260m+ 1.3km)
Alto ▲ Portela 130m (427 ft)
< 🏕 🏠 > Baiona **11.3 km**.

Camiño Portela

100m O Muiño / Soremma — Camiño Portela *Alto* ▲130m — **BAIONA** — río ▼ Miñor — **NIGRÁN**
MOUGÁS 🏕🏠 / 🏠
0 — 5 km — 10 km — 15 km

❚ **Mougás:** *Camping* **O Muiño** €30 ✆ 986 361 600 (PO-550). H° **Soremma** €35-€65 ✆ 986 356 067 Las Mariñas (PO-550). *Camping* **Mougás** €36-€51 ✆ 986 385 011 As Mariñas-Mougás. H **O'Peñasco** / *R Bodas* ✆ 986 361 565 c/ As Mariñas (PO-550). ❚ **BAIONA:** *H°°***Rompeolas** €40 ✆ 615 140 220 Av. Joselín. H°**Parador de Baiona** €150+ ✆ 986 355 000 Av. Arquitecto Jesús Valverde, 3. H°**Carabela La Pinta** €30+ ✆ 986 355 107 c/ Carabela la Pinta. H°**Pinzón** €30+ ✆ 986 356 046 Rúa Elduayen, 21. H°°**Tres Carabelas** €60+ ✆ 986 355 441 c/ de Ventura Misa, 61. H°°**Anunciada** €40+ ✆ 986 356 018 c/ de Ventura Misa, 58. H°°**Pazo de Mendoza** €65+ ✆ 986 385 014 Elduayen, 1. H **Cais** €45 ✆ 986 355 643 c/ del Alférez Barreiro, 3. Hs°°**Santa Marta Playa** €30 ✆ 986 356 045 Camino del Molino 4. ❚ **Nigrán / A Ramallosa:** *Alb.Hospedería* **Pazo Pias** *Priv.[40÷20!]*+ €10-40 ✆ 986 350 654 Camiño da Cabreira,21 A Ramallosa. *Restaurante* Antipodas Calle de la Romana Alta 4. **Senda Litoral:** ● ● ● ● ● H° **Avenida** €40 ✆ 986 354 728 Av. Julián Valverde Nº41 + Nº40. H°**Arce Baiona** €30 ✆ 986 386 060.

BAIONA *i* **0.0** Centro

A Anunciada

A Ramallosa
Pazo Pias
Albergue **1.7** *A*
NIGRÁN
Avenida
Ponte
Romanico
XIII
Arce

AG-57

PO-552

Fonte de Gafos
Fonte de Pombal

Sabaris **3.3**

Plaza

O   E
S

Virxe da Rocha

BAIONA
i **3.7** Centro

Marrucho

A Anunciada

Ponte

S. Maria Afora

AG-57

PO-552

As Cadera

O'Sinal **3.6** Cruceiro

Fútbol

Faro Silleiro

Alto
170m

BAIONA

Castelo de Montereal

Turismo

Pozo Aguada
XV

As Mariñas

Ciclovia

Casa Nena

Mougás
Camping

Soremma H **3.9** Café

A Ermida

Da Vinci

Ciclovia

Pedra
Rubia
O'Peñasco
H Bodas

Camping
O'Muiño

O   E
S

RUTA MÁXICA DE OIA
Castros y Petróglifos

A Cabeciña

O Pousiño

Pedra Lan

O Muiño

PO-552

MOUGÁS
0.0 Albergue Aguncheiro
A

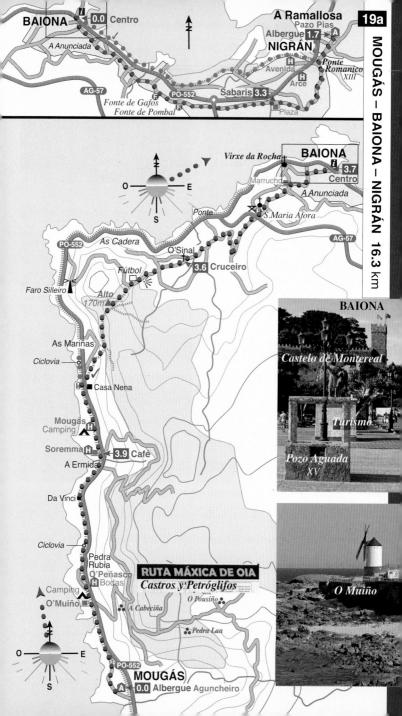

20a *24.9 km – Santiago de Compostela*

A RAMALLOSA *NIGRÁN* – VIGO

Illas Cíes

Porto de Vigo

┅┅┅┅┅	--- ---	8.3	--- ---	40%
▒▒▒▒	--- ---	10.9	--- ---	52%
___	--- ---	1.7	--- ---	08%
Total km		**20.9** km (13.0 ml)		

◣◢◣ --- ---23.5 km (^520m+2.6km)

Alto ▲ Alto Saiáns 180m (590 ft)

< 🅰 🏠 > Freixo *alt.* **11.3** km.

200m · *Alto* 180m
Falucha · *(Freixo)* **Opción** · · · · · · · · · · · · · · · · · · · VIGO
NIGRÁN 100m · · · · · · · · *río Saiáns* · Atanea · · · · Alboios
🅰 · · · Nigrán
P Telleira · rego *Presa*
río Muíños
0 · · · · · · · · · · · 5 km · · · · · · · · · · · 10 km · · · · · · · · · · · 15 km · · · · · · · · · · · 20

■ **Vigo** *Parque de Castrelos:* **Pazo Quiñónes de León** *(Museo Municipal)* ℗ 986 295 070. **Igrexa de Santa María de Castrelos** *románico XIII.* **Vigo Balaídos** *H**** NH* **Hesperia** €40 ℗ 986 296 600 Av. da Florida 60. ■ **Freixo** ● ● ● ● *Alb.*O **Freixo** *[8÷1]* €-donativo ℗ 680 756 664. ■ **Senda Litoral:** ● ● ● ● *H***** **Playa De Vigo** €40 ℗ 986 202 020 Av de Samil 95. *H****** **Pazo Los Escudos** €90+ ℗ 986 820 820 Av.Atlántida.

Alb. y Pazo Pías

Alb. Freixo

ALBERGU

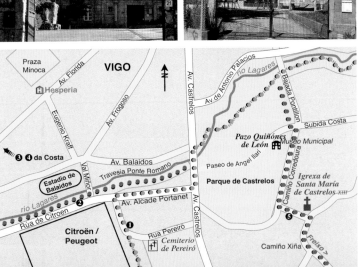

Praza Minoca

Av. Florida

VIGO

🏠 Hesperia

Av. de Antonio Palacios

río Lagares

Balada Portillón

Av. de Castrelos

Subida Costa

Av. Frogoso

Eugenio Krall

❸ ❹ da Costa

Av. Balaidos

Travesía Ponte Romano

Val Miñor

Estadio de Balaídos

río Lagares

Av. Castrelos

Pazo Quiñónes de León 🏛 *Museo Municipal*

Paseo de Angel Ilarí

Parque de Castrelos

Camiño Corredoura

Igrexa de Santa María de Castrelos *XIII*

❷

Av. Alcade Portanet

Rúa de Citroen

❶

Citroën / Peugeot

Rúa Pereiró

✝ *Cemiterio de Pereiró*

❺

Freixo 7

Camiño Xiña

Compostela

22.1 km **Centro** **3.2**
VIGO-BAJA

Uzaiz rúa

H

Catedral S.Roque

Galeones **H** **A** Estación de Autobuses

Kaps

VIGO-ALTA **2.4** **X** **20.9** km

N-120

Av.Beiramar

Opción **4.4** **2.9** **Parque** **5.1** *Freixo*

Parque de Castrelos

Taxi

Bouzas **5.1**

Hesperia **H**

S.Mauro
Xina

Alcabre

Museo do Mar ■ **H** Pazo Escudos

Estadio Balaídos

† Cemiterio de Pereiró

Fonte

Citroën Peugeot

† S.Mauro

Príton **3.1** **Camino Real**

Samil ▲ Samil **H** Samil Playa

Ataque 185m

F Fonte de Ribás

4

2

1 Comesaña

S.André

VG-20

5

Citroën Citroxe

Av.Citroën

F Abilleira

A **5.3** *Freixo*

Opción **4.9**
Río Lagares

Opción **2.3**

Illa Toralla

Bao

Coruxo

S.Salvador XII **Atanea**

Canido
Club Marítimo ■

V20 *Taxi* **A**

Roteas

F Feital

Canido

3.6 **Opción** *Freixo*

Futbol S.Miguel

C.Pirucha ○

Charco
Saiáns
GR-53
Alto 185m

Opción *Freixo*
Semaforo
Ciclovia
Escaleras ○
Porriño

C.Volta
Saiáns

F Bexas

Falucha
Kioso Tito **3.2** **X** **Priegue**
▲ Alto 165m

AG-57

PO-332

Patos **P**

NIGRÁN

Nigrán **P** **3.4** **X** **A Barxa**

Abacial de Nigrán XVII

Monte Ferro

Madorra

Panxón **4.0**

† *Arco Visigótico* XIII

AG-57N

AG-57

America

PO-552

San Pedro

Pazo Pías
Cortixo

Albergue **0.0** **A**

Monte Louriño

Miñor

Ponte Ramallosa VIII

Vigo ALTA: *Hostals:* Hs **Kaps** dormitorio €15-€25: © 986 110 010 Emilia Pardo Bazán 12. Hs **Los Tres Países** © 986 42 04 77 Venezuela 61. H **Solpor** © 986 416 036 c/ Vía Norte 9. *Hotels:* €25-75: H **Ogalia** © 986 222 228 c/ Lepanto 10. H**** **Tryp Los Galeones** €50 © 902 144 440 Av de Madrid 21. Hs **Pio V** €25 © 986 410 060 c/ Alcalde Vázquez Varela 46. H*** **Oca Ipanema** €35 © 986 471 344 Vázquez Varela 31-33. P **Brasil** €30 © 986 413 257 c/ Brasil 48. H** **Celta** €29 © 986 414 699 c/ México 22. H** **Casablanca** €27 © 986 48 27 12 c/ México 7. H **Puerto** €30 © 986 228 245 c/ Urzáiz 83. H*** **Mexico** €35 © 986 431 666 Via del Norte 10.

Iglesia de los Picos *Inmaculada Concepción* © 986 274 622 barrio del Calvario.

Vigo BAJA Turismo Vigo © 986 224 757 Estación Marítima C/ Cánovas del Castillo 3. **Turismo Xunta** *(Galicia)* © 986 430 577 C/ Cánovas del Castillo 22. *Marítima*: Ferry Islas Cíes / Ons €22 July-Sept. ■ *El barrio histórico de Vigo:* ❶ **Concatedral** de Vigo *La Colegiata* neoclásico *XIX*. ❷ **Casa de Arines** *Ceta XV* (Instituto Camões) calle Real. ❸ **Ayuntamiento** *antiguo* Praza da Constitución. *Marítima:* ❹ Monumento a Xulio Verne *(20.000 leguas de viaje submarino; que menciana la Ría de Vigo)*. ❺ **O Castro** *XVII (y Parque Monte del Castro.)*

Hostales Centro: Hs** **La Colegiata** €25-40 © 986 220 129 Plaza Iglesia 3. Hs **Continental** €25-45 © 986 220 764 Bajada la Fuente 3. H** **Compostela** €35-60 © 986 228 227 Rúa García Olloqui 5 *(Praza da Compostela)*. H* **Aguila** €20+ © 986 431 398 c/ Victoria 6. H* **Nautico** €25 © 986 122 440 c/ Luis Taboada 28. H** Del Mar €30 © 986 436 811 Rúa de Luis Taboada, 34. **Hermanos Misioneros** *Enfermos Pobres* €-gratis © 986 451 885 Av. de Galicia 160 (adj. IES de Teis).

Monumento a Xulio Verne

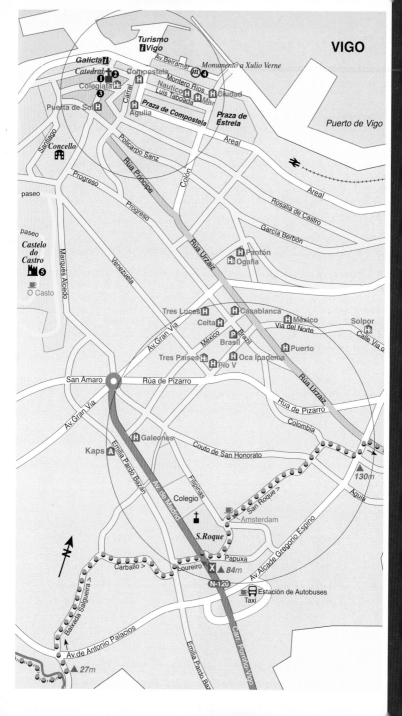

21a *24.9 km – Santiago de Compostela*

VIGO – REDONDELA

··············	--- --- 6.2 --- ---	39%
————	--- --- 9.2 --- ---	59%
————	--- --- 0.3 --- ---	02%
Total km	**15.7** km (9.8 ml)	

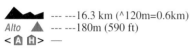 --- ---16.3 km (^120m=0.6km)

Alto --- ---180m (590 ft)

< A H > —

Chapela: *Hs* Bahía de Chapela Av. Redondela 14 (adj. Ponte de Rande ria Vigo – free pickup *transporte gratuito*) ✆ 986 452 780. **Redondela *Centro*:** *Albergue* ❶ **Casa da Torre** *Xunta [44÷2]* €6 ✆ 986 404 196 Plaza Ribadavia. ❷ **A Casa da Herba** *Priv.[24÷3]* €12 ✆ 639 757 684 Praza de Alhóndiga. ❸ **El Camino** *Priv.*[24÷3] €10-12 ✆ 650 963 676 m: 986 639 804 c/ Telmo Bernádez 11. **Alvear Suites** €50 ✆ 986 40 06 37 Pai Crespo 30. *Otros:* *P* **Brasil 2** €27 ✆ 986 402 251 Estrada Porriño 42 / N-550 (-1.9 km).

< Albergue de Torres, Redondela.

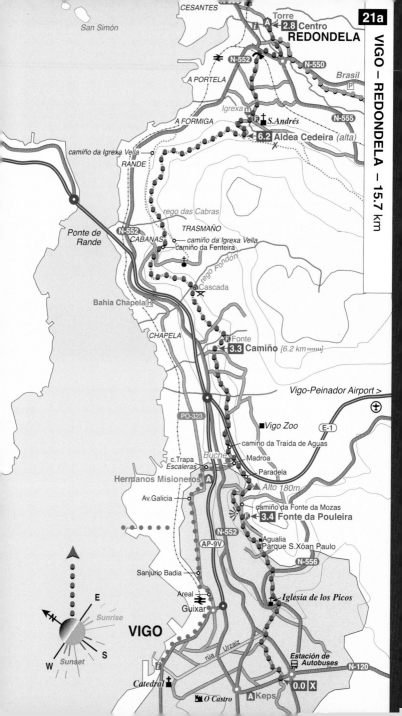

CESANTES

Torre **2.8** Centro
REDONDELA

San Simón

N-552   N-550

A PORTELA   Brasil

Igrexa
A FORMIGA   S.Andrés   N-555

6.2 Aldea Cedeira (alta)

camiño da Igrexa Vella
RANDE

rego das Cabras

TRASMAÑO
Ponte de   N-552   camiño da Igrexa Vella
Rande   CABANAS   camiño da Fenteira

rego Fondón

Cascada

Bahia Chapela

CHAPELA   Fonte
3.3 Camiño [6.2 km]

Vigo-Peinador Airport >

PO-323   Vigo Zoo   E-1

camiño da Traída de Aguas
c.Trapa   Buche   Madroa
Escaleras
Hermanos Misioneros   Paradela

Alto 180m

Av.Galicia   camiño da Fonte da Mozas
3.4 Fonte da Pouleira

N-552

AP-9V   Agualia
Parque S.Xóan Paulo

N-556

Sanjurjo Badia

Areal   Iglesia de los Picos
Guixar

VIGO   rúa Urzaiz

Estación de
Autobuses   N-120

E   **0.0**

Sunrise

N

S

W   Catedral

Sunset   O Castro   Keps

The official literature for the last compostelan jubilee year *año jubilar compostelana* stated boldly on the front cover, 'A Road with an END' *Camino que tiene META*. That may be so – but it is not the end of the road.

Finisterre. Before you leave this corner of the earth why not visit the end of it *Finis Terra*: "… Finisterre is one of the great hidden treasures amongst the many Caminos de Santiago. Only a small proportion of pilgrims arriving at Santiago continue by foot to the end of the road. The way to Finisterre truly follows *the road less travelled* and *that* may make all the difference. We need to search out the waymarks to the source of our own inner knowing. The light, while obscured, lies hidden in our memory – it is no coincidence that the path to Finisterre ends at the altar to the sun *Ara Solis* and a lighthouse." From *A Pilgrim's Guide to the Camino Finisterre.*

USEFUL PILGRIM CONTACTS:

You may be able to obtain further information of the route and a pilgrim passport, record or *credencial*, subject to membership from one of the English speaking organisations listed below. Allow several weeks to process postal applications.

UK: **The Confraternity of St. James**, 27 Blackfriars Road, London SE1 8NY (0044-[0]2079 289 988) e-mail: office@csj.org.uk / *www.csj.org.uk* the pre-eminent site in English with an on-line bookshop.

IRELAND: **The Irish Society of the Friends of St. James**. Based in Dublin, contact through their web site: *www.st.jamesirl.com*

U.S.A. **American Pilgrims on the Camino**. *www.americanpilgrims.com* *also:* Friends of the Road to Santiago *www.geocities.com/friends_usa_santiago*

CANADA: Canadian Company of Pilgrims Canada. *www.santiago.ca*

SOUTH AFRICA: Confraternity of St. James of SA *www.geocities.com/csjofsa*

TRANSLATIONS: *www.freetranslation.com/* or: *www.babelfish.altavista.com*

There are a number of additional web sites (in English) loosely connected with the Way of St. James or with the theme of pilgrimage as spiritual journeying that you may find helpful. These sites provide links with other organisations so you can explore and, hopefully, find information that resonates with you:

Latest News from Santiago and the Caminos (formerly *santiago-today) the pilgrims 'FaceBook'* *www.caminodesantiago.me*

Alternatives of St. James *www.alternatives.org.uk* exploration of ways of living that honour all spiritual traditions. Based at St. James Church, London.

The Gatekeeper Trust devoted to personal and planetary healing through pilgrimage. *www.gatekeeper.org.uk*

The Beloved Community *www.emissaryoflight.com* on-line courses in spiritual peacemaking and peace pilgrimages based in the USA.

Findhorn Foundation dedicated to personal and planetary transformation *www.findhorn.org* with daily reflections from 'Opening Doors Within.'

Lucis Trust incorporating the Arcane School of spiritual education and meditation and World Goodwill *www.lucistrust.org*

Paulo Coelho *www.warriorofthelight.com* with on-line news and reflections from Brazilian author of 'The Pilgrimage.'

Peace Pilgrim *www.peacepilgrim.com* audio and visual reflections of Peace Pilgrim's life and work.

The Quest A Guide to the Spiritual Journey. A practical home-study course for personal and spiritual discovery *www.thequest.org.uk*

BIBLIOGRAPHY: Some reading with waymarks to the inner path include:

A Course In Miracles (A.C.I.M.) *Text, Workbook for Students and Manual for Teachers*. Foundation for Inner Peace.

The Art of Pilgrimage *The Seeker's Guide to Making Travel Sacred*, Phil Cousineau. Element Books

Anam Cara *Spiritual wisdom from the Celtic world,* John O'Donohue. Bantam.

A New Earth *Awakening to Your Life's Purpose*, Eckhart Tolle. Penguin Books

A Brief History of Everything *Integrating the partial visions of specialists into a new understanding of the meaning and significance of life*, Ken Wilber.

Care of the Soul *How to add depth and meaning to your everyday life,* Thomas Moore. Piatkus

Conversations with God *Books One, Two and Three*. Neale Donald Walsch. Hodder & Stoughton

From the Holy Mountain *A Journey in the Shadow of Byzantium*, William Dalrymple. Flamingo

Going Home *Jesus and the Buddha as brothers*, Thich Nhat Hanh. Rider Books

Loving What Is *Four Questions That Can Change Your Life*, Byron Katie. Rider

Handbook for the Soul *A collection of wisdom from over 30 celebrated spiritual writers*. Piatkus

The Hero with a Thousand Faces *An examination, through ancient myths, of man's eternal struggle for identity,* Joseph Campbell. Fontana Press

How to Know God *The Soul's Journey into the Mystery of Mysteries*, Deepak Chopra. Rider

Jesus and the Lost Goddess *The Secret Teachings of the Original Christians*, Timothy Freke & Peter Gandy. Three Rivers Press

The Journey Home *The Obstacles to Peace*, Kenneth Wapnick. Foundation for A Course In Miracles

The Mysteries *Rudolf Steiner's writings on Spiritual Initiation*, Andrew Welburn. Floris Books

Mysticism *The Nature and Development of Spiritual Consciousness,* Evelyn Underhill. Oneworld

Nine Faces of Christ *Quest of the True Initiate*, Eugene Whitworth. DeVorss

No Destination *Autobiography (of a pilgrimage), Satish Kumar.* Green Books

Pilgrimage *Adventures of the Spirit*, Various Authors. Travellers' Tales

Paths of the Christian Mysteries *From Compostela to the New World*, Virginia Sease and Manfred Schmidt-Brabant. Temple Lodge

The Pilgrimage *A Contemporary Quest for Ancient Wisdom*. Paulo Coelho

Peace Pilgrim *Her Life and Work in Her Own Words*, Friends of Peace Pilgrim. Ocean Tree Books

Pilgrim in Aquarius David Spangler. Findhorn Press

Pilgrim Stories *On and Off the Road to Santiago*. Nancy Louise Frey.

Pilgrim in Time *Mindful Journeys to Encounter the Sacred*. Rosanne Keller.

The Power of Now *A Guide to Spiritual Enlightenment*, Eckhart Tolle. New World

Peace is Every Step *The path of mindfulness in everyday life*, Thich Nhat Hanh. Rider Books

Phases *The Spiritual Rhythms in Adult Life*, Bernard Lievegoed. Sophia Books

Sacred Contracts *Awakening Your Divine Potential*, Caroline Myss. Bantam

Sacred Roads *Adventures from the Pilgrimage Trail*, Nicholas Shrady. Viking

Secrets of God *Writings of Hildegard of Bingen*. Shambhala

Silence of the Heart *Dialogues with Robert Adams*. Acropolis Books

The Gift of Change *Spiritual Guidance for a Radically New Life,* Marianne Williamson. Element Books

The Inner Camino *A Path of Awakening,* Sara Hollwey & Jill Brierley. Findhorn Press.

The Reappearance of the Christ. Alice Bailey. Lucis Press.

The Road Less Travelled *A new Psychology of Love,* M. Scott Peck. Arrow Books

The Soul's Code *In Search of Character and Calling,* James Hillman. Bantam

The Prophet. Kahlil Gibran. Mandarin

Wandering Joy *Meister Eckhart's Mystical Philosophy*. Lindisfarne Press

Wanderlust *A history of Walking*. Rebecca Solnit. Verso

Who Dies? *An Investigation of Conscious Living and Conscious Dying*, Stephen and Ondrea Levine. Anchor Books

Whispers of the Beloved *The mystical poems of Rumi*. HarperCollins

RETURNING HOME: *Reflections ...*

When, after a prolonged absence, friends and family remark, *'you haven't changed at all'* I am hopeful they are either blind or following some meaningless social convention. I have spent the last 20 years of my life with the primary intention to do just that – to change myself. One of the more potent aspects of pilgrimage is the extended time it requires away from the familiar. This allows an opportunity for the inner alchemy of spirit to start its work of transformation. It's not just the physical body that may need to sweat off excess baggage – the mind needs purifying too. Our world is in a mess and we are not going to fix it with more of the same. We need a fresh approach and a different mind-set to the one that created the chaos in the first place. Hopefully, this re-ordering of the way we see the world will quicken apace as we open to lessons presented to us along the camino and begin to understand that... life itself is a classroom.

A purpose of pilgrimage is to allow time for old belief systems and outworn 'truths' to fall away so that new and higher perspectives can arise. We may also need to recognise that colleagues and partners at home or at work may feel threatened by our new outlook on life. Breaking tribal patterns, challenging the status quo or querying consensus reality is generally considered inappropriate at best or heretical at worst. The extent to which we hold onto any new understanding is measured by how far we are prepared to *walk our talk* and live our 'new' truth in the face of opposition, often from those who profess to love us. Christ was crucified for living The Truth.

These guidebooks are dedicated to awakening beyond human consciousness. They arose out of a personal existential crisis and the urgent need for some space and time to reflect on the purpose of life and its direction. Collectively we live in a spiritual vacuum of our own making where the mystical and sacred have been relegated to the delusional or escapist. Accordingly, we live in a three dimensional world and refuse to open the door to higher dimensions of reality. We have impoverished ourselves in the process, severely limiting our potential. Terrorised by the chaotic world we have manifested around us, we have become ensnared in its dark forms. We have become so preoccupied with these fearful images we fail to notice that we hold the key to the door of our self-made prison. We can walk out any time we choose.

Whatever our individual experiences, it is likely that you will be in a heightened state of sensitivity after walking the camino. I strongly recommend that you do not squeeze your itinerary so you feel pressurised to rush back into your work and general lifestyle immediately on your return. This is a crucial moment. I have often witnessed profound change, in myself and others, only to allow a sceptical audience to induce fear and doubt in us so that we fall back to the starting point – the default position of the status quo. Be careful with whom you share your experiences and stay in contact with fellow pilgrims who can support new realisations and orientation. Source new friends and activities that enhance and encourage the on-going journey of Self-discovery.

If you feel it might be helpful, please feel free to email me any time at *jb@caminoguides.com* – I cannot promise to answer all emails in writing but be assured they will all be noted and a blessing sent in return. I have developed great empathy and respect for my fellow pilgrims who have placed themselves on the path of enquiry. We are embarking together on a journey of re-discovery of our essential nature and opening up to knowledge of Higher Worlds. We have, collectively, been asleep a long time and while change can happen in the twinkling of an eye it is often experienced as a slow and painful process. It is never easy to let go of the familiar and to step into the new. How far we are prepared to go and how resolute in holding onto our newfound reality is a matter of our own choosing. There is little point in garnering peace along the camino if we leave it behind in Santiago. We need to bring it back into our everyday life. After the camino comes the laundry!

Whichever choice you make will doubtless be right for you at this time. I wish you well in your search for the truth and your journey Home and extend my humble blessings to a fellow pilgrim on the path. The journey is not over and continues, as you will have it be, dedicated to the sacred or the mundane, to waking or sleeping. To help remind us of our true identity, I leave you with the following words of Marianne Williamson, distilled from A Course In Miracles and immortalised in Nelson Mandela's *freedom speech*.

Our deepest fear is not that we are inadequate.
Our deepest fear is that we are powerful beyond measure.
It is our Light, not our darkness, that most frightens us.

We ask ourselves, who am I to be brilliant, gorgeous, talented and fabulous?
Actually, who are you not to be? You are a child of God.
Your playing small doesn't serve the world.
There's nothing enlightened about shrinking,
So that other people won't feel insecure around you.

We were born to make manifest the Glory of God that is within us.
It's not just in some of us; it's in everyone.
And as we let our Light shine,
We unconsciously give other people permission to do the same.
As we are liberated from our own fear,
Our presence automatically liberates others.

Before a new chapter is begun, the old one has to be finished.
Stop being who you were, and change into who you are.
Paulo Coelho – www.warriorsoflight.com

Stay in Touch:

The evolution of human consciousness is gathering apace, one manifestation of this is the increasing interest in taking time out to go on pilgrimage and nowhere is this more apparent than along the camino where facilities struggle to keep up with demand. Information garnered in one month may be out of date the next as old hostels close and new ones open up. Paths are realigned to make way for new motorways and budget airlines suddenly announce new routes (or with the advent of 'peak oil' – closing some). Whilst great care has been taken in gathering the information for this guide it also requires feedback from pilgrims who have recently walked the route to enable it to stay fresh and relevant to those who will follow on after us. Your comments and suggestions will be gratefully received and used to provide up-to-date advice on the free 'updates' page on **www.caminoguides.com** so if you would like to offer something back to the camino or simply stay in touch please e-mail me at:

jb@caminoguides.com

A tithe of royalties from the sale of this guidebook will be distributed to those who seek to preserve the physical and spiritual integrity of this route

Name *Nombre:* _____

Nationality *Nacionalidad:* _____

Passport No: *Número de Pasaporte:* _____

You are encouraged to join your local confraternity who may provide an official pilgrim passport ***credencial do peregrino***. This is essential if you intend to apply for a Compostela in Santiago. You can also obtain an official credencial at the commencement of your journey in either Lisbon or Porto (at the cathedrals or local association offices). Apart from establishing your pilgrim status (essential when staying in hostels within Spain) they make an interesting record of your travels. A pilgrim stamp *sello* (in Spanish) *carimbo* (in Portuguese) can readily be obtained from cathedrals, churches, pilgrim hostels, hotels etc.

To be awarded the ***Compostela***:

• You need to have made the pilgrimage for religious reasons or for a similar motivation such as a vow.

• You need to have walked the last 100 kms or cycled the last 200 kms and to have collected at least two stamps ***sellos*** each day on your credencial as proof. Note the 'two stamp' rule only applies to the last stages within Galicia and is to ensure that only those walking (or cycling) the route without any backup support or transport will be awarded a compostela or certificado.

Those who do not accept a spiritual motivation as part of their reason for making the pilgrimage can obtain a ***certificado***, essentially a certificate of completion.

Date *Fecha:*

Date *Fecha:*

Date *Fecha:*

Date *Fecha:*

Date *Fecha:*

Date *Fecha:*

Date *Fecha:*

Date *Fecha:*

Date *Fecha:*

Date *Fecha:*

12 Caminos de Santiago

❶ Camino Francés 790 km
St. Jean / Roncesvalles – Santiago
· · · · · · · ·

❷ Chemin de Paris 1000 km
Paris – St. Jean via Orléans &Tours
Alt. route from Chartres -
Soulac – Tarnos 170km
· · · · · · · ·
· · · · · · · ·

❸ Chemin de Vézelay 900 km
Vezélay – St. Jean via Bazas
Ext. to Namur (B) & Maastricht (NL)
· · · · · · · ·
· · · · · · · ·

❹ Chemin de Le Puy 740 km
Le Puy-en-Velay – St. Jean
Ext. to Geneva, Konstanz, Prague
· · · · · · · ·

❺ Chemin d'Arles 750 km
Arles – Somport Pass
Camino Aragonés 160 km
Somport Pass – Óbanos
Camí San Jaume 600 km
Port de Selva – Jaca
· · · · · · · ·
· · · · · · · ·

❻ Camino de Madrid 320km
Madrid – Sahagún
Camino de Levante 900 km
Valencia (Alicante) – Zamora
Alt. via Cuenca – Burgos
· · · · · · · ·
· · · · · · · ·

❼ Camino Mozárabe 390km
Granada – Mérida
(Málaga alt. via Baena)
· · · · · · · ·

❽ Via de la Plata 1,000km
Seville – Santiago
· · · · · · · ·

❾ Camino Portugués *Central* 241km
Lisboa – Porto
Porto – Santiago
Camino Portugués *da Costa* 372km
Porto – Caminho
A Guarda – Redonela
· · · · · · · ·
· · · · · · · ·

❿ Camino Finisterre 87km
Santiago – Finisterre
via – Muxía – Santiago 114 km
· · · · · · · ·

⓫ Camino Inglés 110km
Ferrol – Santiago
· · · · · · · ·

⓬ Camino del Norte 830km
Irún – Santiago via Gijón
Camino Primitivo 320km
Oviedo – Lugo – Melide
· · · · · · · ·
· · · · · · · ·